LIZA

BORN A STAR

LIZA

BORN A STAR

A BIOGRAPHY BY
WENDY LEIGH

Research assistance by Stephen Karten

A DUTTON BOOK

DUTTON
Published by the Penguin Group
Penguin Books USA Inc., 375 Hudson Street,
New York, New York 10014, U.S.A.
Penguin Books Ltd, 27 Wrights Lane,
London W8 5TZ, England
Penguin Books Australia Ltd, Ringwood,
Victoria, Australia
Penguin Books Canada Ltd, 10 Alcorn Avenue,
Toronto, Ontario, Canada M4V 3B2
Penguin Books (N.Z.) Ltd, 182–190 Wairau Road,
Auckland 10, New Zealand

Penguin Books Ltd, Registered Offices:
Harmondsworth, Middlesex, England

First published by Dutton, an imprint of New American Library, a
division of Penguin Books USA Inc.
Distributed in Canada by McClelland & Stewart Inc.

First Printing, January, 1993
10 9 8 7 6 5 4 3 2 1

REGISTERED TRADEMARK—MARCA REGISTRADA

Library of Congress Cataloging-in-Publication Data

Leigh, Wendy.
    Liza : born a star : a biography / Wendy Leigh : research assistance by Stephen
Karten.
        p.   cm.
    ISBN 0-525-93515-0
    1. Minnelli, Liza.   2. Actors—United States—Biography.   3. Singers—United
States—Biography.   I. Karten, Stephen.   II. Title.
PN2287.M644L45   1993
    791.43′028′092—dc20   92–25702
    [B]   CIP

Printed in the United States of America
Set in Excelsior
Designed by Leonard Telesca

LIZA
BORN A STAR

She was born in the limelight, destined to live her life under the microscope of the public's endless fascination with her inheritance, her talent, her loves, her traumas and her triumphs.

She is show business incarnate, a glittering superstar who combines the magic of Broadway with the memory of Hollywood's golden era, of her mother, her father and a luminescent age in which the world had seemed more innocent and fresh.

Part of the secret of her appeal, of why her legions of loyal fans cheer for her, root for her and long for her always to survive, lies in the melodramatic saga of her legendary life which has forever veered between the ecstatically happy and the devastatingly tragic.

And although she is adamant that she hates being described as one of the all-time great show business survivors, protesting that she is far too young, has far too many years ahead of her, it is undeniable that her story is worthy of the Hollywood that created her and must, at last, be told.

PROLOGUE
Radio City Music Hall
April 23, 1991

Prices had soared and even in the eleventh hour, just minutes before the curtain was due to go up, outside Radio City desperate fans were offering scalpers untold riches in exchange for a precious ticket.

The paparazzi were out in force, surging forward toward the endless stream of stretch limousines, primed to snap the occupants the second their expensively shod feet alighted on the klieg-lit pavements.

A special entrance, cordoned off with red velvet, was reserved for celebrities, those favored few who stalked into the Music Hall conscious that their very presence heightened the electricity of the evening and intensified the sensation that tonight would out-shine the dazzling Broadway openings of old.

Inside Radio City, the elegant crowd waited expectantly, clutching their programs and jostling one another in an attempt to survey their peers, the gathering of Liza Minnelli fans and intimates. They stared at Lorna Luft, her half sister, forever in her shadow; at Liz Smith, her foremost admirer in the press; at Joe Pesci, the actor with whom she had often been linked; and at the youngest of her illustrious fans, supermodels Naomi Campbell and Christy Turlington. They were all there to cheer for her, even as they whispered about the recent announcement of her plans for yet another divorce and about the new love in her life, Billy Stritch.

The lights dimmed and the buzz of voices fell with them, but there remained an almost palpable energy in the air. And as Liza finally made her entrance, the crowd roared, nearly leaping to their feet. She stood alone onstage, dressed in Isaac Mizrahi's short, sexy, glossy white raincoat designed to expose her fabulous, never-ending legs. Then, as she faced the opening night audience of 6,200 adoring fans, Liza began to tremble.

Normally she felt safer onstage than anywhere else on earth. Performing gave her security and love. But on this night, Liza was so frightened that, as she later confessed (her voice shaking at the memory), she felt sick to her stomach.

But seasoned trouper that she was, she didn't betray herself. She had always been famous for her frenetic energy and the rawness of her nerves, the underlying hysteria in her personality and the transparency of her emotions. Yet onstage, now and forever, she remained the consummate professional, an incomparable and indestructible star.

Her act opened with a ploy designed to create intimacy, even in this arena. Taking binoculars and training them on the audience, she sang "The Nearness of You" with self-mocking irony. She followed up with a rousing "Some People" and an ode to Sara Lee cakes, composed especially for her. But neither the fun of the song nor the obvious enthusiasm of the audience did anything to dispel her stage fright. She had inherited her stage fright from her mother, and tonight, here at Radio City where she had never performed solo before, it was at its height.

She radiated her high-voltage firecracker energy throughout the first act, by turns brassy, romantic, sad, hopeful, heartwarming, vampish, and endearing. Yet her enormous brown velvet eyes never once betrayed her genuine soul-quaking fear.

She was still racked with nerves as she began the climax

of the first act, "Seeing Things," a tribute to her father. Vincente Minnelli had begun his career at Radio City in 1932, the year the fabled music hall first opened. "Seeing Things" was the highlight of Liza's show, a sentimental and touching daughter's valentine to the father she had wholeheartedly loved and idealized. Liza sang the song as slides of her mother, her father, and her as a baby were projected behind her.

As she paid homage to her father, it was clear to those who knew her story well that not only the ghost of Vincente Minnelli hovered over Radio City that night. There were other less cherished ghosts and disquieting memories that Liza naturally chose not to share with her audience, though they would always remain with her.

There was the memory of her first husband, iconoclastic entertainer Peter Allen, whose name was synonymous with Radio City. He had appeared there on a variety of occasions, once dancing with the Rockettes in a sequence that reinforced the rumors about his homosexuality.

There was the memory of the 1976 Radio City premiere of Vincente's last film, *A Matter of Time,* in which Liza had—as a labor of love—starred. The illustrious director (already suffering the ravaging effects of Alzheimer's disease) had valiantly tried to recapture the romantic glory days of his past triumphs like *Gigi* and *An American in Paris,* but had failed so dismally that his last creation was booed by the Radio City Music Hall audience.

Then there was the memory of Liza's Radio City appearance in "Night of a Hundred Stars," in the midst of her substance abuse pre–Betty Ford Clinic days.

Actress Anne Jeffreys shared the stage at Radio City with Liza that night, and her own recollection may partially explain the burning intensity of the startling stage fright Liza suffered years later on the very same stage.

"On the night of the show, all hundred stars had to form a line and kick across the stage. I was standing in the middle of the stage in the line and Liza moved towards me, singing and smiling.

"Then she broke her line, grabbed my arm and whispered, 'Hold me up! Hold on tight!' She was cold and she was wringing wet and she was trembling.

"I knew something was wrong. I had no idea she was heavily into drugs at that time. Clutching my arm, she finished the number. Then she hugged me and said, 'Oh, thank you for holding me up. I couldn't have made it. I just couldn't go another step.' "

Those days were long behind her now, and as Liza ended the first act of her *Stepping Out* show, taking comfort in the memory of her father and all the other people whom she had loved and who had loved her in return, she realized that her nervousness had miraculously evaporated.

Later, she confided, "I took everybody I've ever known with me. Nobody saw them but they were there with me. Sammy and Halston and my mother and my father and my friends and I felt safe and lucky to have known the people that I have known.

"I believe that my mother saw me at Radio City." Then, hastily, lest anyone be left with the impression that her only influence, the only person she had ever cared about, had ever loved, had been Judy Garland, she added, "The first night I walked out on the stage at Radio City, I wasn't by myself."

And she never would be—not just in her own heart but in the minds of the public who adored her, yet still revered the memory of her mother. But tonight, here at Radio City, where she would go on to break all records, she had arrived at the pinnacle of her career, conquering the most spectacular stage in the world and yet again proving that she had triumphed over all adversity fate had flung in her star-crossed path.

Her mother had never appeared at Radio City, so here, at least, the legend of Judy was in abeyance and the legend of Liza glittered brighter than ever. And as the audience rose at the end of the show for a ten minute standing ovation, their thundering applause, their love and their adulation, were finally for Liza—not for Judy. For Liza, the legend whose talent transcended everyone and everything.

CHAPTER ONE

The curtain was raised on Hollywood's newest princess, the daughter of Vincente Minnelli and Judy Garland, at 7:58 A.M. on Tuesday, March 12, 1946, at Cedars of Lebanon Hospital, Los Angeles, California.

Weighing six pounds ten ounces, with dark hair, luminous bright brown eyes, and soft, unmarked skin, from the moment that she took her first breath, she was fated to be a showstopper. Frank Sinatra was her first visitor, Charlie Chaplin's children were her earliest playmates, and Beverly Hills was her personal playground.

With royal show business blood coursing inexorably through her veins, from the start she indisputably belonged to Hollywood. The stage was set for the incredible life and times of Liza Minnelli to begin.

She was Vincente Minnelli and Judy Garland's only daughter and, until she was nearly five, she lived in a world of warmth and security, dominated by two parents who loved each other nearly as much as they loved her.

Vincente Minnelli first met Judy Garland in 1943 when he directed her in *Meet Me in St. Louis*. At the time, she was twenty-two years old, a big star, and a household name. In the four years since playing Dorothy in *The Wizard of Oz* and singing "Over the Rainbow" with heartbreaking poignancy, Judy had appeared in eleven other films. She was Mickey Rooney's endearing little pal, America's girl next door, beloved by millions who thrilled to her singing voice and adored her fresh-faced innocence.

Although she didn't know it at the time, Judy was at the peak of her success. Vincente, in contrast, had all his triumphs ahead of him. He had been a New York director and stage designer at Radio City, then moved to Hollywood, where he directed *Cabin in the Sky* (with Ethel Waters) and *I Dood It* (with Red Skelton and Eleanor Powell). But *Meet Me in St. Louis* was his biggest break, a high budget film starring a major box office draw, Judy Garland.

Vincente was extraordinarily talented, extremely effete (rumors alleged that he had engaged in homosexual dalliances), extremely cosmopolitan, cultured, and sophisticated.

Ostensibly, Judy—now a spoiled and temperamental star with an ever-increasing predilection for all manner of pharmaceutical drugs—had very little in common with Vincente. Yet once filming began, under the hot lights of MGM, they slowly began to acknowledge each other's respective talent and to fall in love. Judy realized that Vincente was creating a work of art with *Meet Me in St. Louis*. And Vincente, in turn, was mesmerized by Judy's charm and vulnerability. They were both artists, both temperamental, both attuned to one another's talent—and their romance was inevitable.

They quickly discovered that they were not totally different after all. Judy had made her show business debut in vaudeville at the age of two and a half as one of the Gumm Sisters, singing "Jingle Bells" in her father's theater in Minnesota. Vincente also came from a show business family, the Minnelli Brothers Dramatic and Tent Shows, and made his stage debut at three and a half in the play *East Lynne*. Both of them spent nomadic childhoods, traveling the country with their families, nurtured on applause and theatrical fantasy.

Vincente was only eight years older than Judy, but with his sophistication, his literary education, and his Japanese valet, he seemed far more mature to her. Initially, he played the mentor: lending her books, schooling her in French literature, in classical music, and in art. It soon became clear to him that Judy was an apt pupil. She was quick-witted and curious and had an innate ability to recognize quality.

He loved her sense of humor, which wasn't based on bon mots but on self-deprecating anecdotes centering around her horrendous Hollywood experiences—of Louis B. Mayer's calling her "a little hunchback," of being overshadowed by shimmering beauties like Lana Turner, and of working with a group of quirky Munchkins in *The Wizard of Oz*.

Like Judy, Vincente, too, was acutely sensitive to mood and ambiance, and he had a wry sense of humor and a marked talent for mimicry that Liza would inherit.

Meet Me in St. Louis proved to be a stupendous success, both for Vincente and for Judy. Their next film, *The Clock*—featuring Judy in her first dramatic role—was equally successful, and the Gallup poll voted her one of the five most popular stars in the country for the third year running.

By now Judy was divorced from her first husband, band-leader David Rose, and in June 1945, she and Vincente were married. Judy immediately became pregnant. She was in the process of making *Till the Clouds Roll By* (in which she sang the classic number "Look for the Silver Lining") and everything conceivable was done to disguise her pregnancy, including placing her behind a sinkful of dishes for the entire number.

Liza was born one day less than nine months after her parents' wedding. By now, Judy and Vincente lived in a pink stucco house on Evanview Drive, which they had refurbished for $70,000 ($500,000 by today's standards) when Liza was born.

Judy and Vincente adored their new daughter, and, unlike many a Hollywood baby, Liza was rarely banished to the nursery or excluded from her parents' daily life. She was constantly petted and cosseted, serenaded, and admired. By the time she could crawl, she would take great pains to pull herself up the stairs every night so she could join Judy and Vincente on the floor above while they had cocktails together.

Liza faced no competition for her parents' love. There were no brothers or sisters to mar her happiness or challenge her supremacy and she was often allowed to sleep in Vincente and Judy's bed. Later, in a memoir she wrote for *Good Housekeeping,* she remembered, "They'd put me in the middle and we'd all go to sleep. But sometimes, during the night in their sleep, Mama and Daddy would hold hands across my stomach or head. I didn't dare move for fear I'd get tossed out. I didn't want that to happen because it was so warm and safe in there."

Liza's sense of safety, like Vincente and Judy's marriage, proved to be an illusion primed to shatter. Judy, accustomed to being Vincente's only "child," was sometimes overcome with an uncontrollable jealousy of his intense love for Liza. And although she was careful not to vent her emotions on her new baby, she once confided that she was terrified that she might inadvertently hurt Liza.

Racked with colitis and cursed with insomnia, Judy once again took refuge in Benzedrine, in Dexedrine, and other drugs that not only served to control her weight but also helped her through agonizing sleepless nights. The drugs induced severe mood swings, episodes of paranoia, and sudden temper tantrums. Her legendary sparkle began to dim and Judy's career, too, began to suffer.

During the making of *The Pirate,* which Vincente was directing, Judy frequently erupted in angry jealous outbursts over his friendship with Gene Kelly, who was starring in the film with her. She escaped from her moods into sedatives, which caused her either to oversleep or to become so lackadaisical that she never bothered to turn up for shooting at all.

She missed days of work and, when she did manage to make an appearance on set, often looked too worn for close-ups. Vincente, still deeply in love with his wayward wife, was tortured on and off-set, unable to cope with her rapid disintegration. For a time, Judy consulted a psychiatrist, but she rarely told him the truth and thus sabotaged the treatment.

She had fallen out of love with Vincente and he, in turn, had no conception of how to handle her, how to cope with her violent mood swings and addictive personality. Totally unequipped to pacify Judy, he either avoided her altogether or, fueled by his own hot temper, launched into full-scale battles with her.

Some of their screaming matches were fought in baby Liza's presence and took their toll on her developing psyche. As a result, even today, those who know Liza well confirm that she can't abide raised voices or loud noises and is even afraid of the innocuous sound of balloons bursting.

In July 1947, Judy was admitted to Las Campanas Sanitarium, in Compton, near Los Angeles. Liza was just fourteen months old, but, according to Vincente, he explained Judy's absence, soothingly telling her, "Momma went away for a little while." He was later to say wistfully, "I felt a steady tone in my voice would assuage those fears about being deserted that plague every child. I was thankful that a very capable nurse protected Liza during those formative years. Between the two of us, we shielded the unhappy truth from Liza until she was able to cope with it."

Vincente was fighting to save his marriage and to rescue Judy from her chemical dependency. He lived as if in quicksand, never knowing what would become of Judy, what would become of both of them. His only constant was Liza, and from the first he turned to her for happiness.

He photographed her night and day, lovingly recording her pixieish personality, her anxiously radiant smile, and her every quicksilver movement. From the first, she experienced life at a higher pitch, so sensitive that sometimes it seemed that her skin was inflamed and unable to protect her from the normal hurts of childhood. She was already an acutely perceptive child, part china doll, fragile with big brown eyes, and part miniadult, observing everything and everyone around her with an intensely focused seriousness.

Even as a small baby, whenever anyone laughed in her presence, she instinctively perceived their laughter was directed at her, and her tiny spirit was broken. Judy delighted in Vincente's sense of humor and he often made her laugh. Whereupon little Liza would burst into tears, believing that both her parents were making fun of her.

It was hardly surprising that life for Liza was a grimly serious matter. She was less than a year and a half old and already had witnessed violent arguments, suicide attempts, and all manner of traumatic situations. Vincente took her to see Judy at Las Campanas and Judy subsequently recalled, "Liza just kept kissing me and looking at me with those huge, helpless brown eyes. I didn't know what to say to her."

Once Judy was discharged from the sanitarium, she went home for a brief spell but was admitted to another sanitarium, the Riggs Foundation in Stockbridge, after a relapse. A short time later, presumed to be cured from her addiction, she was once more released and returned to Liza and Vincente.

Judy went on to make *Easter Parade* with Fred Astaire, which won great critical acclaim. But her career success failed to ease her sense of impending doom over her marriage. Vincente constantly disappointed her. She had searched for a father figure but had married an artist—a man far more intent on creating cinematic art than on providing her with emotional security.

Vincente, too, had based his marriage on an illusion, originally believing Judy to be the perfect woman of his dreams, then discovering that her fragile mental state invariably catapulted him into an addiction-riddled nightmare.

* * *

Whatever their marital woes, Judy and Vincente did their utmost to ensure Liza's childhood wasn't deprived of material benefits, that it matched that of other Hollywood children like Candice Bergen, Zsa Zsa Gabor's daughter Francesca Hilton, and the children of Judy's *In the Good Old Summertime* co-star, Van Johnson.

The Minnellis' parties were legendary. Bogart and Bacall were frequent visitors, Harold Arlen (who wrote Judy's anthem, "Over the Rainbow") played the piano, while Judy sang.

Van Johnson's daughter Schuyler remembers the opulence of those far-off children's parties where nannies gossiped about their employers' chances of winning the Academy Award, while their pampered small charges sampled a variety of delights. "At Liza's parties, she had a little donkey that we all used to ride around on, and a puppet show and screening of all the latest movies. It was all very elaborate."

Even at an early age, Liza wasn't a passive child, just content to be entertained by adults. Instead, she eagerly scrambled to entertain all and sundry. Songwriter Sammy Cahn has fond memories of a tiny Liza imitating Judy by the light of a flashlight—an ersatz spotlight shone on Liza's eager little face by Sammy's obliging small son.

"She had this wonderful personality," recalled one of Hollywood's leading hostesses, Judy and Vincente's friend, Evie Johnson. "Even at that early age, she wanted to be liked. She would do anything to please you.

"Vincente adored her and I never heard him raise his voice to her. Judy was a wonderful mother. In later years she and the children moved near us. We hadn't built our pool yet and so our children Schuyler and Tracy took swimming lessons with Liza. Judy was very caring to my children and, of course, to Liza. Liza was a lovely child."

Given her parentage, her nonstop chatter, her vivacity, and her ease in front of a camera, Liza's show business debut was a foregone conclusion. Liza, herself, in later years observed, "When your mother is Judy Garland, and your father is Vincente Minnelli, film director, you really don't have much choice except to go into the family business."

She was just three years old when her mother and father arranged her professional debut in *In the Good Old Summertime,* appearing in the last scene of the film as Van Johnson and Judy's baby. At the time, Judy made the stilted comment, "Liza can now understand when we talk about our work at the studio. I think acting is a wonderful profession and I know it will bring her happiness."

Judy's press "puffery" remarks carry a terrible and bitter irony. Eventually, she was to be more honest, discussing her own childhood show business debut with writer Peter Evans and confessing, "I've lived off applause ever since. The trouble is, you can't put a big hand away for a rainy day. There's no interest on bravos, baby. I pray that neither Liza nor Lorna is condemned to mama-repetition. I've always had such a tragic talent for fame."

Show business had never brought Judy happiness or stability and she often yearned for normalcy. She would eventually look back on her fractured life and conclude, "Hollywood took away my childhood, took away my leisure."

Yet despite Judy's insights and her own love for Liza, she possessed an inability to learn from the mistakes of the past, to avoid doing to Liza what had been done to her. Ignoring her own history and the aching wounds she had suffered in show business, Judy arranged Liza's debut—partly because her desire to provide a normal life was at war with her consciousness that, even as a small child, Liza had star quality and yearned to perform.

From her earliest days, Liza was surrounded by performers who were more than delighted to encourage an endearingly precocious child star. Sammy Davis, Jr., recollected during a party at Judy's house once seeing the diminutive Liza peeking wide-eyed through the banisters, watching the grown-ups entertain one another by singing at the piano.

Although he knew Judy was strict about Liza's bedtime, Sammy prevailed upon her to let him bring Liza down to the party. Fascinated, she sat on his knee, drinking in the song and dance routines of the various guests. When the entertainment began winding down, she slid off Sammy's knee and, with remarkable poise, launched into a current hit song.

According to Sammy, Liza stole the show. He turned to Judy and informed her that Liza was destined to become a star. Melodramatic as always, Judy said, "You know what we've done, Sammy. We've thrown her right in the middle of the Atlantic. She'll either swim or drown." When he left Judy's house that night, Sammy Davis, Jr., was totally convinced that Liza Minnelli, no matter what, would become a star.

And the very first time Liza went on to join Judy on stage at the Palace Theater, dancing in front of a live audience while Judy sang "Swanee," she would never forget "waves and waves of applause washing over us, and I also remember wondering whether my pants had shown while I was dancing." She had basked in the glow of limelight and experienced the seductive warmth of mass love. She was ten years old, and from then on any other destiny would seem mediocre to her.

For now, Liza had to contend with reality. In the summer of 1949—the same year in which Liza made her cinematic debut—her mother was undergoing shock treatment after having attempted suicide a number of times. For a spell, Judy was admitted to Peter Bent Brigham Hospital in a bid to withdraw from drug addiction.

She weighed eighty pounds and, although she was hospitalized and under supervision, undeterred she still managed to smuggle pills into the hospital. Nevertheless, after four weeks, Judy was pronounced cured.

Yet once released from hospital and in the care of the distraught Vincente, Judy was yet again unable to control her addiction to diet pills and barbiturates. Often, she begged her friends for Seconals, for something to help her sleep. And if they refused, she resorted to other means. Zsa Zsa Gabor remembers, "The first time I saw her, we were at Bogart and Bacall's house in Holmby Hills and Betty took me into one of the guest rooms and begged me, 'For God's sakes, darling, watch Judy, because if she goes into the bathroom she'll eat up every single pill I have in there.' "

Vincente was unable to cope with Judy, and Judy no longer loved him. In the last days before the marriage ended, she revealed to her friend Van Johnson her fears that Liza's security would soon be shattered. With tears welling up in her huge brown eyes, Judy said, "What do you tell a three-year-old? 'Don't get hooked on the marzipan, kid, because someday, somebody is gonna snatch it all away?' I can't rain on her parade."

Liza's life with her mother and father was over, and as in the most tear-jerking show business sagas, her childhood had an unhappy ending that destroyed her world. On December 22, 1950, Judy Garland walked out on Vincente, leaving him alone with Liza. The contrasting happiness of the holiday season served only to accentuate Liza's passionate sorrow at her abandonment. To this day, when she hears a recording of Judy singing "Have Yourself a Merry Little Christmas," she is compelled to leave the room before she dissolves into tears, explaining, "I guess because it was so hopeful."

CHAPTER TWO

Judy Garland and Vincente Minnelli were divorced in early 1951, having spent most of their money on psychiatrists and medical care for Judy. They were adamant that although they were divorcing one another, they definitely were not divorcing Liza. Yet, because they went in separate directions, Judy and Vincente continued to love Liza in very different ways as well. Their love for her was undisciplined, uncoordinated, dispensed without rhyme or reason, brimming over with contrasting values and colored by their differing individual life-styles.

According to the custody agreement, Liza was to spend six months with her mother and six months with her father. At the age of five, she was now the inhabitant of two worlds, a pint-sized diplomat shuttling between two universes, both ruled over by two very different gods who did their best to love her as she deserved.

With Vincente, she became a Hollywood princess and she lived in a tinsel-covered ivory tower. Noting that Liza relished his new status as a bachelor father, Vincente, in his personal life always a passive, ineffectual, but kindhearted man, brought her up to the best of his ability. Overwhelmed by his all-consuming love for Liza, he proceeded, throughout her childhood, to devote the best of himself to her: his finely tuned artistic sensibility, his creative talents, his gifts as a storyteller.

By the time Liza was five, Vincente had already taught her the song "Love for Sale." In years to come, he taught Liza other, similarly sophisticated love songs. His selection of literature for his little daughter was equally eclectic. "He'd read to me about Colette and her men when other children were being told about Heidi and her goats," Liza remembered, many years later, in a voice that brooked no criticism of Vincente's fathering techniques.

Vincente never forgot Liza's horror at being laughed at, and now that he and Judy were divorced and she no longer sapped his energy, he did all he could to prevent her ever being subjected to laughter again. He couldn't bear anyone hurting her, even in error.

One Halloween he designed a costume for Liza and took her trick or treating, assuring her that she would frighten people to death. Despite his assurances, everyone laughed at the sight of the miniature witch with the sparkling saucer-sized brown eyes. And although Vincente steadfastly told her that the neighbors' laughter merely cloaked their fear, Liza was upset. It was only when Vincente took her to Gene Kelly's house and Gene pretended to be terrified that Liza was mollified.

Liza craved love and Vincente stopped at nothing to satisfy that craving. Years later, when her childhood was long over, Liza and Vincente would both take great pleasure in the telling of an anecdote that demonstrated his slavish devotion to her.

As the story goes, one day when Liza was four, Vincente drove for over an hour to take her to the Ice Capades. But once they arrived, Liza informed him she didn't like the dress she was wearing. Undaunted, Vincente drove all the way home, waited while she changed, and then drove back again. Given that the extra two-hour drive must have meant

that by the time they arrived the second time, the Ice
Capades would have been nearly over, the whole anecdote
seems highly apocryphal.

Its meaning, however, was crystal clear: when Vincente
was with Liza, he did everything humanly possible to en-
velop her in a tidal wave of love and attention. His love cast
a spell on her. He was the first man who would ever love her,
and for the rest of her life she would search in vain for another man whose love for her would equal Vincente's.

Liza's life with Vincente revolved around the studio. Zsa
Zsa Gabor, who made *Lovely to Look At* with Vincente, recalls, "We would film at MGM and I would look up at the
boom and see this tiny little girl with enormous brown eyes
staring down at me. That was Liza."

Makeup artist Charles Schramm, who was at MGM for
thirty years and worked with both Judy and Vincente and
then with Liza (on *Tell Me That You Love Me, Junie Moon*),
remembers Vincente as being condemned to the classic dilemma of the divorced father. Trying to work yet desperate
to entertain his hyperactive little daughter, he would take
her to the studio and then entrust her to the care of the
makeup artist. "She would come down to the makeup department, and I would give her some clay to work with. She
was just a little girl being taken care of by her father's secretary, because there was no one else to look after her."

The bond which Vincente formed with Liza was unshakable, a product of his loneliness, guilt, and longing for a
soulmate. To Liza, the image of her father was (and remains)
that of a loving magician whose power and personality were
meshed with the magic of Hollywood and with motion
pictures.

When she was five, she imperiously demanded, "Daddy,
I want you to direct me." Vincente's mind was currently
occupied by the sets for *An American in Paris,* and at first,
he didn't grasp the significance of his diminutive daughter's
ingenuous request. Then Liza elaborated, "I want you to get
mad at me and shout just like you get mad at other people."

Vincente's temper became part of his appeal for her,

something that did not displease her. Looking back, she said, "He'd take me on the set when he was directing, and he'd yell a lot; he was like working with Caesar. At night he couldn't remember it. I'd say, 'Daddy, you yell so badly,' and he'd say, 'I did? When?' He didn't yell for effect. He did it to get things done. I never felt intimidated. He'd never put me in that position."

When she was older, Liza said that she was bored at MGM, only liked watching musical sequences, and had no interest whatsoever in acting. Nevertheless, Vincente, treating her as his equal, even when she was a small child, gave her tips on acting, advising, "Always listen to the director." Liza never forgot Vincente's advice, in the future telling all and sundry, "I'm just the director's daughter," clinging to the phrase as if it were a talisman.

For now, at least, she was the director's *only* daughter. And she luxuriated in every second of Vincente's attention, guarding him as passionately as if she were a grown woman fearful of losing the one man she had ever loved.

With an innocent lack of insight, Vincente gleefully recorded in his autobiography that at Liza's sixth birthday party, "Some little girl came over and she sat on my lap and I kissed her. And I didn't notice that Liza was watching and she came over and punched me on the nose. It was so completely unlike her. The attitude was 'that was for nothing. Now watch it!' " Vincente's tone is indolently amused and he is unaware that Liza's raging jealousy verged on the unhealthy.

Every year he presented her with five costumes designed by Adriane or Irene Sharaffe and scaled down to fit her. To her delight, Liza's costumes were replicas of those worn by actresses in such films as *An American in Paris*, *The King and I*, and *The Band Wagon*.

There are those who claim that Vincente was an absentee father, that Liza has idealized him beyond recognition. Whatever the truth, the most tangible proof she had of Vincente's love, his caring, and the special place she retained in his heart were the costumes he had so lovingly created for

her. Even as an adult, when discussing Vincente, Liza painstakingly detailed the costumes. They symbolized his love for
her, his creativity, and the fantasy world into which she and
Vincente so often retreated together.

Vincente photographed Liza in her costumes and, even
as a small child, she understood what those photographs
meant, clung to them, and accorded them pride of place in
her tiny universe. George Hamilton's mother, Anne, was a
close friend of Judy's and from the time that Liza was born
felt an instinctive need to mother her. To this day, she has
fond memories of Liza's sweet-natured consideration for others. "Once, when she was seven years old, I remember she
was showing me photographs that were taken of her in all
the little costumes that Vincente made for her. Suddenly,
she looked at me and said, 'Are you tired?' She was so sweet
and considerate. I don't think she has a mean bone in her
body."

In late September of 1952 Liza was taken to the set of *The
Band Wagon*. Years later, in her tribute, *Minnelli on Minnelli,* Liza said she was unable to pick her own personal
favorite of Vincente's films, but that she loved the scene in
The Band Wagon in which Fred Astaire sang and danced,
ecstatic that he'd just had his shoes shined. To Liza, that
scene demonstrated her father's belief, "Everybody searches
for a little magic."

Forever after influenced by Fred Astaire, she would one
day ask Halston to design clothes for her that would make
her look like a female version of Fred Astaire. Watching
Astaire in *The Band Wagon* was also the basis of her ambition to be a dancer. Very early on, she studied at Nico Charisse's dance class and was always improvising to records
and giving musical and dance performances with her friends,
Amanda Levant and Gayle Martin.

She learned all her mother's stage routines and, free of
inhibitions, eagerly belted out Judy's songs like "Button Up
Your Overcoat" using a pine cone as a microphone.

On stage and off, when she was with her father, Liza was
outgoing and friendly. Yet, even at this early age, she was
wary of other people and their underlying motives. When

Vincente was making *The Long, Long Trailer*, with Desi
Arnaz and Lucille Ball, Madge Blake (who played Lucy's
aunt) met Liza and later wrote to Vincente praising her.

Madge Blake's letter reveals a great deal about Liza.
Madge describes her as talented, well mannered, and lovely
but notes that when she asked Liza where she went to
school, Liza instinctively didn't answer and, instead, went in
search of Vincente. Madge, a teacher herself, surmised that
she had been instructed never to answer personal questions
posed by prying strangers. Liza was seven at the time.

Her father was her protector and her shield, her teacher
and her mentor. "I was always a daddy's girl. He was so
wonderful, supportive, patient," Liza remembered nostalgi-
cally. "He made me feel the prettiest, the best little girl in the
world." Vincente was everything to Liza. And, until his life
changed once more, she was everything to him.

The flavor of Vincente's relationship with Liza is best
captured by Liza herself. When Vincente began writing his
autobiography Liza pointed out that the book lacked her
perception of him. So Vincente invited her to contribute
something to the book. Although she was writing in the late
seventies, Liza (a gifted writer) was with flawless accuracy
able to recapture her childhood memories and the voice of
the child she had once been.

Liza's two pages focus on the years between Vincente's
divorce from Judy when she was six and his remarriage
when she was eight. She evokes a routine suffused with love
and security. She is staying with him in his Hollywood home
in her room, "decorated to accommodate a passing fairy
princess," and Vincente in his room, "which smells of to-
bacco, warm colors, and thinking of all kinds."

She writes of Vincente at the studio working with Astaire and Charisse, and of dinners alone together as Vincente
tells her about Paris, and Colette. The essay ends as she and
Vincente part at eight thirty, when she is whisked away by
Judy's driver, and she says good-bye—"good-bye. I've always hated that word."

In his autobiography Vincente says, "I smothered her

with love. If I spoiled Liza outrageously, the fairy tale quality of our relationship achieved a balance with the starkness of her life with Judy. Much as Liza loved her mother, Judy represented duty and worry. I required nothing but love."

Despite Vincente's rationalizations, it was clear that his relationship with Liza, dominated by motion pictures and by his own need to spoil her unceasingly, emphasized escapism to such a degree that, as an adult, the most magnetically alluring form of reality for Liza would always be escape.

CHAPTER
THREE

Judy, never one to tolerate loneliness, quickly replaced Vincente in her life. Soon after the divorce, she became involved with Sid Luft. Luft was a piratical character, an entrepreneur, a brawler, and a gambler in the game of life. "He's a survivor, he's really a charming rogue. That's the way he describes himself," said Judy and Sid's daughter, Lorna, who would one day characterize her parents as "The Richard Burton–Elizabeth Taylor of the musical world." Everyone who saw them together agreed that in Sid Luft, Judy Garland had finally met her match. He was powerful and unstoppable, and, inasmuch as anyone could ever handle Judy, Sid was able to handle her. His attempts, however, would often lead to situations in which hate would predominate over passion and would ultimately damage their love.

Judy was now suspended from MGM and in 1951 was booked for the first of her many comebacks, this time at the London Palladium. Though already on the verge of marrying Sid, Judy did not neglect Liza, spending £434 (the 1951 equivalent to $12,000) on transatlantic telephone calls to her. Judy said proudly at the time, "Ever since I left home, either Liza or I have telephoned each other every day. It may have cost me a pound a minute since April, but it has been well worth it." The English papers also reported that Judy carried a folding metal photograph album of Liza wherever she went.

Vincente believed it was vital that Liza witness Judy's incredible talent firsthand so that she would understand the bright side of the rainbow. With that in mind, he stifled his innate longing to keep Liza to himself, and dispatched her to England, where she and her nanny spent a happy week with Judy, basking in her mother's triumphant reception in the country that had always loved her.

On her return, six-year-old Liza learned of Judy's marriage to Sid via the six o'clock news, discovering that the wedding had taken place three days earlier. And although her lower lip quivered tremulously, she drowned her sorrows by escaping into the familiar indulgence of an Eskimo Bar. Ice cream had always been her addiction and, as she grew older, she would often seek solace in food. Like Judy, throughout her life she would suffer from weight fluctuations, most dramatically at thirteen when she ballooned to a gargantuan 165 pounds. And, later in her life, her varying weight would continue to be a problem; designer Halston dealt with it by manufacturing every outfit he designed for her in three different sizes.

Liza's emotions about her new stepfather are not on record, but Vincente was happy about Judy's marriage, believing that Sid would bring her a measure of security. More than that, he was delighted that Judy and Sid had moved to California to begin production of *A Star Is Born*, which George Cukor was directing, and that Liza could live with them.

He desperately wanted Liza to have a good relationship with Judy, but the truth was inescapable. "Judy was most often doting with Liza, but there were times when neglect was inevitable; thankfully, I would now be around for Liza to turn to during these difficult times." It was undeniable that Liza's young life was already overshadowed with burdens. A

year after Judy's marriage to Sid, Vincente sadly acknowledged, "She was only seven, but onerous responsibilities
were already being delegated to her. In many ways, she
played mother to Judy's daughter."

Psychiatrists indicate that any child, even one as young
as Liza, senses a mother's feelings, which ultimately color,
and sometimes even become, her own. And no matter how
reassuring his tone, how steady his words, how all-embracing his love, Vincente was incapable of shielding Liza from
Judy's emotions.

For much as he would succeed in diverting Liza from the
truth by creating for her a wonderland filled with fantasy,
art, and beauty, ultimately Vincente would fail. Although he
did all in his power to enhance the sensitivity and creativity
she had inherited from him and from her mother, the dark
side of her inheritance would mark her future irrevocably.

Although Sid was far better equipped to cope with Judy
than Vincente had been, his relationship with her was inevitably marked by her drug use and her highly strung, often
hysterical personality. He did his utmost to dissuade her
from using pills and—just like Vincente before him—fought
a losing battle against her addictions.

As a result, although Judy's love for Liza was strong, it
was always overshadowed by Judy's own personal problems, which invariably took precedence. Even Liza, who
throughout her life has always taken immense pains to embellish Judy's image, in a rare and unguarded moment un-
willingly conceded, "My mother never gave up anything
for me."

Consequently, Liza, like many children of alcoholics,
schooled herself in the gut-churning art of maintaining appearances, at all costs. Evie Johnson was one of Judy's closest friends and remembers Liza as a small child. "When
things went wrong for Judy, Liza would worry desperately
and try to cover for her. I remember going over to Judy's
house and being greeted by Liza, looking really nervous saying, 'She's not down yet. But she *will* be down. . . .' "

During six months of each year when she inhabited

Judy's world, Liza alternated from being Judy's nurse, protector, secretary, to being defender of her public image. Once, a schoolmate derisively described Judy as a fat pig. Liza trudged home from school, crying all the way. When Judy asked what was wrong, she avoided answering but then finally broke down and blurted out the truth. Judy may have had her demons, but when it came to her children, to helping them cope with the hurts that life inflicted on them, she was a fighter, invincible, unshakable, and determined to impart her fighting spirit to Liza.

Taking her demoralized little daughter in her arms, Judy told her to wait until the very next time that her foe repeated his attack, instructing her then to "look him dead in the eye and say, 'My mother can get thin anytime she wants to, but your father couldn't get talent if he took twenty years of private lessons from Sir Laurence Olivier.'"

On November 21, 1952, Judy's second daughter, Lorna Luft, was born. Always adept at pleasing adults, at saying what was required, and at displaying a range of appealing emotions, Liza had repeatedly voiced a desire for a sister. She was six and a half now and had hitherto been an only child. If the birth of her new half sister undermined what little sense of security remained for her, Liza did not exhibit any signs of sibling rivalry.

As years went by, Liza's only complaint was that she sometimes had to babysit for Lorna. Other than that, she treated her new little sister with great affection, quickly accepting Lorna into her world. There was no rebellion, no tantrums, nothing. When it came to her life with Judy, Liza knew nothing else but acceptance.

Soon after Lorna's birth, Judy's fragile emotions plunged and she once again turned to pills. Sid Luft valiantly tried to dissuade her from taking them, but, like Vincente's, all his attempts disintegrated into violent arguments. Finally, when Lorna was just a few weeks old, Judy locked herself into her bedroom and cut her own throat.

Sid, a man who loved control and normally exercised it, was in the midst of a horrifying nightmare. Quickly calling a doctor, he watched appalled as Judy was given stitches. Yet

less than a week after her suicide attempt, he threw a gigantic party for Hollywood's most prominent glitterati and
watched admiringly as Judy—her scars covered by her high-
necked dress—sang with the same innocence and freshness
that had warmed the world's heart in *The Wizard of Oz*
nearly fifteen years before.

When Liza was seven, Judy and Sid moved into a big
Norman-style chateau next door to Lana Turner. And although Lana's daughter, Cheryl, was two years older than
Liza, they became firm friends. In her memoir, *Detour: A
Hollywood Story* (written with Cliff Jahr), Cheryl reminisced, "We were both well-known star babies with Sunday
fathers and outrageous mothers, so we understood each
other and could share problems.

"I was impressed by how much she knew about her
mother's career and personal problems. She had seen every
one of Judy's movies."

It was unusual for Liza to confide anything about Judy's
personal problems to anyone, so it must have come as a
welcome change for her, at seven, to be able to pour out her
heart to a friend. Trained to be loyal and to keep the family
secret of Judy's addiction to drugs and alcohol, Liza only
cracked momentarily when she suggested to Cheryl Crane
that she and Cheryl trade mothers. Amused, Lana and Judy
agreed to go along with the experiment, but it soon faltered.

In those days, Hollywood was still a village and the news
of Judy's descent into drugs and alcohol had spread rapidly.
No matter how badly Liza wanted to shield Judy's frailties,
no matter how valiantly she attempted to hide the facts,
close friends and neighbors inevitably observed the truth.
Evie Johnson confirms that although Judy was a wonderful
mother, Liza's life with her and Sid was an immense strain
on the child. "Liza had a very difficult time with Judy. Judy
was protective of her, but she and Sid had big fights. She
used to come to my house and tell me he was trying to
kill her."

During one stormy night, Judy nervously paced the
floor with Evie Johnson by her side, trying to quiet her.
She made a shocking admission: her marriage to Sid Luft

was so tempestuous because she had fallen in love with ur-
bane British actor James Mason, her *A Star Is Born* co-star.
And Sid knew it.

Evie says, "Judy told me all about her crush on James
Mason. I don't know if Mason reciprocated, but I do know
that she hung around him as much as possible." According
to Evie, Judy, ignited by the possibilities she perceived in
Mason's smoldering eyes, did her best to elude Sid. In the
process, she sometimes drank herself into oblivion and
ended up on Evie Johnson's doorstep.

Ruefully, she remembers, "Sid would call my house a lot,
and ask if Judy was there. Judy, knowing he was on the line,
just shook her head and motioned, 'No, no, no' to me. So I
told Sid Judy wasn't with me, that I didn't know where on
earth she was. Then I'd do everything in my power to get her
sobered up. And when she finally recovered, I'd make her a
wonderful breakfast.

"Liza was a godsend to Judy. She was a very good,
charming little girl," says Evie Johnson. "When things were
going well for Judy, Liza would be a little homebody, clear-
ing the table when we went for cocktails."

Judy's mothering alternated between strictness and
emotional outbursts of love. Although the horrors of her
drug dependency inevitably colored her relationship with
Liza, Judy nevertheless strived to teach Liza values and
made an effort to give her life some degree of normalcy. She
was determined that Liza would not degenerate into a typical Hollywood brat and emphasized the importance of good
manners. Although Humphrey Bogart, Lauren Bacall, and
Lana Turner became Judy's neighbors, Judy played down
their profession to Liza and, later, to Lorna and Joey, refusing to allow them to see films during their childhood. Liza
once told a confidante, "People think that because my
mother had so many problems, my childhood with her was
nothing but drama. That isn't true. Mama was very strict and
brought me up with a lot of discipline."

Judy veered between martinet and crazed addict, and
Liza lived through all her various incarnations. The disciplinarian mother intent on imbuing her daughter with man-

ners and all the accoutrements of good breeding could, in a
flash, be transformed into a drugged harridan spewing out
threats of suicide.

As years went by, Liza would become adept at judging
which of her mother's suicide threats merited serious attention and which were merely desperate pleas for love. And
although Liza's instinct has always been to protect Judy's
image and salvage her offstage reputation, even she has
conceded that as a child (more times than she cares to remember) she was compelled to burst into a room and save
her mother's life. Then, when Judy was saved, her equilibrium restored, she would once more become the good
mother. Confused, traumatized, and insecure, Liza naturally
consistently sought refuge with her father.

CHAPTER FOUR

In 1953, seventeen-year-old half-French, half-Italian Christiane Martel was named Miss Universe and was offered a contract at Universal Studios in Hollywood. Christiane was from Nancy, in France, and her parents were apprehensive about sending their cherished young daughter to Hollywood alone. As a result, Christiane's twenty-two-year-old sister, Georgette, also classically beautiful, traveled and lived with her while they waited for their parents to join them in America.

Vincente had always been fascinated by France and all things French (a taste Liza would also acquire) and he was bowled over by the statuesque and dark Georgette, her "Frenchness," her openness, and her charm. Although she was glamorous enough to be a movie star, she shocked Vincente by disdaining the movies and categorically refusing to attempt to storm Hollywood. It quickly became clear to him that unlike Judy, Georgette was stable, sensible, an efficient money manager, and an ideal wife for a bachelor father grappling with life alone.

Vincente and Georgette married on February 16, 1954,

while he was directing *Brigadoon*. Liza now had a stepmother.

When Lorna was born, Liza had reacted to her birth with
equanimity. She was used to sharing Judy, first with Sid Luft
and now with Lorna. But Vincente was different. Liza had
always come first in Vincente's life and her hold over him
had been unchallenged. So it is understandable that she reacted to his new wife with a mixture of rebellion and wild,
uncontrolled emotion, hitting out as best she could at the
woman who had partially replaced her.

Long since remarried, the second Mrs. Minnelli recalls
the trials and tribulations of life with her former step-
daughter.

"I tried to treat Liza as if she were my own daughter.
When her father was around, she was very sweet to me, but
when he was out of the room, she would say terrible things
to me. I wasn't thin and Liza would look at me and say,
'You aren't really as fat as everyone says you are.' She was
not nice."

Georgette was able to ignore Liza's well-aimed barbs,
tried to understand her loneliness, and did her utmost not to
assume the clichéd role of wicked stepmother. "I took care of
her when she was sick. But when Vincente came home, she
would lie to him and complain bitterly that I'd left her alone
all day."

Liza equated love with getting her own way and Vincente continually capitulated to her every whim. Georgette
remembers, "As a child, Liza would want people to love her
very much. But she was just as set on getting her own way.

"I tried to be very diplomatic, but it was useless trying to
discipline Liza. If she didn't get her own way, she would have
terrible tantrums—screaming fits like a nervous breakdown.

"Vincente felt very guilty about Liza and wanted her to
be happy no matter what. He was afraid that if he didn't
make her happy, she wouldn't want to come to stay with
him. We had parties for twenty of her friends and we
wouldn't know what to do next to please them all and to
please Liza.

"Vincente always treated Liza as if she were a star. He saw her as a star because she really was very talented. He gave her everything he could. But when she couldn't get what she wanted from Vincente, she would cry and scream. I think most of the time she was acting. She knew she would get what she wanted if she screamed and cried. She was very intelligent—a strong character, even then, who knew exactly how to get what she wanted.

"She always wanted to stay up and watch a movie until midnight. Even after that, she had problems falling asleep so Vincente would stay with her and read her stories until she finally did."

Georgette employed a gourmet cook and Liza, instinctively grasping that meals were of vital importance to her new stepmother, retaliated accordingly. "Liza loved ice cream and ate that more than anything else. Vincente agreed to everything she wanted. And Jeanette, the nanny, was terrified of upsetting her. So when Liza demanded that she eat all her meals in her room, Vincente automatically allowed her to," says Georgette. "Liza's room was decorated all in white and Liza would eat all the food with her hands. When she had finished her dinner, the wallpaper was smeared with grease, the bed cover drenched in ketchup, with chocolate stains everywhere. I think she did it on purpose."

Liza wasn't Georgette's only problem. A practical, down-to-earth woman, she quickly discovered that marriage to the iconoclastic Vincente was fraught with obstacles. She was unnerved by his constant preoccupation with work, by his propensity for getting up in the middle of a meal and disappearing to another room, where, without a word to her, he proceeded to spend hours reading.

Then there was the matter of money. Vincente had never been concerned with finances, but Georgette was determined to change all that. She not only arranged an MGM pension for Vincente but made it clear that she intended that they both live on a budget. Vincente rebelled—particularly during Liza's jealous tantrums. Terrified that Liza would leave him and run home to Judy, he would rush out to the nearest toy store and buy her anything she wanted. When Georgette saw the price of the toy, she was not amused.

In April 1955, she gave birth to her own daughter, Christiane, whom she and Vincente affectionately dubbed Tina Nina. One of Georgette's first visitors after Tina Nina's birth was Judy, who came bearing gifts and congratulations. Georgette remembers, "Vincente was in another world. He was a dreamer. But Judy was really nice. She was happy being with Sid Luft so she had no reason to be jealous that I was now married to Vincente. I felt sorry for her. Vincente told me how MGM made Judy work so much when she was very young. They thought she was too fat and made her take diet pills. Then, because of the diet pills, she couldn't sleep at night so she would take sleeping pills."

If Judy was happy that Vincente had started a new life with a second family, Liza was not. On March 29, just a few weeks before Tina Nina was born, Judy had given birth to Joey Luft. Liza had coped admirably with the advent of yet another sibling. But this time, the new child was Vincente's.

From the moment that Tina Nina was born, Liza would cling to her identity as Vincente Minnelli's only daughter with the ferocity of a drowning woman clinging to a life raft. And she could hardly be blamed, for while Judy ricocheted from drug dependency to weight problems, from alcohol to depression, only Vincente was consistent, only Vincente was there for her. At the time she could not have known that she would never relinquish her place in Vincente's heart, nor that her power over him would never diminish. All she knew was that she now shared her father with another daughter.

But fate intervened and Liza only had to suffer the specter of Tina Nina's living with her father year round for four years before they separated. Georgette and Vincente divorced after five years of marriage, and Tina Nina went to live in Mexico with her mother, her grandparents, and her aunt. After the divorce, according to the custody agreement, Tina Nina spent two to three months a year with Vincente in

California. This was often during the time when Liza was staying with him, since she only lived half the year with him, and the other half with Judy.

Today, Tina Nina, the mother of Vincente Minnelli's two grandchildren, Vincente and Xeminia, lives in Mexico City. Her life has always been lived far from the spotlight, far from her half sister Liza, far from the benefits and tributes to her late father to which she has never been invited. As far as Hollywood and the world in general are concerned, Vincente Minnelli only had one daughter—which may well be just the way Liza wanted it. Yet despite Liza's tendency to ignore her half sister's existence, Tina Nina's memories of Vincente Minnelli's other daughter add an extra facet to the portrait of Liza's extraordinary childhood:

"My earliest memories of Liza are of her waiting for Daddy every night and, when he arrived, showing him what she had learned during the day, the new songs, the new steps; she was very talented. She was very hyperactive and full of energy. She had such big brown eyes, always searching for something.

"Daddy had beautiful costumes made for both of us at MGM. I remember Liza in one of those costumes, a long red strapless dress. We always played make-believe games, sang songs and read books together. Daddy always had the most wonderful art books. He loved them so much and we learned to love them too.

"He always told us stories. He was such a loving father. He would never say no to anything we wanted and he would never spank us. He spoiled us both.

"He never told me if I ever did anything wrong. I remember him asking me where I wanted to go to lunch. When I said it didn't matter, he said, 'I really want to please you. Even if you have to flip a coin, you have to make a decision, because later on, when you are older, some young man will ask to take you out and he will want to please you and he will want to know.' "

Although Tina Nina was nine years younger than Liza and remembers her mostly as an adolescent, she learned very early on never to mention the name Judy Garland to her.

"I knew that the subject of Judy was a very delicate one. Daddy and Liza would say things to each other like, 'Mama did this in that movie,' or, 'Remember when she sang that song.' And Daddy told me that Judy was a wonderful person. He never talked badly about her, ever."

Aware that Liza often suffered with her mother, becoming inextricably intertwined in Judy's ups and downs, Tina Nina felt a great deal of compassion for her half sister and says, "I knew how hard the situation was on Liza. She would live with her mother for six months and help her through all her inner conflicts. Then she would live with Daddy for six months and he would be working and trying to pay attention to her at the same time.

"Liza was much more at ease, much closer to Daddy than I was. She had her mother, but although Judy had her ups and downs, Liza had her on a pedestal. But Daddy was her stability and Liza was practically in love with him. She worshipped him and he worshipped her. He didn't have a family, other than an aunt. All he had was Liza. He gave her so many things and she says he, and not her mother, taught her to sing.

"It was a special family, Daddy, Liza and I. I always thought of Liza as my sister and Daddy did everything he could to encourage our relationship. When I was in Mexico, I would always write to Daddy and when he got my letters he would call Liza immediately and read them to her.

"Years later, she told me that she felt so jealous of me when I was with her and Daddy, and that she had hated it when Daddy had called her and read my letters. But that was normal. Daddy was all she had. He was alone and she was alone. They only had each other.

"Daddy and Liza were so close that she would get jealous when I arrived. Sometimes she pretended to be sick. Then Daddy rushed into her room and comforted her. I remember her lying in bed and crying, 'Daddy, you don't care about me. You only care about Tina Nina. I'm jealous of Tina Nina.' I felt so guilty.

"Other times she would be very sweet to me. When I arrived, she would kiss me and we would be glad to see each other. Then we would have the usual problems sisters have. Once I remember she was taking a picture of the dog and I wanted to be in it and she locked me into a room. But all that was normal. She was used to having Daddy to herself all the time."

Although Liza and Tina Nina stayed in touch as adults, their relationship was severed when Vincente died and Tina Nina challenged his will. Yet Tina Nina still, even today, considers Liza her sister and thinks back to their times together with a degree of fondness.

"Was Liza a happy child? She was very full of energy, but I don't know if she was happy. She was always dancing and acting in front of the mirror. It was a fantasy world, make-believe all the time. But that fantasy world helped her survive a life that was very difficult. And I couldn't really tell when Liza was acting and when she wasn't."

CHAPTER FIVE

Just before her twelfth birthday, Vincente took Liza to a dinner party at Lee Gershwin's house on North Roxbury Drive in Beverly Hills. The atmosphere was rich with the resonance of some of the world's most famous voices, all close friends of the Gershwins. Roger Edens played the piano after dinner, Gene Kelly and Frank Sinatra sang, then Roger asked Liza to sing. Gene Kelly recalled, "Until that time I thought Liza was a sweet gawky kid with big open eyes just like her father's. But she had something." When Gene suggested Liza appear on his television special (which was scheduled to air on April 24, 1959), Vincente asked Judy's permission. Judy agreed. Together Liza and Gene sang "For Me and My Gal," the same song that Gene had first sung with Judy in 1942.

During rehearsals, Liza picked up the dance steps quickly, and after the show (in front of a live audience), Gene marveled at her coolness, her lack of stage fright, her performing as if she was a seasoned veteran. As he later observed, "I don't think it harmed her having two talented parents, but I don't think you can say it gave her talent."

After the performance Liza told Vincente that her debut had been fun but her first love was still dancing.

She and debonair actor George Hamilton (who had had a small part in Vincente's film *Home from the Hill*) were neighbors and friends. She and George danced together for Vincente, regaling him with all the latest rock and roll steps. Liza was infatuated with George and he became her first teenage idol.

George Hamilton's mother, Anne, and her other son, David, visited the set of *Home from the Hill*, where she observed Liza during her agonizingly awkward ugly duckling years and remembers, "We were all in Paris, Texas, and Liza was down with her father and a nanny. She was on the set. Liza was crazy about George. She had a crush on him. One day, on the set, she was watching George do a scene and was chewing gum while she watched. Suddenly, a bit of chewing gum got caught in her hair and she was so embarrassed. I said to the nurse, 'The poor child has chewing gum on her hair. Do something about her hair; cut it off!' "

George's brother, David, says, "I remember her on the set with Robert Mitchum and George Peppard. They were all sitting around and Liza was massaging George's neck while he was relaxing. She was so sweet and nice to everyone. But they never dated. She was too young."

Once filming was over, Liza returned to L.A., where Vincente was still the center of her life, Tina Nina, an occasional visitor, and her mother, the source of drama, excitement, and worry.

But despite everything, Judy insisted that Liza concentrate on her studies, and once said, "What I missed most when I was a child star was an education. It wasn't a bit of good going into a cabin to do twenty minutes of history with a private tutor and then coming out to sing a song. I've never had time to play. I have a daughter, Liza. Like all the children, she'll go through college. She can do what she likes when she's got an education, but not before."

Judy oversaw Liza's education with a fanaticism that catapulted Liza from school to school so that in the end, she attended fourteen schools in all. In the summer of 1960, she arranged for her to spend a few months in Annecy, France, where she shared a pension with six other American girls and learned French, the language which her father loved so much and which would prove useful to her career in the future. Liza was lonely and took comfort in the nearby (but inaccessible) presence of singer Bobby Darin, who was performing in the next town. And although she never managed to meet her current teen idol, his very existence sustained her in her solitude.

While on holiday in Rome during the same summer, the film producer Sam Spiegel and his wife, Betty, introduced Vincente to Denise Gigante, a flamboyant Yugoslavian socialite who had been married to a wealthy businessman. Denise was glamorous, glittering with a tremendous allure. "I knew Denise for years. She was a beguiling girl, always very attractive, very ambitious. Vincente was nuts about her," recalled the late socialite Doris Lilly.

When Liza's French course was over, she visited Vincente in Paris, where, at the Georges V Hotel, he introduced her to Denise. Secure in her place in Vincente's heart, Liza was prepared to grant her father's current dalliance a brief audience. But, to her surprise, Denise did not fawn all over her. Always exotically elegant, with blond streaked hair which she often twisted into a braid, at their first meeting Denise was wearing a black broadtail suit and low-heeled black shoes. Liza, in contrast, was sporting a Brigitte Bardot look with white patent leather high heels (which Denise noted were dirty), full felt skirt, and a tight white angora sweater.

Ever sensitive and instantly aware of the negative impression that she had made on the stylish Denise, Liza apologized for looking terrible, whereupon Denise vowed to graft some glamour onto Liza's somewhat bedraggled appearance.

On December 31, 1960, Vincente and Denise were married at Anne and Kirk Douglas's house in Palm Springs, with actor Laurence Harvey as best man. Denise, now Liza and Tina Nina's stepmother, made an instant impact on their

lives. Until Vincente's marriage to Denise, Tina Nina's
grandmother always accompanied the little girl to California. But, according to Georgette, "Denise wanted to assume
control of her new household completely, so she asked that
Tina Nina's grandmother not come with her again and she
also fired the gourmet cook I had hired."

"As a child, I didn't like Denise. I was kind of scared of
her," says Tina Nina. "For a time my mother wouldn't send
me to Daddy because she didn't know Denise. But she knew
Daddy and she knew how incredibly weak he was with
women. Denise tried to be nice to me. Maybe she *was* nice,
but I was shy. I wanted to be with my Daddy. But I never
expressed my feelings whatever."

Nor, it seems, did Liza now. For Denise was not subjected
to the same histrionic displays of jealousy Georgette before
her had encountered. Although Liza's love for Vincente was
still strong, she was maturing into an adolescent with her
own interests, goals, and plans for a show business career.
Denise remembers, "From the moment that we met, Liza
and I developed a wonderful relationship. She was charming
and I used to say she was 'my girl.' "

In contrast, Tina Nina, whose happiness depended on the
goodwill of her new stepmother, was left to struggle with her
negative emotions about the third Mrs. Minnelli. Tina Nina
remembers, "Denise always wore pajamas all the time. She
tried to be nice, tried to be funny, but she scared me. At the
time, I never spoke to Liza about what we really felt. Liza
was the kind of person who never talked negatively about
anyone. But I couldn't go up to Daddy and say, 'Daddy, I'm
afraid of Denise.' I kind of knew what he was going to answer. I couldn't say the same to Liza because ten minutes
before, Liza had just said how wonderful Denise was, but I
didn't know if she really meant it."

Whatever Liza or Tina Nina's feelings, Denise set about
transforming Vincente's hitherto quiet life into a more lively
existence. Commented Doris Lilly, "Vincente was famous
and Denise was extremely elegant, social and had many
friends from international society.

"She and Vincente had a pretty house just off Sunset

where Denise used to throw a lot of dinner parties and make a great deal of pasta or take friends out to elegant dinners. It was a good marriage for him; she made a very good home for him. She entertained for him. She had nice friends from all over the world."

Denise herself adds, "Merle Oberon and Rosalind Russell were my friends and Mrs. Samuel Goldwyn was my mentor, but Vincente was very shy and never went out. Before we met, the only friends he used to see were Ira and Lee Gershwin and Oscar Levant."

At first, Denise endeavored to alternate the social whirl with an element of peace and quiet, explaining, "I keep perfectly silent unless my husband wants to talk. At home I make sure that there are no outside noises like doors banging or telephones ringing. I encourage him to unwind." Vincente concurred, "My wife is a very relaxing influence." Always stylish and original, Denise soon became one of Hollywood's leading hostesses.

At the time of Vincente's first meeting with Denise, Liza was living in London with Sid and Judy. They had rented a house at 213 Kings Road, Chelsea, and Liza attended Dixon and Wolfe Tutorial College on 25 Victoria Street. Mrs. Daly, who taught Liza and is now retired, remembers Liza as an average student. "She was friendly and polite to everyone. When she eventually became a star, I was really surprised, because at school she was like all the other girls. I had no idea she was so talented. Her only problem, I think, was that one or two of the girls tried to make friends with her just because her mother was Judy Garland. But Liza coped with it all splendidly."

Coping, by now, had become Liza's specialty. Aside from having to cope with her father, her new stepmother, and her half siblings, she was also compelled to cope with the three faces of Judy: Judy, the good mother, who aspired to give Liza the education she had never had; Judy, the addict who needed drama, drugs, and drink; and Judy Garland, the legend, mobbed by adoring fans wherever she went.

Adept at deciphering Judy's every move and reacting

accordingly, Liza comforted, protected, and guided her mother through the vicissitudes of her stormy marriage to Sid Luft. And although the London press, as always, idolized Judy, one or two journalists couldn't help remarking on her nails, which were bitten to the quick, and on Liza's, which were in the same condition.

Liza loved London, gorged herself on bangers and mash, and window shopped all over town. In the course of one shopping trip, she hired a London taxi and during the journey was informed by the chatty driver, "Now I know you. You are the daughter of—I'll get it in a minute—Deanna Durbin."

"Stop the cab," shrieked Liza, "I'm getting out."

She guarded her mother's legend fiercely, applauding more loudly and fervently than the most zealous fan when Judy opened at the London Palladium. That night, Liza not only sat next to the duke of Windsor (who knew all of Judy's songs and sang along with her) but at the after-show party marveled at the magnitude of her mother's ability to dazzle and to play the diva par excellence.

Judy played many roles and Liza witnessed every one of them. She adored the divine Judy, the Judy who could break your heart minutes after having warmed it blazingly. And she worshipped and nurtured the tragic Judy, the Judy who needed more love than any other human being and who craved it from everyone she knew, especially her own daughter.

In return, Judy did her utmost to be a caring and loving mother to Liza. She promised her that on the day Liza became a woman, they would toast the occasion together. But when Liza finally began menstruation and Judy attempted to live up to her promise, mother and daughter discovered that an ever vigilant Sid Luft had locked up all the liquor. So they ended up toasting the event with cooking wine, laughing uproariously. Judy always transformed everything into a game. It was you and me against the world, Judy and Liza together, *egoisme à deux,* closer to sisters than to mother and daughter.

But there was no consistency, not then, not ever. The

traumas of Liza's life with Judy were made public three years later, in a Santa Monica courtroom in October 1964, during Sid and Judy's fight for the custody of their children, Lorna and Joey. Verne Alves, a Luft associate, described a night in May 1961 that typifies the manic, wild state Judy often got into and Liza was forced to deal with: "Following a performance in Philadelphia, I went to sleep in an adjoining room of their hotel. She had started drinking earlier in the evening. She suddenly became very noisy and was screaming and hollering accusations. She was running from room to room without any clothes on. She kicked at the television and behaved in such a manner that it terrified me. All the time, I was trying to catch her, she was bouncing off the walls. And the last thing I did was to capture her before she got out of the window."

He also told of a time when Judy had been in a hotel room for a few days with a throat ailment: "She summoned all her employees into her hotel room, one at a time and fired them all, including myself. Following these mass firings, she got out of bed and fell to her knees. It was the last time I saw her for two or three years. In a normal day she drank or used five or six bottles of alcohol."

During the same case, when questioned by Sid Luft's lawyer, Saul Bernard, housekeeper Rhonda Chiolak said of Judy, "She often locked herself in her room all day and didn't come out until 4:00 P.M. for breakfast. She was often screaming and had to be calmed down."

There was also Judy, the teacher, an unparalleled professional whose advice to Liza would stand her in good stead throughout her own acting career. In 1961, in *Judgment at Nuremberg,* Judy played the part of a German girl who was a witness in the trial of an old man whom the Nazis had accused of having had sex with her. The man was innocent and had always treated Judy's character as a daughter, while she had always viewed him as a father figure. During filming, Judy gently explained to Liza that she had found the necessary emotions for the part by reaching deep into her soul and imagining those same unjust charges having been made against her own beloved father, Frank Gumm.

Judy's Method acting paid off and she went on to win an Oscar nomination for Best Supporting Actress. The press, however, preferred to focus on Judy the neurotic mother, rather than on Judy the accomplished actress, reporting that when she flew home from Toronto after *Judgment at Nuremberg,* she sat next to Sid Luft on the plane praying and clutching photographs of her children.

She loved them passionately and congratulated herself for not spoiling Liza and her other children and staying true to her firm belief that spoiled children wouldn't get along in the world. Again and again she asserted that she was very, very proud of their honesty, and of their ability to love and to be loved.

In January 1961, Liza attended New York's celebrated High School of Performing Arts, which was immortalized in the film *Fame*. Then, later that year, she worked in summer stock at the Hyannisport Summer Playhouse in Massachusetts. Her official title was that of apprentice. She received no salary but gloried in playing bit parts in *Flower Drum Song, Wish You Were Here,* and *Take Me Along*. She loved acting; there was no more talk of a dancing career.

Vincente and Denise, Judy and her agent, David Begleman, all went to see one of Liza's performances at Hyannisport together. Denise recalls, "We all flew out together. My relationship with Judy had always been very harmonious. In fact, I met her two years before I met Vincente, when actor Rosanno Brazzi introduced us. She had a fabulous talent and was great fun. And I liked her very much. Really, though, Vincente had a far greater influence on Liza than Judy did. There was never any question that she was his daughter, even down to the soles of their feet. Vincente and Liza had identical hands and feet."

Vincente observed, "Judy and I were two enormously explosive people. Any actor or actress who is any good has temperament and the director makes allowances. But if they happen to be married, it can become unbearable. Now we are no longer married, we are perfectly good friends. We all thought Liza was wonderful." Judy added, thoughtfully,

"Liza will one day be better than I ever was as an actress."

Once summer was over, Judy moved to Mamaroneck in Westchester County, New York, and Liza was enrolled at Scarsdale High School. She spent six months there, although she wasn't always happy. Scarsdale was as wealthy an area as Beverly Hills but Liza found the other girls at the school more snobbish than her Hollywood friends, and with her quick wit and highly developed sensitivity, complained that they weren't very bright. Moreover, many of them had attended the school for years and Liza, the new girl in town, felt rootless and ill at ease.

Acting proved to be her salvation. She threw herself into rehearsals for the school production of *The Diary of Anne Frank,* in which she had been cast as the lead. The play premiered on December 8, 1961, and Judy and Sid went to see the show. Afterward, wonderstruck at the emotion Liza brought to the part, Judy raved, "I've always known she was a marvelous dancer but she dazzled Sid and me with her performance. She was very professional about rehearsals, took direction only from her director and wouldn't let Mama butt in with free advice."

"Liza, at that time, was not what one would consider a scholar. She was not academic and was much more interested in performing," recalled Robert Hazeltine, today still a teacher at Scarsdale High, in Liza's day technical adviser to the theater group. "She was an awfully nice girl, I thought, very enthusiastic about the theater. With lots of energy in that score. She displayed a lot of talent."

CHAPTER SIX

She was fifteen but, as precocious as she was in most areas of her life, Liza (apart from her crush on George Hamilton and her long-distance passion for Bobby Darin) had never been in love. Now, she started dating, but, like everything else in her life, Liza's dating began unconventionally.

Tom Cooper was a twenty-one-year-old singer from Kansas who as a teenager became obsessed by *A Star Is Born* and made his own eight-millimeter-one hour version of the film, featuring local actors. Judy heard of the film and then contacted Tom asking to see it. Impressed by Tom's enterprise, she and Sid subsequently befriended him. Later, in January 1962, Tom met Sid at the Hollywood Golden Globe Award nomination party and the conversation turned to Liza. "I was about twenty," he says. "I was chatting with Sid and I had seen Liza's picture in a movie magazine so I mentioned, 'You know Liza is starting to get grown up; she's a very pretty girl.'

"Sid said, 'Really, you think so? In that case, I want you

to date her. She doesn't have many friends. I want you to call her tonight. Will you promise?' "

Feeling helpless in the face of Sid's strong pressure, yet curious about Liza, Tom agreed. And as he says ruefully, "I was almost forced into dating Liza by Sid." Sid's involvement in Liza's romantic life may have been intrusively bizarre. But in time, Judy would follow suit and arrange a date for Liza that would have far-reaching consequences.

As promised, Tom telephoned Liza that same night. "Liza came to the phone and I said, 'Your Dad told me to call.' She didn't seem in the least bit shy and grouched, 'He's always trying to fix me up.' But she didn't seem that disturbed and went on to ask me to tell her all about myself. I told her I was singing at the Hilton, and the second I got the words out, Liza cried, 'Oh wow, you're a professional singer!! I want to meet you because I want to be in show business.' I said, 'Maybe next week, we can—' but Liza interrupted me and asked, 'What are you doing tonight?'

"She was very unpretentious, very eager, very enthusiastic, but one of her problems was that she didn't think she was pretty. Also, she didn't want people to know she was Judy's daughter. She was very up-tight about that. I think that she felt that people might want to be her friend because Judy Garland was her mother. I think that at certain times she even felt that about me."

Tom paints his relationship with Liza as the kind of alliance formed by Judy and Mickey Rooney in countless MGM musicals. "Liza and I went out almost every night for five months. First I picked her up at the house, and then we would go out on the town, to restaurants and places where we could get in," he says, adding, "Liza loved watching shows because she wanted to be an entertainer and wanted to be in show business.

"She was not your normal fifteen-year-old who can hardly articulate two intelligent words. Liza was so much fun, so eager, and she was so enthusiastic about my singing. When we went out, she would cajole, 'Come on, Tommy, you sing me a few songs, and then I'll sing some songs to you.' And we would sing together. Often she'd say, 'Now you try this rare Garland song that I haven't heard before.' She was thrilled whenever I discovered a song that she didn't know."

Liza's innocent carefree evenings with Tom provided a crucial counterpoint to much of the rest of her life during 1962. Judy and Sid's love affair had evolved into bitterness and, in the first week of April 1962 they separated. Judy became embroiled in the first of a series of custody fights over Lorna and Joey. The stress was too much for her high-keyed temperament and, on April 17, 1962, Judy was in a New York hospital suffering from nervous exhaustion.

Bullishly determined to retain custody of his children, Sid wrested Lorna and Joey away from Judy. Discovering that the children were with him at the Stanhope in New York, Judy begged Liza to intercede with Sid so that he would allow her to take Lorna and Joey to London, where she was due to start shooting *I Could Go On Singing*. Liza, never yet able to refuse her mother anything, confronted Sid at the Stanhope and, her eyes burning with intensity, her slim hands fluttering nervously, pleaded with him to let the children go. But he remained immovable. Then Judy's body-guards swung into action, holding Sid helpless as Liza, Lorna, and Joey scrambled into a waiting limousine. Three days later, Judy was alone at the Savoy Hotel in London. The children had been sequestered in a hideaway at a secret location just outside London, protected by bodyguards.

By May, they were back with her at the Savoy, watched over twenty-four hours a day by bodyguards Judy had employed. Weakened by her battle with Sid, she whimpered, "I don't know why Sid says I am an unfit mother. The children love me. I hear he may be coming over to Britain to try to take them away from me. He will never do that. There is no chance at all of a reconciliation."

Digressing from the custody fight, in a conversation with her friend, Noel Coward, Judy summed up her philosophy of mothering: "I came into show business after the real great days and before television. Really, it was awful, vaudeville, you know, so there was nothing very inspiring. But my children are being exposed to all the best. I want them to be exposed to theater. I think it's rather stupid to be involved in making movies or whatever and just leave your children every morning. I take them along with me.

"They have been backstage in the wings. They know what I do when I go to work. And you know it isn't a bad atmosphere. It's fun for our children to go to the theater. And I think that as long as I have a good relationship with them and our home life is a good one, the entertainment world can't possibly hurt them. I don't know whether any of them will become entertainers or not.

"My oldest daughter, Liza, is talented and sort of stuck on the business. She started to dance when she was five. And she's a brilliant dancer, really. But now she's grown up with the best of talent. Her father, who is a very talented man, has exposed her to the very best of the theater, so she does have taste and she does have talent."

Liza was scheduled to tour Italy and Israel in *The Diary of Anne Frank* with the Scarsdale High students. But before she left, Liza spent time with Judy in London during the filming of *I Could Go On Singing* with Dirk Bogarde. The film, directed by Ronald Neame, was a soap opera style saga telling the story of an international superstar, Jenny Bowman, an alcoholic singer, a great survivor, determined that no matter how tragic her life, the show will always go on. The plot of *I Could Go On Singing* is the most autobiographical of all Judy's films, focusing on not only a singer's obsessive ambition but her tortured love for her child—a love which is doomed to be swamped by the unresolvable demands of her career.

"Judy was at the end of her tether during the filming. She used to stay up all night because she couldn't sleep, then, around five in the morning she would take a sleeping pill. Naturally, after that, she was unable to get up at seven and get to the studio on time. She would make all kinds of excuses. But all along, Liza was a support to her," remembers the then long-suffering Ronald Neame.

"Judy made endless attempts at suicide, always leaving the door open for somebody to rescue her, and her temperament, her unhappiness, all rebounded on Liza in a big way. But Judy still cared about her and Liza was never neglected. She seemed very sensible, very bright, outgoing, warm and happy.

"In return, Liza was always warm to Judy and behaved towards her in the most natural way possible. She was very good around her.

"Liza's talent was already apparent. I remember being with her at Dirk Bogarde's house and her singing to us. You could tell that she had a voice and a talent that was beginning to emerge."

Judy clearly loved Liza but, when it suited her, wasn't above using their relationship as fodder for emotional black-mail. Neame recalls, "In the last two weeks before shooting was scheduled to end, all I needed was to shoot a scene centering around Judy in order to finish the picture. One morning, she phoned me at 3 A.M. and said she wasn't coming in. I asked her why and, her voice full of indignation, she stormed, 'Well, my daughter Liza is more important to me than your f——— picture!'

"I said, 'Well of course she is, but what has that got to do with anything?'

" 'Well,' she announced, 'Liza's flying to Israel tomorrow at eleven and I am going to the airport to see her off.'

"And I wailed, 'Oh, Judy, do you really have to see her off?'

"Judy was adamant, 'Yes, I definitely do. Liza is more important than anything else in the world to me.'

"I pleaded with her to get her hair and makeup done at home, then take Liza to the airport (which is only twenty minutes away from Shepperton Studios where we were shooting) and then get back to the studio for the afternoon. She hesitated for a while but in the end agreed to meet at the studio at twelve.

"Of course, Judy didn't arrive. And when we called her, I discovered that she was asleep and had left word that she wasn't to be disturbed until two. And she hadn't seen Liza off at all because she hadn't even gone to the airport."

* * *

Despite her mother's failure to take her to London airport, a crushed Liza made it to Athens, Greece, where on
July 3 she joined the *Anne Frank* tour. The tour lasted for
over a month and provided Scarsdale High teacher Robert
Hazletine with further opportunity to observe Liza at close
range.

He says, "None of us knew she was a talented singer
and dancer because, up until that point, all we had seen her
in was *The Diary of Anne Frank*. Then, when we were in
Tel Aviv, all of us, Liza and the cast, went out together one
evening to a café for soda and ice cream. Liza went off to
the ladies room, and while she was away from the table,
somebody drank her soda. When she came back, I said,
'Well, you are just going to have to sing for your supper, I
guess.' She gulped and then said, 'OK.' Then she went up
on this bandstand and, before we knew it, started singing
'San Francisco.' No one outside the café knew that Liza was
Judy Garland's daughter and the amazing thing is that as
soon as she began singing, a big crowd gathered around to
hear her. Her presence was so strong that she commanded
instant attention.

"I also remember coming back from Florence to Rome on
a train and Liza happened to be sitting opposite me. All the
other kids were exhausted and had gone on to sleep so I
started chatting to her. I said, 'You know, Liza, I've always
loved the movie *A Star Is Born*, in which your mother sang
a song called "I Was Born in a Trunk." ' And Liza cried
enthusiastically, 'Oh yes, I know that!' Then I asked her to
sing it for me, and she said. 'Sure.' That was one of the most
amazing experiences of my life, listening to Liza singing to
me on that train traveling through Italy. She was a sweet
girl."

It isn't difficult to imagine Liza's chagrin at first being
cajoled into singing for her supper and next being further
mortified by the request to sing one of her mother's songs.
But then and always, Liza exhibited an inordinately strong
desire to please, to be pleasing, and, at that stage, hadn't yet
mastered the ability to refuse to replicate her mother's most
famous performances.

The philanthropist Dorothy L. Silverstone, who led the trip to Israel, centered more on Liza as a teenager than on the connotations of her relationship to Judy. "She was just a delightful girl. Offstage, she was also happy and friendly. She was so interested in everything. Whenever we stopped to look at any historical sights, Liza just ran from place to place, full of enthusiasm. She was very, very sweet, and she played the part of Anne Frank very sincerely. One of Israel's ministers was in the auditorium and said afterwards he had never seen a young actress give such a moving performance. She was so good."

In Israel, Liza's portrayal of Anne was so heartfelt that a reporter for the newspaper *Maariv* asked how she could understand Anne. Her reply reflects her sensitivity, as she thoughtfully answered, "Every young girl has the same problems with parents, with the lack of parental understanding. Every young girl has her first love."

Then she mused, "The audience here is quite different. At the moment in the play when the Germans come to pick up the Frank family, I looked at the audience and do you know what they seemed like—like the Germans were coming to pick them up too."

After Liza returned from her successful tour of Israel, Judy didn't deviate from her plan to give her a good, if eclectic, education and, with that goal in mind, enrolled her in a course in French civilization at the Sorbonne in Paris.

She was now sixteen. Eager and warmhearted, she remained somewhat childlike. Up till now, she had escaped relatively unscathed by the press, who were always ravenously hungry for stories about her mother. But in November 1962, Liza suffered her first public brush with illness. At London's Heathrow Airport, while waiting for a Paris flight, she felt faint, was treated by the airport doctor, then was detained at the airport for five hours until she recovered. The next day, Liza's airport incident was widely reported. She was Judy's daughter, the daughter of tragedy, and, to the ever vigilant media, even the smallest mishap in her life assumed staggeringly monumental proportions.

When she returned to Paris, Liza's stay there was brief. For once, she voiced her feelings. Although Vincente had attempted to inculcate her with his own love of Paris, Liza, at this point in her life, was not enamored of the City of Light, telling her mother that she felt unhappy and lonely there. Judy relented and, after just one term, agreed that Liza leave the Sorbonne. She left at the end of 1962, didn't graduate from high school, and never attended another school or university again. Her formal academic education was over.

I Could Go On Singing was released in England in January 1963, just two months after Judy had filed for divorce from Sid Luft. Liza's life, too, was undergoing a radical transformation. After a confrontation with Vincente at his suite in the St. Regis Hotel in New York, during which she proclaimed her intention to become an actress, Vincente, who would have supported Liza in any career, gave her his blessing. So did Denise, who added the caveat, "If you study hard in New York and do well, I will give you my white leather mink-lined coat." Liza had admired the coat the very first time the elegant Denise had worn it and, her heart set on an acting career, knew that the coat would soon be hers.

In Los Angeles, Liza broke the news of her decision to Judy. Judy first cautioned her, "I don't have to tell you what pressures you are going to be under. You've seen what's going to happen to you." Liza observed that she had, but "I'd also seen a little bit how to avoid them." Ever intuitive, Judy, knowing the extent of Liza's ambitions, the ferocity of her drive, gave her blessing. She did not, however, volunteer her money, making it clear that she would not finance Liza's bid for stardom.

Her speech completed, Judy heaved a sigh of relief. Next, with the instinct for drama that had helped make Judy Garland great, had elevated her to fame, fortune, and legend, she offered Liza a cigarette. And then mother and daughter, for the first time in their lives, smoked together. Since the age of five, Liza had lived her life on an adult plane, dealing with adult emotions, adult dramas, adult inconsistencies. She had never been a child, had always been an adult. Now, finally, in a grand gesture, her mother at last acknowledged the truth.

CHAPTER SEVEN

Hollywood was the logical starting point for the career of the daughter of Judy Garland and Vincente Minnelli. Instead, Liza focused on the Great White Way: "I wanted to be on Broadway. I didn't want to be a movie star. It was kind of virgin territory, the theater; not Hollywood, not the movies. It was not any place my parents were ever attached to."

When Liza first arrived in New York, in the new year of 1963, Frank Sinatra, aware that she was struggling to survive, with fatherly concern sent her five hundred dollars. Liza returned the check, too proud to accept hand-outs. Nevertheless, it was undeniable that her name would automatically gain her instant admission to any audition in town and she knew it, in a typical burst of honesty observing, "It's both a help and a hindrance to be the daughter of a big star. It's good because people will always see me and hear me. But there's always that thought of measuring up. It's a very funny feeling."

She auditioned for Arthur Whitelaw, the producer of an upcoming revival of the 1941 musical comedy *Best Foot For-*

ward, and won a secondary role in the production. "It's not just a matter of trading on famous names," said Arthur Whitelaw. "We had six kids from show business families who auditioned for us. Liza was the only one with talent. When she first auditioned, she was a scared kid. She sang in a very small voice. As she has gained in confidence, she has gained in talent."

Liza's talent, like her mother's, was laced with a high-strung nervousness. "Her hands were shaking so that I had to hold them just to stop them from shaking. She was so vulnerable I instinctively wanted to protect her," recalled then–press agent, writer Lawrence Eisenberg, who met Liza just before her seventeenth birthday.

Eisenberg wasn't alone in being touched and disarmed by Liza. So was the show's director-choreographer, Danny Daniels, who forged a lifelong professional alliance with her which still endured in 1991, when he directed her in *Stepping Out.* Throughout her life, she was to melt the hearts of those who worked with her. Part waif and part high-voltage bundle of energy, she was a prime candidate for adoption by anyone whose life she touched.

When Liza first arrived in New York, she lived on West End Avenue with actress Paula Wayne, who was also appearing in *Best Foot Forward.* "I was big sister when she needed it most," explained Paula, adding, "Liza, you must understand, never traded on being Judy's daughter. She worked like a dog."

In those early days in New York, she took voice lessons from David Sorin Collyer, one of America's foremost voice teachers and a talented singer-actor in his own right. Sorin Collyer had taught Bette Midler, Chita Rivera, and countless other singers. Liza worked with him for two years, during which time he judged, "She needed a fuller voice as she would get hoarse when she sang. So I taught her how to sing without forcing her voice down where the cords would rub together. I taught her to keep her larynx and her tongue down."

As Liza's teacher, he was constantly aware of her mother's voice reverberating through the years and says,

"The difference between Judy and Liza's voices is that Judy had a sweeter, softer voice. In contrast, Liza is a belter. Vocally, Liza does a lot of things that Judy did, and we didn't try to eradicate Judy from her voice. Like her mother, Liza is a wonderful actress and puts intense emotion into her singing."

During this period, Liza shared an apartment with another young actress, Tanya Everitt. Later, she would date Tanya's brother, a twenty-year-old dancer named Tracy, then appearing in *How to Succeed in Business without Really Trying*. Tracy and Liza met at a theatrical party in December 1962 and attended the same acting class in New York. But her strongest affinity, from the first, was with Tanya, who remembered, "We knew each other for a week when we decided to live together. Ly and I were very much alike. We didn't know a damn thing about money and just kept spending it until our accountant took us in hand. We were kooks, but in a funny way."

Tanya may depict their existence as simple, easy, and free of any responsibility, but in reality, Liza was already weighed down by the demands of her career. Booked to appear on the Jack Paar show, just before the *Best Foot Forward* premiere, always tentative about picking clothes, she took the plunge and went on a shopping spree, buying a navy blue outfit with accordion pleats and a blouse, then went to Lilly Daché for a hat. There, she was interviewed by drama writer, critic, and editor of *Week in Review* Jerry Tallmer. About this early press interview of Liza, he wrote, "One thing she unmistakably shared with her mother, in a way, on her own, is that immense vulnerability. It reveals itself, at least under these circumstances, in the pauses, the little low apologetic giggle, the breath between phrases."

During rehearsal, Liza fractured her foot but gamely soldiered on until the rehearsal was over. Immediately afterward, she was rushed to a hospital, the broken bone was diagnosed, and her leg was put into a cast. When she reached Judy, in tears, she begged her to contact the Jack Paar producers and break the news of her accident to them so that they could replace her on the show. Judy proceeded to give

Liza a lesson in turning the negative events of life into the positive, counseling, "Be sure to wear a cast. People will love it." Judy's vulnerability was her trademark, suffering the leitmotif of her life, and she knew how to exploit it.

Judy threw a party for Liza's seventeenth birthday at Le Club. According to guests, that evening, in anticipation of her first professional triumph, Liza was deliriously happy, bubbling over with joie de vivre.

Judy arrived decked out in rhinestones, sequins, and feathers, then danced and sang the night away. Yet, once again, her facade masked an ever increasing number of problems. Judy was still toying with the idea of going back to Sid and was staying at the Plaza, where she often suffered bouts of depression. During those bleak moments, Judy turned to Liza, who was then staying with venerable publicist Eleanor Lambert. Lambert, who was close to both Judy and Liza, recalled, "Liza just sort of took over, you know? She treated Judy like a child and wooed her back to sanity and humor, and you know they were darling together. They made jokes and she raised Judy's spirits. They had a light manner toward each other, very gay and quick, never tough. Liza was always sort of maternal towards Judy; she adored her and kindly took care of her."

Although *Best Foot Forward* was an off-Broadway production, the first night on April 2, 1963, rivaled any Broadway opening. Long before curtain time, fans, desperate for a glimpse of Judy, gathered outside the theater with police on hand to control the eager crowds. But Judy never materialized.

Later, Liza claimed that Judy hadn't attended the first night for fear of upstaging her, but that wasn't the real truth. In his book *Weep No More My Lady* (written with Ann Pinchot), Judy's last husband, Mickey Deans, quotes a backer who was in the audience the first night that *Best Foot Forward* opened. According to Mickey, Judy had promised to come to the show and bring Lorna and Joey. Liza had accordingly arranged for three seats in the front row to be reserved for them. They never showed up and, distraught, Liza telephoned Judy.

"The young backer, who happened to be in the office, surmised that Liza was terrified that something had happened to Judy. She listened, looking more and more distressed, 'But Momma, I told you it was tonight!' She seemed to be close to tears. But as the conversation continued he had the feeling that in a subtle way the mother-daughter roles had been exchanged and Liza was consoling Judy. 'Don't feel badly, Momma,' Liza said. 'You can come tomorrow.' " Mickey reflected, adding, "Mostly Liza tries to remember the nice things about everybody, particularly about her mother."

Liza had successfully conquered off-Broadway, and as promised, her stepmother, Denise, presented Liza with her white leather mink-lined coat, in recognition of her success. Although she didn't have the leading role in *Best Foot Forward,* she had garnered a great deal of attention, particularly for her rendition of the song "You Are for Loving," written specially for her by Hugh Martin and Ralph Blane, who also wrote "The Trolley Song" and "The Boy Next Door" for Judy.

Labeling her debut "auspicious," Lewis Funke noted in the *New York Times:* "There's a little of Judy in Liza. She is even perhaps a mite shorter, the curve of her nose is definitely a reminder, and there is the same hoydenish quality to be noted at times. Her voice has some of the touching quality that has been a trademark of Judy Garland and, like her mother, Liza seems capable of letting that voice go all out in a crescendo of emotion."

In the *New York Post,* Richard Watts, Jr., wholeheartedly agreed: "Miss Minnelli has a secondary role, but she has enough to do to indicate her talent in the part of a girl of flirtatious instincts at the prep school prom. She reveals an appealing quality, a wistful sense of comedy, and a small but attractive singing voice that has haunting overtones of her mother."

Liza herself said, "I realize that all my professional and

personal life, I'll never be able to be disassociated with my mother. I really wouldn't want to be. I guess someday, I'd like to be thought of as Liza Minnelli, who happens to be Judy Garland's daughter, but who also happens to be Liza Minnelli. I know I sound like Mother when I sing, but I don't intend to do it. It just happens. Sometimes when I hear my voice on a record or something I'm really surprised at how much it resembles hers. It's kind of, well, spooky. But we've always clowned around at home, singing and dancing together."

In another one of her many press interviews given around the time of the opening, her Bambi eyes sparkling, she eagerly confided, "I'm staying with Mother out here until this show is completed. But Mother is more like an older sister or a good friend than a mother. It's more fun that way. Yet when I need her advice or help, Mother is always there."

On April 3, 1963, Judy and Sid belatedly attended Liza's professional debut and Judy praised her fulsomely, commenting, "Liza is the first one of us to do this. I never had a Broadway show. All I had were variety shows."

Liza was paid just $45 a week for her role in *Best Foot Forward,* and she eventually supplemented her income by making a series of television appearances. On June 3, 1963, Liza was booked on *The Tonight Show.* Judy was so excited by Liza's television appearance that she and a group of friends, including Carolyn Jones and Aaron Spelling, all watched the show at Sid Luft's office.

Just a week later, Liza taped *The Judy Garland Christmas Show* with Jack Jones, Lorna and Joey, Tracy Everitt, and Mel Tormé. Tormé, in his book *The Other Side of the Rainbow,* later asserted, "Liza had inherited a great amount of talent and seemed overwhelmed at the thought of appearing on the show with her mother, whom she openly adored. Judy loved her kids actively and passionately and her devotion was returned in kind."

He also remembered Judy's passionately declaring to him, "I've got Liza, Lorna and Joey, and you know something? They're really all I need. They're the only people who care for me. They don't give a damn how much money I've got or whether I'm working or starving or being applauded or sued. They just love me. So, I'm happy to just be with them."

Coyne Steven Sanders wrote a book called *Rainbow's End* about *The Judy Garland Show* series. Liza cooperated with the project, perceptively observing of her mother, "She understood that her vulnerability in performance was something that we all recognize in ourselves. She knew how to portray somebody in flux, somebody in pain. She understood it deeply enough to portray it.

"She created the legend. She did it, and she knew exactly what she was doing. And it instilled a great need in people. She'd say, 'Don't correct anything, let the legend build, it's going to build anyway—and if you fight it, you're going to drive yourself nuts!' "

Liza's presence on the show helped Judy a great deal. Liza was awestruck at performing in the same show as her mother, but Judy didn't attempt to upstage her—not this time. Generously, she gave Liza all her support and it was returned to her manifold. Choreographer Danny Daniels, who worked closely on *The Judy Garland Show* with both Liza and Judy, staging "Put on a Happy Face" for them, revealed, "Because Liza was fast, she picked everything up, and when Judy couldn't remember, Liza would say, 'No, Momma, left foot.' "

The Judy Garland Show was taped in California. Judy was living in a house on Rockingham Drive, in Brentwood, West Los Angeles. In early September, Liza left the cast of *Best Foot Forward* and joined Judy in California.

On November 15, Liza suddenly ran a high fever, a kidney stone was detected, and she was rushed to Cedars of Lebanon Hospital. She was in the midst of her convalescence when President Kennedy was assassinated. Judy and JFK had formed a mutual admiration society, as Judy periodically phoned the president for advice on how to handle backstage politics and, before the conversation ended, the president invariably asked her to sing "Over the Rainbow" for him.

Now, as Judy and Liza watched the events surrounding the assassination unfold further on television, Liza, controlling her own tears, sensed that her mother was on the verge of breaking down. Judy became almost feverish and then began kicking and screaming like a wild animal. Frantically, Liza tried to calm her. In his biography of Judy, written with Liza's cooperation, Gerold Frank writes, "Liza wrestled with her as she flung herself about, tried to throw herself against the wall, Liza pleading, 'Momma, don't, don't, please don't, you'll hurt yourself, he wouldn't want you to hurt yourself.' " As night came, Judy, exhausted, fell into a deep sleep.

By January 15, 1964, Liza had recovered from the excruciating pain of her kidney stone attack and was eager to work again. She was offered the chance to tour in *Carnival* and joyfully accepted. Judy, partly prompted by her concern for Liza's health, but primarily by her own relentlessly strong will to keep Liza with her in California, did everything she could to prevent her from opening at the Mineola Playhouse on January 28.

Consequently, she released a statement on January 18, 1964, that Liza would not be appearing in *Carnival*. Simultaneously, her attorneys dispatched a telegram to the show's producers saying that, given Liza's bad health and the fact that she was a minor, her mother had deemed that she should not appear. Liza spent days in tears, torn between obeying her mother and pursuing her own desires. Nonetheless, despite threats from Judy that she would drag her off stage, on January 28 at the Mineola Playhouse and then, on February 11 at the Paper Mill Playhouse in Millburn, Liza Minnelli appeared in *Carnival*. Judy never interfered with her daughter's career again.

CHAPTER EIGHT

Admitting defeat and relinquishing her bid to control Liza's professional destiny, Judy instead made a bid to resuscitate her own faltering career and, in the spring of 1964, toured Australia with the latest man in her life, Mark Herron, a young actor whom she would marry in November 1965 and then, after just six months, divorce. Herron was ten years younger than Judy; in his book *Judy and Liza,* writer James Spada commented, "Newspaper reports referred to him as everything from Judy's traveling companion to a homosexual, a male nurse and a gigolo."

Although *Variety* reported that in Sydney, the audience accorded Judy the greatest ovation in Australian show business history, by the time she opened in Melbourne, she had begun a downward spiral. On stage, in full view of her audience of worshipping fans, she floundered badly, forgetting lyrics she'd been singing all her life and, when she remembered them, singing off-key. After forty-five minutes, her voice gave out completely. Suffused with humiliation, her head nonetheless held high, Judy swept off stage amid a deafening chorus of boos.

She and Mark fled to Hong Kong (then currently being lashed by ninety-mile-an-hour winds generated by typhoon Viola) and took refuge at the Mandarin Hotel. Sid Luft, caught up in his custody battle with Judy, had very recently publicly revealed that Judy had made twenty-two suicide attempts. In Hong Kong, on May 31, 1964, shell-shocked by the way in which the raucous Melbourne crowds had treated her and frightened by the destruction wrought by Viola outside, Judy Garland tried to kill herself for the twenty-third time.

In critical condition, she was rushed, sirens blaring, to Hong Kong's Canossa Hospital, just three blocks away from the Mandarin. Dr. Harry Colfer, the doctor attending her, said that the end was near. Judy was in a coma, struggling for life in an oxygen tent. It was a familiar struggle, but her spirit was formidable and although her emotions were fragile, her body retained the capacity for regeneration. Hour after hour, Mark watched over her, fighting back his tears until, finally, she came back to life.

Unaware that the danger had passed, the press, believing that Judy was still at death's door, were gathered at the hospital, primed to report her predictable yet tragic demise. Late at night, Mark managed to elude them, slipping out of the hospital to the Hong Kong Hilton praying that he might be distracted from the drama swirling around Judy. Noticing a sign advertising "The Allen Brothers and Adrienne appearing nightly at The Crow's Nest," Mark whiled away a few hours and watched the act.

Much later, Peter Allen reminisced, "Mark caught our act, and the next day he went to the hospital to see Judy and she whispered to him with her last breath, 'What did you do last night?' He said, 'As a matter of fact, I went out and saw this fabulous act.' Well, Judy was furious he went out and enjoyed himself while she was lying in the hospital. She ripped out all the tubes, put on a scarf and went to the hotel to see us."

Elated by the Allen Brothers' performance, Judy informed the twenty-year-old Peter that he reminded her of Fred Astaire and praised him warmly. However, Peter, who didn't know a great deal about Judy, just that, in his own words, "She sang very loud," initially was not particularly gratified.

Nevertheless, he didn't refuse Mark and Judy's invitation to spend the rest of the evening with them. After the show, Mark and Judy took him out on the town, to some of the shady after-hours clubs in Kowloon. At one of them, tempers became heated and Judy, as always entirely caught up in the mood of the moment, flung a billiard ball at a fellow drinker. Then she and Mark launched into a blistering argument, which reached a crescendo on the ferry during their journey back to Hong Kong.

Suddenly, inexplicably, the ever mercurial Judy demanded that Peter sing. At first he protested that he only performed in harmony with Chris, but finally, his protests quelled by Judy's entreaties, Peter sang, "The Music That Makes Me Dance" from *Funny Girl*. And Judy was happy once more.

From that moment on, Chris and Peter Allen were swept up on the roller coaster of Judy's life. Every night, for the rest of her stay in Hong Kong, Judy was to be found at the Hilton, wildly applauding the Allen Brothers' act and sometimes even singing along with them.

She had always been far too self-involved to play Pygmalion before, but she was bowled over by the Allen Brothers and gushed, "Peter and Chris are without a doubt the best act I've ever seen. They have such vitality, exuberance and warmth that I find quite irresistible. If you need one word which sums them up, it is simple: talent!"

Eventually Judy made up her mind to manage Chris and Peter, inviting both boys to travel to Tokyo (where they were booked to open on June 23 at the Hilton) with her and Mark on the *President Roosevelt*.

On board, Peter, Chris, and Judy entertained the passengers with their singing. At the time, the Tokyo-based newspaper of the American army, *Stars and Stripes,* carried the following report: "After traveling from Hong Kong to Tokyo with the controversial rainbow girl, the Allen Brothers knew exactly what to do. They joined her in a rendition of 'I Wish You Love' and had the surprised customers pounding the tables."

There are those who say that Peter, who was gay, was physically attracted to Mark. Others claim that his sole interest was in Judy, in her charisma, her personality, her warmth, and her ability to make him into a star. Irrespective of Peter's motives, he and Judy were twin souls. Like her (and Liza), Peter possessed a verbal facility and a ready wit. Moreover, he loved the old Hollywood musicals and was an all-around entertainer whose act, even at this early stage, radiated promise. Given Judy's oft-professed belief in the Allen Brothers, her offer to manage them seemed plausible. Yet Peter Allen, who had survived a harsh childhood riddled with hurt and disappointment, didn't believe in fairy godmothers and had no great expectations. By now he knew exactly who Judy Garland was, had investigated her past, understood all about her present, and as a result, when Judy left him and Chris in Tokyo, he firmly believed he would never in his life set eyes on her again.

In London, on June 18, 1964, Liza made her first appearance on British television on *The Cliff Richard Show.* Before the show, she conducted a press conference. Chain smoking and looking thin, Liza mentioned that the previous night she had gone to a nightclub where she had given an impromptu performance. As an afterthought, she added, "They weren't my mother's songs I sang. Oh no. Please be clear about that. I sang 'Birth of the Blues' and 'Make It One for My Baby and One More for the Road,' not 'Over the Rainbow.'

"I don't try to copy my mother. I definitely do not want to live my life secondhand. And I can't say whether I could ever sing as well as her because she's not a person I would make comparisons with. She's such a fantastic personality."

A journalist asked Liza whether she'd gone straight to
the nightclub from the plane. "No," she replied unthink-
ingly, "I went home first."

"Home?" ventured the puzzled journalist.

"The Savoy," said Liza, before gasping, "Oh my good-
ness, what did I say? Home? Oh, that must have sounded
terrible." A journalist was heard to comment that it was a
little sad.

After her stay in England, Liza flew back to America,
where she spent the summer appearing in *The Fantastiks*
with Elliott Gould. In the process, Elliott and Liza became
firm friends; Gould reported to his then-wife, Barbra Streisand, that Liza wasn't sufficiently selfish. And, in Elliott's
own words, "She was as interested in my work as in hers."

Still in London, Judy spent a summer that was far from
glowing. Toward the end of July, she, now forty-two, was
admitted to St. Stephen's Hospital in Chelsea. A statement
issued by W. Mayne Butcher, secretary for St. Stephen's
Hospital, announced, "Miss Judy Garland was admitted to
the Casualty Dept. of St. Stephen's Hospital suffering from
minor injuries to her wrists." Judy was released and was
then put under sedation at the Cumberland House Private
Nursing Home in North London.

On the surface, it appeared that her personal life was
stabilizing, with her marriage to Mark Herron still to come.
Yet professionally Judy was afraid. Her voice had lost its
sweetness, and she was no longer remotely reminiscent of
the Dorothy of so long ago. The London Palladium had consistently been the scene of her greatest triumphs and now
she was terrified of disappointing her devoted fans, of a repetition of her abortive Melbourne performance.

Ever manipulative and resourceful, even in the face of
her deepest fears, Judy formulated a solution. After hearing
Liza's first album, *Liza! Liza!* Judy was impressed by her
burgeoning talent. Just as in the days of her 1956 Palace show
when she shooed little Liza on stage to perform with her and
thus divert the audience's attention from her somewhat sub-
standard performance, Judy once again conscripted her

daughter to rescue her and invited Liza to share the Palladium stage with her. Liza, dimly aware that Judy's proposal smacked of exploitive sentimentality, refused. But Judy had always possessed a chess player's instincts for tactics, no matter what the cost or who the victim. Intent on overriding her daughter, Judy persistently ignored all of Liza's refusals and announced the date of the joint Palladium appearance. Once the tickets were sold out, it was impossible for a dismayed Liza to withdraw.

Prompted by her own reasons (which would later become apparent to everyone around her), Judy invited her protégés, Chris and Peter Allen, to fly to England and see her perform there at the London Palladium and sent them two Japan Airlines tickets. Judy fervently hoped that Lorna and Joey would also be on hand to witness her Palladium triumph, but the ever-battle-ready Sid Luft thwarted her. On October 28, 1964, a Santa Monica court ruled that Judy and Sid must share custody of Lorna and Joey but simultaneously refused to grant permission for the children to fly to London to see Judy and Liza's Palladium opening there.

Peter and Chris arrived in London on November 8 and that same evening were on hand to witness Liza's first adult appearance at the London Palladium. From the audience's vantage point, that night at the London Palladium was emotional, nostalgic, as the packed house stamped, cheered, and roared their approval when Liza sang eight solo numbers and twelve duets with Judy. Afterward one critic raved, "At times one had the incredible sensation of seeing and hearing in Liza the Judy Garland of twenty-five years ago."

Liza, however, had a completely different perspective. For the Palladium show didn't merely mark her debut as an adult performer (as well as her first meeting with Peter Allen) but also came to symbolize for her a kind of filial high noon in her relationship with Judy.

From the beginning, she had never wanted to appear in the show. She said later, "It was awful; the show came out so stupid and sentimental and I looked like a complete idiot." By denigrating herself, Liza, generous as always, underplayed the evening's real drama: the disturbing emergence of Judy's blatant competitiveness with her own daughter.

Whenever she has discussed the trials and tribulations of living with Judy, Liza has studiously neglected the dramas, the destructiveness, the conflict. But in telling of this, the night of their Palladium performance, Liza has always told the unvarnished, unmitigated truth, no matter how damaging it might be to Judy—perhaps because, for once, Liza's pride in her own evolution, her own painfully wrested victory, overshadowed her innate tendency to protect her mother.

Twenty-seven years after that momentous night at the London Palladium, during an appearance on the "Donahue" show, she reconstructed what happened. "Life was always speeded up in my family. We went through in two hours what most mothers and daughters go through for years, which was that sense of 'wait a minute, you know, there's competition here.'

"And it was funny because when that show started, I'd never done anything. So it starts out and I hear her say, 'Ladies and gentlemen, Liza Minnelli,' in a great, proud voice. And I come on and I sing and the audience really likes it and I hear her backstage going, 'Yeah, baby!! go, baby! go, yeah, baby!'

"Then I sing the second song and there's more applause and she says 'Yeah.' I thought, 'Keep going, Minnelli, keep going.' Now, my mother walked off the stage; Judy Garland walks back on the stage. It was, like, competition, but with enormous love, but with the sense of 'I'm dealing with a power out here,' from both of us.

"And like I said, I had nothing to lose, so in the end, we walked off the stage together and she said, 'Great, baby. It was just great.' And she patted my behind. She said, 'I'll see you in the dressing room.' And I started to walk and I turned around in time to see her running back out on stage for another bow, and I went, 'No you don't.' And I went right with her."

* * *

From that moment on, Liza would always grapple with the dilemma, all the more bitter for a loving daughter, of either equaling and perhaps eclipsing her mother in both success and happiness or opting out of the entire contest altogether and thus surrendering her own chance for fulfillment in her chosen field. But she was born to entertain and she could do no less. She could not afford the luxury of joining the legions worshipping at Judy's star-spangled altar. So for Liza, the choice was clear: compete and win or be obliterated.

That night at the Palladium, the symbiotic relationship between Judy and Liza was torn asunder forever, and it is no wonder that Liza turned to another relationship with which to replace it. Waiting in the wings was Peter Allen—the ideal candidate, a new ally who would be by Liza's side as they both grew up together.

Peter Allen was born Peter Woolnough on February 10, 1944, in Tenterfield, Australia. Unlike Liza, he was raised in a small town with a population of only ten thousand. But like her, he did not come from a conventional background. During his early childhood, his father was away at war and he was brought up solely by women, his mother, his grandmother, and his aunts.

They may have been raised on different continents, thousands of miles apart, but from the first, Liza and Peter were born scene stealers. Ten-year-old Liza danced to "Swanee" at the Palace Theater, New York, and Peter as a small boy in Australia put on black face and sang "Mammy," winning first place in countless talent contests.

He loved music and musicals, mastered the piano by the age of ten, and, miraculously, was then able to play by ear any popular song requested of him. He enrolled in dance classes, played piano in local bars, and, by the age of twelve, was already earning his living as an entertainer. Just as adults in Hollywood were disarmed by lovable little Liza, any adult who came into contact with Peter, too, was smitten by his charm and precocious sophistication.

Yet his function was not merely to garner applause, to find mass love, but to help his family through hard financial times. His mother, Marion, declared with pride, "Peter was being paid 30 shillings a night [about $3.00 in American money] and he had three nights at the hotel, so that meant a fortune to us."

When he was thirteen, Peter took a job in a sheet music store where he worked during the day and by night played in pubs. If the young Liza found solace from the harsh reality of Judy's alcoholism in Hollywood musicals (some of which she had watched being filmed), Peter also clung to the identical illusions, spending every weekend at the cinema, drinking in the glory of countless musicals—none, apparently, starring Judy Garland, since he had little knowledge of her when they met.

His need for escapism increased when his father shot himself. Peter's mother, Marion, has characterized her late husband as "a mean brutal man, the town drunk," and says that he also battered her and Peter. When his body was found, it was left to Peter to clean up the bleeding remains from the bedroom floor. He was only thirteen years old, but the experience of Peter Woolnough Allen, an adult long before his time, was very close to that of Liza May Minnelli, another child whom fate had also forced to become old before her time.

Peter and Liza were both adult children of alcoholics. Liza, as a teenager, had constantly endeavored to hide the truth about her mother's bouts with drinking and drugs and her suicide attempts from prying eyes. Very young, she became mistress of many facades, protecting Judy's image and suffering anguish while unkind strangers taunted her with her mother's frailties.

Although Peter and Liza were born into different worlds, their life histories, their mythologies, meshed. Their traumas were similar and so were their wounds. Liza's story, to this day, has always remained the story of a child forever struggling to uphold a parent's reputation, to hide the truth, and to remain loyal, no matter how deep the disgrace, no matter how dramatic the disintegration.

When his alcoholic father was alive, Peter's public persona was consistently bright, charming, loyal, and protective. When Peter's father died, he, too, was compelled to deal with the specter of a black sheep parent. Peter's father, Dick, was so notorious for his drunken behavior that no one in the town would agree to be a pallbearer for his coffin. Peter's innocent happy nights playing for an admiring pub crowd ended abruptly, because when he took his seat at the piano, so many people stared and pointed at him that their gossip drowned his music and he was ultimately forced to quit.

Just as adversity drove Judy, Liza, Lorna, and Joey closer together, so it did Peter, his mother, and his sister, Lynne. Two weeks after his father's suicide, Peter, Lynne, and Marion Woolnough auctioned their furniture and left Tenterfield forever.

The Woolnoughs settled in Lismore, in eastern Australia, where Peter's mother cleaned a hotel and waitressed. Peter gravitated to Surfer's Paradise, in Sydney, where he tried out his unique brand of singing and dancing at the local clubs.

There, at the age of fifteen, Peter met Chris Bell, himself part of a singing duo, "The Two Shades." Backed by Chris's father, an anomaly who managed his son's career with the fanaticism of the most dedicated of stage mothers, Chris and Peter joined forces, renaming themselves the "Allen Brothers."

The Allen Brothers' career took flight in Sydney, where they won a popular following among the locals. There, too, at the Chequers Nightclub (which would, in years to come, become the scene of a pivotal meeting between Liza and another man), Peter encountered the American singer Frances Faye, whose flamboyant act captured his imagination. Frances, for her part, was titillated by Peter (a natural-born protégé) and included him in her life, unveiling to him her skill at winning and holding an audience, her partiality for smoking dope, and her admiration for the revolutionary comedian Lenny Bruce. Peter was fascinated by Frances's wildness, a wildness which fortuitously prepared him for Judy.

After the show, Judy introduced Liza to Peter Allen, saying, "This is the boy I've been telling you about. Peter, this is my daughter I've been telling you all about. You'd be perfect for each other." Though Peter was gay, Judy firmly believed he was the man for Liza. Even though she had once made the comment that she was terrified that Liza would suffer from "Mama repetition," Judy sensed that, as women, they were similar and needed the identical type of man.

Although Judy's emotional stability was always fragile, none of her biographers has ever doubted her intelligence. Looking back on her own life, she may well have concluded that as she (with a homosexual father) instinctively gravitated toward men who (with the notable exception of Sid Luft) may not have been gay but definitely did not exude masculinity, Liza would do the same.

She knew that Liza loved Vincente as much as she, in a different way, had once loved him herself. And that although Vincente was a man who loved women and adored being married, he was also distinctly effeminate in style. Peter Allen was not dissimilar from Vincente and, from the moment that she first set eyes on him in Hong Kong, that similarity had captivated Judy. And it is highly likely that she reasoned that Liza, too, would be equally enthralled by Peter.

Peter Allen would be the first man (apart from her father) whom Liza ever loved, and the first in a line of entertaining, outgoing, colorful men who would become part of her life. He was the first in the brother-figure category of men she would love. Yet Liza, like Judy with Sid, would also be drawn to another, entirely different type of man as well: the mentor/father figure. She had never been convinced of her own desirability, just as Judy had never been convinced of hers. And in pursuit of validation in the eyes of the world, she would sometimes be drawn to older men of fame and influence.

The men in her life would consistently be divided into the entertaining, sometimes effeminate brother figures and the powerful, successful mentors. And she would spend most of her life seeking love and reassurance from all of them.

CHAPTER
NINE

After the Palladium show, Judy, Peter, Liza, Chris, and entourage left the theater for Ad Lib, then London's trendiest nightclub. The night was long, the company—the Beatles, Rudolph Nureyev, and Dame Margot Fonteyn—glittering, but jet-lagged after his arduous flight from Australia, Peter promptly fell asleep right there in the midst of the most star-kissed gathering in all of London. Liza watched him sleeping and smiled with complicity. The next evening, when Peter played "Hello, Dolly!" at George Sanders's birthday party, with Vivien Leigh and Judy singing a duet (Judy sang, "Hello," and Vivien, "Dolly"), Liza's eyes met Peter's and they moved closer to each other. Amid all the razzle-dazzle, they felt that they alone were the only two people in the room who were real.

At the weekend, they made their escape from all the excitement surrounding Judy and flew to Paris, where Vincente was in the process of directing Elizabeth Taylor and Richard Burton in *The Sandpiper*. *What's New, Pussycat?*

was being shot at the same studio, and Peter and Liza had lunch with Richard Burton, Elizabeth Taylor, Peter O'Toole, Woody Allen, and Ursula Andress. But Peter, with his uncanny British style of reserve, remained strangely unmoved by his surroundings, stable amid all the tinsel, down to earth amid all the starriness. And Liza liked that.

Just as Judy had adored Peter's sense of humor and his passion for music, so did Liza. He, in turn, was beguiled by her vitality, her sense of humor, her verve and enthusiasm. And, beneath it all, he knew they were soulmates, two lost kids, both adults before their time, who had learned to survive without many visible scars. It was no wonder that they would, for a time, find magic in one another and cleave together.

Liza Minnelli and Peter Allen became engaged on November 26, 1964, less than three weeks after they first met. The engagement took place at Trader Vic's in the London Hilton. And when Peter presented Liza with a white and gold engagement ring, Judy cried. The following day, the London papers gleefully reported the engagement.

Studying photographs of Liza around the time of her whirlwind engagement to Peter, she is invariably pictured with Peter and Chris, her arms around both of them, looking wide-eyed and innocent, exuding joy and optimism.

Peter, always eager to define his emotions as accurately as possible, said, "Liza was like my sanctuary." And some time afterward in a *New York Times* interview with Joanne Stang, Liza, too, crystallized her feelings for Peter and their commitment: "The reason Peter and I get along so well, the reason I'm engaged (because I don't usually commit myself to anything), is that Peter is exactly like I am. The funny thing about him is that we were always such good friends, before we kind of fell in love.

"You see, he knew Mamma. He'd been through all the tensions that happened around Mamma, which are not created by her, but by other people. So he could say to Mamma, 'relax,' and she'd listen to him. She adores him. But one afternoon we were with her when a reporter broke into the house, and Mother got upset and said, 'Get out.'

"I was very nervous because I didn't know whether Peter and Chris had ever seen anything like that before. Peter was just sitting at the piano and I sat down beside him and he smiled and said, 'Nothing like a little drama at the end of the day.' And that made me laugh and from then on, we became allies."

The day after their engagement was announced, Liza flew to New York to audition, for the fifth time, for the lead in George Abbott's musical *Flora, the Red Menace,* and Peter and Chris started touring for Judy as her opening act, appearing with her first at the Diplomat in Miami and then in Toronto and Las Vegas.

Sometimes, the experience of being Judy Garland's opening act proved daunting for the Allen Brothers. On some nights, they would complete their act but Judy could not be found. Instead, a doctor came on stage and announced to an angry audience that Judy was indisposed and would not be appearing, leaving the Allen Brothers to cope with the ensuing riots. Remembering the days when the Allen Brothers were virtually thrown to crowds of howling, disappointed fans, Peter recalled, "Actually the cult was annoying. It became the entire thing and it was a nuisance, because you couldn't see her work and when she did, she was brilliant."

At the end of the year, on December 28, Lorna and Joey, detained in California by Sid against Judy's will, were finally reunited in New York with Liza and Judy. They met Peter for the first time and immediately adopted him as a cross between brother and father figure.

In early 1965, Peter went on tour with Judy again while Liza waited anxiously for news of *Flora, the Red Menace.* The venerable director and co-author George Abbott was not enthusiastic about casting Liza, favoring Eydie Gorme for the part of Flora. "Liza Minnelli is not right for the part," he said. "She's not what I had in mind and I don't think she'll be able to carry it." Irrespective of Abbott's opinion, impresario Harold Prince asked her to read again, and she knew she had done well. The next morning, her agent phoned to say that she had the part. Liza and her roommate Tanya went wild jumping around the room, alternating between laughter and tears.

The title character was a young art graduate in 1933. The musical comedy was co-written by Lester Atwell and George Abbott, with music by composer John Kander (who had been the arranger for *Irma la Douce* and *Gypsy*) and lyricist Fred Ebb.

Fizzing over with excitement, Liza began rehearsing for *Flora* and, in the very early days, encountered a man who would play a large part in her career. Fred Ebb, a New Yorker eleven years her senior, in an interview with *Time* magazine published in May 1972, recalled his first meeting with Liza. "I remember this shy, awkward girl coming into the room. She looked awful, like Raggedy Ann. Everything was just a little torn and a little soiled. She just sat there and stared at me, and I stared back."

As the years went by, Fred Ebb would grow to understand Liza as well as if he had created her himself—as, in a way, he had. Along with his collaborator, composer John Kander, Fred packaged Liza through lyrics which, during her entire career, have not only mirrored the vicissitudes of her life but have also hinted at the shadow cast over her by Judy.

From the first, Fred instinctively understood the density of that shadow. Long after their first meeting, he said, "Liza has a deep need for complete trust from anyone who doesn't need her for anything. Liza, like her mother, can't be alone easily and she knows it. In every situation, Liza always looks for a person, usually masculine, to depend on, to be close to."

On a professional level, Liza's relationship with Kander and Ebb duplicates that formed by Judy with Harold Arlen and lyricist E. Y. Harburg, who were responsible for "Over the Rainbow," when she was seventeen, and the song "I Could Go On Singing" when she was in her twilight forties.

Fred Ebb was enthralled by Liza, bewitched by her to the extent that she once confided to a close friend, "I can always wrap Fred around my little finger. He is so good natured." She has consistently paid tribute to Ebb's influence on her

career. Many years after their first meeting she acknowledged, "I've had fabulous guidance from Fred Ebb, who has
been my Svengali since I was seventeen. He's really guided
my career brilliantly."

Their association remains extremely beneficial to both,
financially and emotionally. Fred Ebb has said of Liza,
"She's an extremely positive force in everyone's life. She's
the first to encourage, sympathize and offer her help. Liza
just believes that everything is going to turn out well.

"She flatters an audience. She really cares for them; she
makes people want to look after her. She's everybody's kid
sister, every guy's dependent girl. Liza's never idle. She
never stops. She just has a rage to live."

During the *Flora* rehearsals, Liza (her fingernails extremely badly chewed) eagerly proffered lots of ideas. She
was nervous, but now that she had won the part, she had
nothing more to fear. In a complete volte-face, George Abbott later rhapsodized of Liza, "I'm afraid you'll think I'm
sounding off because of *Flora,* but I think she's the most
wonderful girl, very vital and devoid of any pettiness. She's
always on the job, she has an unerring instinct for what's
true and right, and she's a quick study. I find her a delight."

Years later, Abbott further reminisced, "She was really
very amiable, no problem. She was a very agreeable girl. It
was obvious that she had a lot of talent. She had a marvelous
personality."

Flora, the Red Menace, opened on Tuesday, May 11, 1965,
at the Alive Theater. Opening night telegrams arrived for
Liza from Lillian Gish, Barbra Streisand, and Elliott Gould.
Vincente telegraphed, "All best wishes for my wonderful
girl. I love you so very much." And from Judy, "My darling
baby, I know you will be brilliant as always tonight. Don't be
scared, just get out there and kill them. I love you, Momma."

This time, Judy managed to attend the opening, wearing
black chiffon and diamonds. With tears streaming down her
face, she proclaimed Liza a truly great star, glowing that, "I
cried and laughed at the same time in the wrong places, I was
so proud." Vincente, too, was proud, enthusing, "I knew she

was talented but this—this was great." Peter Allen did not attend the first night of his fiancée's triumph. He was playing a series of club dates and battling to make his own mark in show business.

After the show, Liza, Judy, and Vincente celebrated at Ruby Foo's, with Judy and Liza singing duets. It was nine years since Judy sang "Swanee" at the Palace Theater and ten-year-old Liza danced in the background. Tonight they sang the song together and, for that one night, at least, were equals.

The show ran for eighty-seven performances, garnering tepid reviews. Yet for the most part, Liza was hailed as Broadway's brightest new star. Critic John McClain wrote, "Liza Minnelli, who looks like a charming little rabbit designed by Walt Disney to look like Judy Garland, her mother, is a big new star on Broadway today. Young Miss Minnelli has her mother's voice and timing and delivery and a special quality of her own growing out of her plaintive little personality which has been beautifully exploited in the music of John Kander and the lyrics of Fred Ebb."

Newsweek, however, was highly critical of Liza, commenting, "Liza Minnelli is engaging, but far from accomplished, and it is unpleasant to see her rushed into a big Broadway show at 19, as though she were another Barbra Streisand. But Miss Minnelli lacks Miss Streisand's equipment. Her voice is thin, her movements stiff, her presence woolly and uncertain."

Despite *Newsweek*'s acerbic opinion, on June 13, Liza became the youngest performer ever to win the Tony Award for Best Actress in a Musical. The ceremony took place at the Astor Hotel ballroom, where, ironically, the award was presented to her by Bert Lahr, who had played the Cowardly Lion in *The Wizard of Oz.* Yet, as always, a cold fog dampened her joy. For in the hour of Liza's greatest triumph, Judy was languishing in a Los Angeles hospital intensive care unit, suffering from what was described as "an emotional upset." According to an eyewitness, Liza remained completely poised and never once alluded to Judy's illness dur-

ing what should have been one of the greatest nights of her
life.

Interviewed for *Life* magazine, Liza proved that she was
beginning to master the art of the press interview. She
talked a great deal about Judy and how much she loved her,
then changed the subject with a decisive "And now back to
Liza." Yet despite her fruitless attempt to control this and
other interviews, most of the press reports centering around
Flora invariably stressed Judy before enthusing about Liza's
freshness and spontaneity.

But below the surface of that much-touted spontaneity,
even this early on in her career, all her dealings with the
press were governed by an underlying wariness. After all,
she was Judy's daughter and had witnessed firsthand what
she perceived to be the cruelty of the press. In a May 1965
interview with journalist Elaine Dundy, she issued a mock-
caution, "I liked the questions, and if you write a bad interview I'll bop you over the head next time I see you."

At that point, her fashion sense was completely un-
developed and mostly she tended to wear pants and a loose
blouse, claiming that she loved blue jeans and sneakers
without laces, wasn't the frilly type but owned thirty-five
hats. Fashion maven and society columnist Eugenia Shepherd commented, "Liza couldn't happen any time but today.
She's so 1965 that she makes even those teenage bombshells
from Europe look like last year's girls."

On September 14, 1965, Liza began her first nightclub
tour of America, which would include appearances at the
Camden, New Jersey's Latin Casino; the Sahara, Las Vegas;
the Coconut Grove, Los Angeles; and the Deauville, Miami
Beach.

The tour began in the Blue Room of the Shoreham Hotel
in Washington, D.C. "In those days, Liza was a lanky, doe-
eyed, almost knock-kneed little girl. She was always very
open, very bubbly, very up, always a little excited and a little
hyper. On the tour, she was always looking for answers, for
a way to do things to make her performance more effective,"
remarked dancer Robert Fitch, who met Liza during *Flora,*

the Red Menace and toured the nightclub circuit with her and fellow dancer Neil Schwartz.

Fitch recalls, "She raised money for her first nightclub act through Stevie Phillips, her agent, through Kander and Ebb's connections. Then Peter, with his innate good taste, advised her. Liza succeeded on her own, without her mother and father, because she was a hard worker. She did her best not to involve her parents in her career. She loved them but she didn't want to ask for help.

"Above all, she didn't want to show favoritism to Vincente over Judy or vice versa. She wanted to be fair to both of them. But sometimes it was desperately difficult for her. Liza could always relax more at her father's place than at her mother's. Judy was very hyper, always dramatic. When we were in Los Angeles, Liza stayed with her father, but didn't want her mother to know." With her lifelong experience of the volcanic elements that periodically threatened to erupt and overwhelm Judy's volatile nature, Liza was understandably gun-shy.

According to Fitch, Judy's temperament nearly ruined Liza's September 14 Shoreham opening night. He says, "Liza had a phone call from Judy, just before her very first show. Liza was nervous and the first thing her mother asked was, 'Are you making fun of me in your act?' Now, at one point, Liza introduced a song by saying, 'This is a song I taught my mother.' So when Judy asked that question (and I was holding Liza's hand because she was so nervous) she couldn't answer.

"After the call, I persuaded her to phone back and convince her mother not to worry. She ended up saying, 'Momma, I appreciate what you went through and I am trying to do that now and I'm beginning to see how difficult it is. Wish me luck.' Judy did and it was fine."

In May of the following year, at Liza's Coconut Grove opening in Los Angeles, Fitch was present during another crisis.

"All of Hollywood turned out to see Liza's opening. Her mother sat in the audience on the left with Mickey Rooney and Vincente sat on the right with his entourage. The room

wasn't balanced like a theater and it was an awkward place
to perform.

"Just before the overture, Liza (who was extremely nervous about appearing in Hollywood in front of all her friends
and family for the first time in her life) suddenly developed
a new fear, 'Oh, God. Do you realize that I perform most of
my act and sing most of the songs on the side of the stage
closest to Mama. Daddy is going to think I am favoring her.
We got to change the act!'

"I said, 'If we change it now, it's not going to work out.
Your mother and father will just have to realize that the act
is the act.' She was going through a paranoia, a nervous
paranoia. But we got Liza over that hurdle and she pulled
herself together and was ready to go on stage.

"The opening of the act was always heralded by a drum
roll followed by the announcement, 'Ladies and Gentlemen,
Miss Liza Minnelli.' Just before Liza was due to step out on
stage, Neil and I were in the wings holding her hand when
we heard the drum roll and then the words 'Ladies and
Gentlemen, Miss Judy Garland.'

"My stomach plunged. Then the voice falteringly said,
'I'm sorry, I mean, Miss Liza Minnelli.' All of Hollywood was
there that night and the entire audience laughed and applauded. Liza was stunned and turned absolutely white. She
looked at us with absolute terror in her eyes. There was
nothing we could do, so we said, 'Smile!' She went on anyway and gave a great performance."

Offstage, she and Peter hadn't yet set a wedding date. By
all accounts, they lived relatively separate lives, as Peter and
Chris appeared in predominantly gay clubs and Peter pursued his own chosen life-style. Nevertheless, he and Liza
maintained a Manhattan base: a three-room eighteenth floor
apartment on East 57th Street, with navy blue walls, Lucite
sculptures, a baby grand piano, and good paintings. When
questioned about marriage, Liza defensively declared, "Oh
yes, we're very much in love. Marriage? Of course, but that's
all the paperwork—visa and working permits if he's to stay
in America. Kids? Oh yes, I hope so, when we marry. But not

straightaway—after all, I'll be a kid myself for a few years yet. Peter's very sweet. Before one show he brought me these pearl earrings. Before another show, he bought me a dozen carnations, each wrapped in a separate box with a separate note that finally spelled out, 'I love you dear.' But most of the time we're together we just sit on the couch reading and watching TV."

In October 1965, a double album of the previous year's Palladium concert, entitled *Judy Garland and Liza Minnelli 'Live' at the London Palladium,* was released. The album was a hit and her career continued to steam ahead. In the week of November 28, 1965, Liza starred in ABC's hour-long musical comedy special, "The Dangerous Christmas of Red Riding Hood," as well as appearing with Arthur Godfrey and Roger Miller on "CBS Ice Capades of 1966," another hour-long special.

On February 9, 1966, she made her debut at the Persian Room at the Plaza Hotel. Her father and stepmother, Denise, were on hand to lend her support. Denise recalls, "Liza had three costume changes but I didn't like the dress she was wearing in the last change. So I let her borrow one of my dresses, a black Galanos."

Liza sang thirteen songs in fifty-five minutes and was an unqualified success. In the *New York Times,* critic John S. Wilson enthused, "Miss Minnelli's act is a buoyant blend of dancing, comedy and song. As a singer, she is at her best in subdued settings that permit her acting ability to supplement her vocalizing and that avoid frenzied endings—notably in a child's song, 'You've Let Yourself Go,' which begins as a comedy cliché, and is gradually transformed into touching reality."

After the show, Denise Minnelli gave a big party to celebrate Liza's triumph. She remembers, "Liza told me she was disappointed by the first night parties she had had up till then. So she said, 'Next time, I want you to be in charge.' I promised I would. And I was true to my word and gave her the most glamorous opening night party possible." Denise assembled a glittering guest list to applaud Liza's opening, including Barbara Walters, the duchess of Westminster, John Richardson, and C. Z. Guest.

Liza repeated her Persian Room triumph at London's Talk of the Town, after which the London *Daily Mail* critic praised, "She bewitches with her versatility, her vibrant, belting performance." Liza spent two weeks in London, staying at a flat in Chelsea, before flying to Paris with Neil Schwartz and Robert Fitch.

At sixteen, Liza had been unhappy studying at the Sorbonne. But now, just three years later, Paris would be the scene of great success and the advent of a new influence in her career and in her personal life.

Liza was seventeen when she first met Charles Aznavour, the man destined to be both her mentor and, even to this day, her father figure. In fact, with his small wiry frame, his large eyes framed by dark bushy eyebrows, Aznavour is very much the same physical type as Vincente. At the time of their meeting, he was in his forties, unmarried, and after his years as Edith Piaf's protégé, had endured many days and nights of life with a prima donna, and, on meeting Liza, applied some of the knowledge he had gained from observing Piaf.

Of Liza, Aznavour noted, "I knew she would be a star. But she has no discipline in life. She needs that discipline to stay where she is. Her heart rules everything, but that is a problem of singers and artists alike. They become too emotional in their romances. They have to find someone who could understand them, make love to them in the right way, and yet not stifle their personality."

From the start, Aznavour understood Liza, and throughout the years, she turned to him for friendship and compassion, even in 1990, after the breakup of her third marriage. There are those who claim that their relationship was far from platonic, but neither Aznavour nor Liza has ever confirmed that they were romantically involved.

The most that Aznavour cryptically concedes of their relationship is encapsulated in the following comments: "She is very special. There exists between us what we call in

France, an *amitie amoureuse*. It is less than love. But more than friendship. Less than sexual, but more than platonic. Which means we can rub cheekbones together. When I first met Liza I was not married at the time, and the first things that struck me were her never-ending legs and that fascinating face!"

Liza has never discussed Aznavour the man, but since the first time she saw him perform when she was only seventeen, she has clearly always been impressed by his artistry. "I thought it was the greatest thing I'd ever seen! That somebody could sing a song and it was like a little movie, that each piece had a life of its own, that it was acted. It's miraculous! He does a song called 'In My Chair,' where there's a wife singing about losing her husband at a party, sitting there watching another woman taking her husband away. I loved all that.

"The only real concert performing I'd ever seen was like Frank Sinatra, a very American style of performing, which I admired, but I didn't think I was terribly good at. Because I liked Broadway, I liked characters. So when I saw Aznavour do that, I thought, 'Oh now, wait a minute. That's the way to do it.'"

Liza appeared on a double bill with Aznavour at the legendary Olympia in Paris in June 1966 and brought the house down. Gradually, she was maturing as a performer, appearing on equal terms on stage with her former idols—first her mother and now Charles Aznavour, then, in later years, Frank Sinatra and Sammy Davis, Jr.

During the Olympia run, impresario Bruno Coquatrix, who ran the Olympia, also became a father figure to Liza, advising her to make her act more informal, to take chances, to experiment. He said of her, "I love Liza. I find her just a bit exaggerated in every sense. Her little pains become big, her little joys, great. She's *une excessive*."

CHAPTER TEN

In October 1966, Liza moved on to England and her first film, *Charlie Bubbles,* starring with the respected British actor Albert Finney (who rocketed to fame playing the title character in *Tom Jones*), who was also directing. Liza played an American secretary with aspirations of becoming a novelist. Finney cast the film in Los Angeles, auditioned hundreds of actresses, then picked Liza because, as he says today, "She was perfect for the role."

Ever the director's daughter, during the five-week shoot in Manchester, England, Liza called Finney "Boss" and readily took direction from him. Monitoring her somewhat histrionic performance, Finney tactfully advised her, "You have a face that registers everything. It's not veiled enough. Do half of what you're doing."

Producer Michael Medwin remembers that Liza's face, her unique quality, almost prevented her from getting the part in the first place. "She was hired very much against Universal's wishes. They wanted Albert to cast a chocolate box blonde in the part. Albert is very perceptive as an actor and director and he saw a passionate, dedicated quality in Liza that he wanted. It was a magical piece of casting and she was an absolute delight to work with."

Despite Universal Studio's reluctance to cast Liza (a reluctance which would later be shown by other studios also set on casting stereotypical blondes), Liza's secondary role in *Charlie Bubbles* was a worthy film debut and, in the *New York Post,* critic Archer Winsten said, "Liza Minnelli's version of the ambitious young American woman is something that sounds as if recorded in documentary style."

In December, Liza returned to America, effervescent with emotion. There, she informed Peter that, with his talents for words and music, he should write songs. Remembering that Albert Finney's son was named Simon, she flashed, "I love the name Simon. Write me a song called 'Simon.'" At this stage in the Allen Brothers' careers, Judy was no longer their manager. Chris and Peter had been on *The Tonight Show* twenty times, where they gave very polished performances of songs like "Puff the Magic Dragon." But Peter was dissatisfied and simmered with unresolved ambitions. So he followed Liza's advice, thus launching a songwriting career that produced countless hits, including "Don't Cry Out Loud" and "Quiet, Please, There's a Lady on Stage."

In turn, Peter reciprocated and helped Liza develop her voice, advised her on her dealings with her agency, and shaped her stage act. Although Liza and Peter never sang together, he still gave her confidence and encouraged her to believe in herself. "Peter gave her some leadership and protection and a sense of guidance that I think she needed. I think he certainly loved her and she loved him," notes producer Lester Persky, who knew Peter and Liza during the early years of their relationship.

Liza was twenty years old, and, despite her possible romantic link with Aznavour, marriage to Peter was a foregone conclusion. "When Liza came to the house with Peter, she seemed very happy. They did seem to get along very well. At least, for appearance sake," Tina Nina says.

Only Denise was against the marriage, warning Liza that

she was too young, that she should wait before committing her life to Peter. She says, "I felt Liza should concentrate on her career and not rush into marriage. I liked Peter very much, but didn't want her to marry him, because she was far too young. I told Liza that because I didn't approve of her getting married so young, I wouldn't go to the wedding. And she was very upset."

Nevertheless, on March 3, 1967, just before her twenty-first birthday, Liza married Peter Allen in the Park Avenue apartment of her agent, Stevie Philips. Vincente drove Judy to the wedding, artist Paul Jasmine was best man, and the guests included Van Johnson and Yul Brynner. Liza wore a lace wedding gown for the ceremony and afterward, for the reception at the Central Park West home of her business manager, Marty Bregman, wore an Elizabethan style gown designed specially for her by Vincente.

Ostensibly, Liza and Peter's union had all the hallmarks of young love and happily ever after. Seeing the ecstatic couple leaving the church, an onlooker may well have sighed enviously, anticipating the marital bliss that awaited them. The reality, however, was very different. A confidential source (who was very close to Liza and to whom she revealed the information) has claimed that her marriage to Peter wasn't consummated on the wedding night because he was out having sex with a gay lover.

Now she and Peter were Mr. and Mrs. Woolnough and, although they had been living together sporadically since soon after their first meeting, initially Liza found her new role unnerving. "I couldn't adjust to normality. I was used to only screaming attacks or obsessive love bouts, rivers of money or no money at all, seeing my mother constantly or not seeing her for weeks at a time while she was away on locations," she confessed to writer Muriel Davidson of *Good Housekeeping.*

There were breakfast, lunch, and dinner, marketing, and shopping. Routine was totally alien to her, and she later remembered forlornly, "Peter was there, rock steady. I kept waiting for something to happen; something could take away my tranquillity. It was, I guess, a sort of breakdown in reverse. I had everything I always wanted and I just couldn't believe it. But Peter made me believe.

"Peter and I are intellectually balanced now. He's more emotionally stable than me, whereas I explode at the little things in life. We've found out so much about one another."

Peter reminisced, "We both sought each other out. We'd grab each other and go disco the night away. We were literally climbing through the snow to carve our initials out on the top of Plaza fountain. It was total Scott and Zelda."

Women's liberation hadn't yet made an impact on her and Liza assumed she was supposed to cook for Peter and do his laundry. But, always unconventional, it seems that Peter finally persuaded Liza to forget about traditional role playing and instead, for the first time in her young life, think about enjoying herself. He remembers, "Every night for three years, and I don't mean for four or five nights a week, every night, we were up till dawn. We had to get home by six. Wherever we were, I'd say, 'Liza, we have to get home.' So we could be asleep before that terrible half hour on television when the late show had gone off at six and nothing came on till six thirty. We had to be asleep before that test pattern.

"I don't think we ever slept. We were out dancing till dawn in those years, and it was considered very decadent because people then were into moving to the country and planting trees. Liza and I had great times. There are few originals in this world and I had one."

Peter was more brother than husband to Liza, more companion than lover. But to Judy, he was the quintessential son-in-law, solicitous and courteous. Mature before his time, he not only paid Judy's bills and answered her fan letters but also guided Lorna, then fifteen, and Joey, thirteen, through all manner of storms. He helped them through nights when Judy exploded into rages, screaming, smashing mirrors, flinging things, and then, finally, throwing Lorna and Joey out into the menacing New York night.

Understandably, they sought refuge with Liza, who, after years of enduring the same torturous dramas, was unabashed. She and Peter would spend most of the night working with Lorna and Joey, trying to understand, trying to be kind to Judy, trying to analyze her as objectively as possible. Around three in the morning, Judy would invariably telephone; on learning that Lorna and Joey were there, her voice would splinter with insecurity and jealousy.

Burning with hostility, she would react imperiously and slam down the phone. Half an hour passed, then Judy would call again, this time in a totally different mood. Her voice was no longer that of a hysterical, unbalanced woman but the measured tones of a disciplinarian mother, demanding that her recalcitrant children return home to her immediately, whereupon the long-suffering Peter would escort Lorna and Joey home, both terrified at what awaited them. Peter, too, must have been apprehensive, knowing that, as always, Judy would greet him as if he had singlehandedly kidnapped her children.

Liza would continue to treat Judy gently and to talk about her mother in the most glowing terms. But, in reality, Judy had become a burden to her. Since as far back as she could remember, she had protected her mother with the utmost tenderness. But now that Liza finally had her own life, her career and her marriage, she made an attempt to sever the cord. True to her nature, Liza avoided a direct showdown with Judy and instead used serpentine tactics to deal with her. First, she cautioned her doorman not to admit her mother unannounced. And, according to Judy's housekeeper, Alma Cousteline, whenever possible, "Liza always avoided talking to her mother."

Luckily for Liza and all concerned, in August 1967, at the end of her four-week engagement at the Palace Theater, Judy found a new anchor, a new promise of happiness— Mickey Deans, night manager of the fashionable discotheque Arthur.

Mickey, a man in the Sid Luft mold, muscular, rough, tough, and dangerous to know, was the second masculine type who had attracted Judy's fancy. She found him magnetic and compelling and began to spend all her time with him. In turn, Mickey was able to observe Judy in different circumstances and to monitor her attitude to the children. "Judy was ecstatic when the children were with her; she was tender and loving with them, and whatever mistakes she did make were innocent of the drive and ambition that had marked her mother's treatment of her." According to Mickey, Judy discerned of Liza, "Liza has more love to give than anyone I know."

On January 8, 1968, in New York, Liza opened an act about which Earl Wilson later remarked, "Liza Minnelli became a truly great big star at the Waldorf Empire Room." Judy, suffering from a virus that night, didn't see the show, but Lorna, Joey, Faye Dunaway, Ethel Merman, Arlene Dahl, Joel Grey, and Ed Sullivan were all on hand to see Liza sing "Mammy."

"When Liza was appearing at the Waldorf, Judy would be there every night. Judy, at that time, was just like a person who was dying to be on stage and who wasn't on stage. So Liza used to bring her up on stage during her closing, and the people, of course, would go totally crazy, and then they'd go off stage together," said drummer Jerry Fischer, who worked with Liza at the Waldorf and in other shows for some years afterward. "Liza is the most talented lady I've ever known. And probably the one with the biggest heart. Very generous. Very sweet. Very good to her people, and very good to her fans."

Although Judy's vocal powers were long past their zenith, she still continued to command worship whenever she appeared. In 1968, too, she acquired a new acolyte, one who would benefit from and embellish her legend and who would, in the future, perform with Liza in a hauntingly tear-jerking show.

Impersonator-singer-actor Jim Bailey met Judy in 1968, when she went to see his act, in which he impersonated her. "She got up on stage and the audience went out of their minds," he says. "When the curtain closed, she threw her arms around me and said, 'You know, I never knew I was that pretty.'

"Then she came into the dressing room, and we sat and talked for a long time. She said that she was very lonely, and asked me if I would call her and she gave me her phone number. We talked many times.

"She watched me perform as Judy Garland and afterwards advised me, 'Now you can't do all the same things, you can't do all the same movements all at once, you have to spread them out.' I think she was sort of giving me tips and training me. I don't know if she had a premonition that she wasn't going to be with us much longer, but we would be having a conversation, and in the middle of it she would make a hand gesture and explain, 'Now at the end of so and so, I do this.' I never questioned; I listened. When I look back on it now, I think in her own way, she was passing things on to me.

"She was a nocturnal person and she invited me out to her house in Brentwood a couple of times. So I spent some time with her very late at night. I listened to wonderful stories—she was so full of humor—and I just listened. She did say that Liza was going to be big one day, that she was going to be a big star. She always had that feeling about her. And she said, 'How could Liza go wrong, with me as her mother and Vincente as her father?' She was definitely proud of Liza, but I think she sort of missed her. I'd ask where Liza was and when she was coming back and Judy would look sad and say, 'Not soon enough. I wish she were here now.' "

In June 1968, Liza toured Australia and became embroiled in the first of a long series of sexual scandals that would dog her career. She was young, overflowing with passion and emotion, and somehow those qualities conspired to inveigle her into situations which often linked her to the wrong man at the wrong time.

At the time of Liza's tour, John Gary Gorton was Prime Minister of Australia. Middle-aged and married, with a crooked smile and big hands, he was not a particularly attractive man. Unpopular among groups who were opposed to his having involved Australia in the Vietnam War, the controversial Gorton was nonetheless extremely powerful.

When Liza appeared at the Chequers Nightclub in Sydney, Gorton was in the audience. He brought a bottle of champagne to her dressing room after the show—whereupon, legend has it, Liza and Gorton then proceeded to spend an inordinately long amount of time alone together behind the locked door.

Afterward, an Australian newsletter, *Things I Hear*, reported that Gorton was injured when he tried to kiss Liza. His political opponents seized on the implications that Gorton, a married man, was romantically entangled with Liza. The resultant furor was so intense that allegations of impropriety were made against Gorton in the House of Representatives in Canberra and he was eventually forced to make a statement denying any truth to the rumors linking him with Liza.

The Gorton-Liza situation became a cause célèbre in Australia. When word spread to America, Liza issued a statement: "I'm very shocked to hear there have been any allegations. I was very honored by Gorton coming to see the show. It's just as if our president came. It was wonderful. Gorton came backstage with a bottle of champagne. He was with a lady and some friends. I think he has a very manly appearance. He has the sort of face of the people."

Although no one except the protagonists will ever know whether Liza and Gorton engaged in some sort of sexual encounter in her dressing room at the Chequers Nightclub, Liza would ultimately reveal a taste for exhibitionism, for having sex in semipublic locations where, for her, it seemed that the possibility of discovery only lent yet more frisson to the experience.

CHAPTER ELEVEN

Back in America, Liza threw herself into work again, starring as Pookie in *The Sterile Cuckoo,* directed by Alan J. Pakula. She had campaigned vigorously for the part after reading John Nichols's novel. On discovering that Pakula had an option on the book, she contacted him, breathlessly telling him, "I've read the book and I want you to know that I'm absolutely convinced that I am the person to play the part."

Liza's self-confidence paid off and Pakula (whose directorial debut this was) cast her in the part. Looking back, in an interview with the late Tommy Thompson, he remembered, *"Sterile Cuckoo* was one of the happiest times in my life, a great deal because of Liza. I've never seen anybody get more joy out of working, and it's contagious. One of the great delights of Liza is that she is unashamed about her need for affection and her delight in it."

Shooting commenced in September 1968, at Hamilton College in upstate New York. Once again, she was the director's daughter, following Pakula's every instruction, calling him "Boss," and begging him, "Hey, Boss, tell me the story again." Obligingly, Pakula would tell Liza the *Sterile Cuckoo* story, just as a father does to a young child, even beginning the telling with the words, "Once upon a time," just as Vincente used to when he soothed Liza and Tina Nina with bedtime stories.

Although *Charlie Bubbles* had been released, it had been filmed in England, so Liza had never worked with an American film crew. On the first day of filming in upstate New York, they burst into spontaneous applause at her performance. Pakula said admiringly, "They were absolutely stunned. They didn't know from Liza Minnelli. They knew Judy, but they didn't know Liza."

Liza's co-star in the film, Wendell Burton, was transfixed by Liza. He said, "She's one of the nicest people I've ever met in my whole life. She's a hard worker. She took the film very seriously but didn't have an out of shape ego.

"We stayed at a motel in Rome, New York, and there was a little grocery store next door. The owner of the store recognized Liza and said, 'Hey, you know, you should come by my place.' Liza asked, 'Where do you live?' and he pointed to his house. Liza said, 'O.K.' and we went over to the grocery store owner's place and spent a few hours there with him. Liza was extremely accessible to regular people. When they wanted autographs, she was always willing to give them and was always completely open to carrying on a conversation with her fans.

"Liza was so unself-protective in that sense. But at the same time, there was no question that she knew that she wanted to be a great actress and a star and she was determined to achieve it. She was a very smart and focused professional, but at the same time she was not aloof or in any way irregular."

When the film was released in October 1969, Liza's performance as Pookie Adams was highly praised, even by her detractors: Kathleen Carroll wrote in the *New York Daily News,* "Like Pookie, Miss Minnelli is irritating at best. Her voice is too nasal. She looks like a Raggedy Ann Doll. But no matter. She has a plaintiveness about her that tugs at the heart and a sincerity that more than compensates for her inexperience as an actress."

Respected critic Pauline Kael hailed Liza's performance as a great success, raving, "Liza is just about perfect!" An Oscar nomination was inevitable.

The new year of 1969 found Liza in Paris, where she had been asked to host a party thrown in Paris by Menley and James, the Philadelphia cosmetics manufacturers, to celebrate the introduction of their new makeup. The party was held at Drug Store 13, and the list of two hundred and fifty guests was impressive: Gloria Swanson; the duke and duchess of Windsor; Bettina, the onetime fiancée of the late Aga Khan; Emilio Pucci; Diana Vreeland; the Vicomtesse Jacqueline de Ribes; Mrs. Herve Alphand; Jerry Zipkin; Rex Harrison; and Yves St. Laurent. Another famous guest was expected, about whom Liza, clad in brown sleeveless top and pants, expectantly gushed, "I'm waiting to see Brigitte Bardot."

Nightclub owner and chanteuse Regine wore a little black Piaf-style dress and sang three numbers. Young British singer Mary Hopkin sang "Those Were the Days." Then Liza sang the hit song "I Will Wait for You," a song from the popular film *Umbrellas of Cherbourg.*

With sister-in-law Lynne Allen by her side, Liza played hostess and sipped scotch and Coke, and on spying *Vogue* photographer Baron Arnaud de Rosnay, blurted out, "Hi, Baron!" But that night, she could do no wrong. She spent an hour in the receiving line, smiling with glazed eyes, and everyone who met her was enchanted by her verve and freshness. That year, Paris reverberated with the phrase and concept of "Yea! Yea!", co-opted from the Beatles by the pop-crazed Parisians. It epitomized all that was young, energetic, and enthusiastic. Liza personified "Yea! Yea!" and Paris loved her.

At the beginning of 1969, too, Judy married Mickey Deans in a Roman Catholic ceremony in London. "I think he was very gracious and patient with Judy, who was going through a very difficult time," said Ann Pinchot, who worked closely with Mickey on his book *Weep No More My Lady*. She added, "But I don't think he saw the girls very much. Judy was going through such a difficult time, I don't think she wanted to see the girls very much, either, which was very sad."

Mickey was now Liza's third stepfather, living with Judy in London, and halfway across the world over in Los Angeles, Vincente's marital status, too, was changing. To his chagrin, he was estranged from Denise, who had fallen in love with tycoon Prentis Hale. "Vincente was happy with Denise, and I think his heart was broken when she went off with Prentis Hale," said society columnist Doris Lilly, who was an intimate of both Vincente and Denise.

Tina Nina agreed. "Daddy loved Denise very much and Liza told me that he had a very hard time getting over her because she hurt Daddy so much."

According to Doris Lilly, the divorce was friendly and Denise subsequently played a major part in suggesting Vincente become involved with British publicist Lee Anderson, who was divorced first from socially prominent French millionaire Eugene Suter and then from cattle rancher Marion Getz.

Soon, with Denise's active encouragement, Lee was living with Vincente. "Everybody was rooting for Lee to marry Vincente," commented Doris Lilly. "They were together for a very long time until he married her. And then, of course, she did the right thing, with the urging of Denise and everybody else, in marrying him."

Denise herself adds a footnote: "Lee is a very nice lady. Vincente really needed somebody to take care of him and Lee was marvelous at looking after him."

In February 1969, Liza traveled to Puerto Rico and, in a bar named Ocho Puertos, fell in love with a stray mongrel whom she dubbed *Ocho*. "He's some dog," she raved. "Sometimes I see him looking at me and I know exactly what he's thinking, 'We're making it now, but don't depend on it.

Someday I'll probably leave.' " In the meantime, Liza smuggled Ocho back into America with no papers and took him home to Peter, who also loved him. And, as time went on, Liza grew even more attached to the dog and was soon given to boasting that his daily diet consisted solely of caviar, chicken livers, and sirloin steak.

Ocho's existence didn't remain totally trouble-free, though. Soon after his arrival in America, in March 1969, Liza was appearing in Miami when Ocho had an unpleasant encounter with Liza's wardrobe mistress, Rita Stander. Today, Rita Stander's former attorney says, "Little Ocho decided to get a piece of fat Rita and bit her real bad on her arm."

Claiming that her injury now made it impossible for her to execute the seven-second change necessary to her career as a wardrobe mistress, Rita Stander subsequently sued Liza and was awarded $7,500 damages. Ocho's teeth were all extracted and he remained the love of Liza and Peter's life.

On June 22, 1969, Liza and Peter were in Southampton when the phone call from Mickey Deans came informing her that Judy was dead. She was forty-seven years old. Liza broke the news to Vincente; through his shock, he nevertheless noticed that Liza gave the appearance of being in total control. And although Vincente decided not to attend the funeral, Liza, still deferring to his judgment as always, consulted him throughout all the heart-numbing funeral arrangements.

An inquest was held in London on June 25, culminating in a verdict of accidental death by an incautious self-overdose of barbiturates. On June 26, Mickey Deans, accompanying the body, flew into Kennedy Airport. He was met by Peter and Liza, who drove him back to their apartment in Manhattan, where they talked till dawn. With them was Kay Thompson, Judy's closest friend, a multitalented iconoclastic cabaret star and Liza's godmother. She had not only starred in the nightclub act "Kay Thompson and the Williams Brothers" but was also the gifted writer who created *Eloise at the Plaza*.

Fortuitously, Kay was in town and took control of the situation, mothering Liza, reminding her that Judy had had a wonderful life. Kay held Liza close in the moments when the enormity of her loss shuddered through her.

From that moment on, Kay became Liza's mother figure, her mentor, her companion, and her inspiration. Kay had been a legend at MGM, and Judy, who was indisputably influenced by her singing style, had formed an extremely intimate relationship with her. In his book, *Judy Garland,* author David Shipman has alleged, "Another alternative for her [Judy] was homosexuality, and throughout her life she was to have affairs with women. One of these was Kay Thompson, and there were few on the MGM lot who did not know about it." Liza's response to those rumours is not known.

One can only surmise that if she had, indeed, heard and believed that her mother had had lesbian affairs, Liza's feelings for Judy would not have been diminished. Throughout her life, she would identify herself with the gypsys of Broadway and, like her mother, would relish in her homosexual following and her homosexual friends. There was also the matter of her gay relatives; it was well known that her grandfather, Frank Gumm, had been gay, her father's heterosexuality had always been in question and then, of course, there was Peter Allen, her husband. In any event, from the time of Judy's death, Kay also became a major force in Liza's life; Liza, to this day, not only loves but supports Kay financially. She said in 1978, "Kay is an older woman but she's got even more energy than I have. Dances like a fool, marvelous woman! She writes two books at a time and is always decorating or directing something. No. Because of her, I certainly don't fear old age."

With Kay by her side, Liza flung herself into arranging the funeral, dulling her feelings in details and instructions to everyone concerned. Later, she confided, "I don't know how to say this but in a curious way, I felt an elation. When Momma died, I went into shock—but not for long. I said to myself, 'Right, here we go—death. O.K. What does death entail? Burial. I'm going to have to bury Momma.' So, instead of a depression, I went into an elation period. I was going to do it right by J.G."

Judy had been a star, a legend, and the mother she had loved more than anything else. Liza marshaled all her strength, bringing into play all the directorial skills Vincente had somehow, perhaps by osmosis, imbued her with. It was as if she had subconsciously resolved to approach her mother's funeral as if she were directing yet another MGM extravaganza for which she and she alone was responsible.

Sid Luft had wanted Judy to be buried in California, but her children disagreed because Judy had always loathed California, felt far more comfortable on the East Coast. They settled on Frank Campbell's funeral home in New York.

In her will, Judy had stipulated cremation, but Liza, Lorna, and Joey didn't accede to her wishes. Gerold Frank writes that initially it was Sid, Lorna, and Joey who didn't want her to be cremated, and that Liza had capitulated. Mickey Deans contradicts Frank and (in a statement that would be somewhat corroborated when her father, Vincente, died) says that it was, in fact, Liza who refused to allow Judy to be cremated.

Judy was laid out wearing a gray crepe gown, silver slippers, and a silver brocade belt decorated with pearls. On her wrist (as she had once requested of Liza when discussing her funeral) Judy wore her favorite bracelet, which Kay Thompson had given her for good luck when Liza was born.

Over twenty-two thousand people filed by the open mahogany coffin and paid their last respects to Judy Garland. The coffin was covered in a blanket of yellow roses, ordered by Liza, and the service was conducted by the Reverend Peter Delaney. Three hundred and fifty of Judy's closest friends attended the service, including Mickey Rooney, Ray Bolger, Katharine Hepburn, Sammy Davis, Jr., Otto Preminger, Dean Martin, and Lana Turner.

Mickey Deans, who had been married to Judy for just six months, was the only one of her husbands to attend. James Mason, at Liza's request, spoke the eulogy. Mason quoted Liza's tribute to Judy, which she had written in the white heat of her devastating loss. It provides a flavor, not just of

Liza's love for Judy but of Liza's passionate and ever protective commitment to her:

"I wish you could mention the joy she had for life. That's what she gave me. If she was the tragic figure they said she was, I would be a wreck, wouldn't I? It was her love of life that carried her through everything. The middle of the road was never for her. It bored her. She wanted the pinnacle of excitement. If she was happy, she wasn't just happy, she was ecstatic. And when she was sad, she was sadder than anybody.

"She had lived eighty lives in one. And yet, I thought she would outlive us all. She was a great star and a great talent, and for the rest of my life I will be glad to be Judy Garland's daughter."

During the funeral, Kay Thompson stood with her arms around Liza, Lorna, and Joey, comforting them as they all stood together and sang, "The Battle Hymn of the Republic," and tears streamed down Lorna's and Joey's faces. Only Liza, a twenty-three-year-old facing the most tragic of all of life's experiences, remained serene and dignified.

She would, long afterward, admit that in the aftermath of the funeral, once the activity had ceased and she faced the realization that Judy was truly dead, a doctor had prescribed Valium to deaden the pain of her loss. Many years later, recalling the havoc ultimately wrought by that very first prescription, she also remembered the initial relief. "I was so grateful that someone had given me an order, made a decision for me, that I did exactly what I was told. That was when it started."

CHAPTER TWELVE

The day after the funeral, Liza flew back to Boston, where she was filming *Tell Me That You Love Me, Junie Moon,* directed by Otto Preminger. Although she said, "I'm glad to be working, it keeps my brain going," finances also necessitated that Liza earn a living. Judy left nearly $200,000 in debts, and Liza was determined to pay back every penny. Frank Sinatra helped to a hitherto unrevealed extent, but Liza understood that now, more than ever, work was her only deliverance.

She took only one day off from shooting, the day of the funeral. Then she was back in Boston, staying at a motel with the rest of the cast and crew, completing the ten-week shoot. Her role was a demanding one, particularly as she was playing a girl whose face was cruelly disfigured after being splashed with battery acid thrown by a sadistic lover.

Charles Schramm, the makeup artist who not only did Judy's makeup for *The Wizard of Oz* but for her funeral as well, also designed Liza's blood-curdling look for *Junie Moon*. He remembers, "It took me an hour and a half to apply Liza's makeup because it had to look as if her entire face had been burned on one side. When I originally discussed the makeup with Preminger, he told me he wanted it to be horrible to look at but that it wouldn't be seen much in the film.

"Then, when I did the makeup, Preminger liked it too damn much and insisted showing Liza's disfigured face in every scene. I think it was shown too much. I don't think Liza liked that at all. Her face was not a beautiful face to start with and she always tried to do the best to create a better image.

"I felt really sorry for her. At the end of the day, she had to go through the ordeal of my ripping all the makeup off. She didn't complain, though. But I saw her later and she told me that she is glad that the film isn't being shown today.

"Otto treated both of us well, though. Oh yes. He fired six or seven people during the picture. But because Liza was the star of the picture, and her looks depended on me, with me it was 'Mr. Schramm,' all the way. He was very respectful of me. If I had walked off the set, there would have been no picture."

Although Preminger's legendary temperament was never directed at Liza or at Charles Schramm, Preminger did encounter serious problems during the *Junie Moon* shoot. He shot a scene in the Blue Hill Cemetery in Braintree, Massachusetts, in which Liza was shown nude from behind. Whereupon a Mrs. Margaret Forganaro, of Randolph, Massachusetts, the widow of a man buried there, brought a legal complaint against Liza and Preminger for creating a nuisance.

Liza wrote a letter to Mrs. Forganaro protesting, "I wasn't nude anyway. I had the front part of a bathing suit pasted on up here and down there and it was night, and it was beautifully lit, and it was a middle distance shot, and they had artful shadows and they only shot my back anyway." Liza implored, "If she would only look back into my life for the past few months, she would know that I couldn't do anything like that."

Although Peter was there for Liza to lean on, providing stability and security for her more than ever now that her mother was dead, the marriage—such as it had been—was clearly over. Peter and Chris were still struggling while Liza was well on her way to stardom. Years after their split, Liza attempted to detail the reasons for their final breakup: "Peter and I began to argue all the time. I hated Peter's friends and he disliked mine. We were going through *A Star Is Born* together. I was always trying to make things like I was Myrna Loy and he was the Thin Man. When we got married, we were equal in terms of career success and I went up and he went down. We almost broke up when I started making it big."

As in most post mortems of once-happy relationships, Peter's version is diametrically opposed to Liza's, as he claims that if they had both been equally successful, "it would have ended earlier. It would have been two raging-on-the-way-uppers. We would have seen less of each other than we did. We decided to try living apart and it turned out that we liked that much better. I have no regrets. In fact at some point we dragged each other up to adulthood."

On a more specific note, Peter pinpoints the holiday season of 1969–1970 as triggering the final demise of their marriage. "I think that Christmas was the final thing, the start of the big rift between us," he remembered. "We stayed with Vincente in Hollywood. I really liked him. But every night there were parties with all these old movie greats. Liza can enjoy that sort of thing. They've all known her since she was born, and knew her mother, and she makes herself enjoy it as an expression of loyalty to her mother. But I nearly went out of my mind. Everyone was so old. There was Jimmy Stewart and Cary Grant and Gregory Peck and all that age group. And they're so dull to talk to. They've given up any mental stimulation and their brains have turned to butter. I said to Liza, 'I can't bear one more night of this butter talk they go on with.' "

In April 1970, Peter and Liza agreed to a formal separation. Soon after, Liza was nominated for an Academy Award for her performance in *The Sterile Cuckoo,* but just before the event, she had a motorcycle accident and had to have twenty-five stitches. Charles Schramm disguised her injuries with careful makeup and Vincente escorted her to the Oscar ceremonies. Liza didn't win, but after the ceremony, a solicitous Peter telephoned to inquire how the East Coast branch of the Hell's Angels were doing. On the surface, they were on good terms. As Peter affirmed, "Liza can still get to me when tears spring to those big brown eyes. I'll be her friend for ever and ever."

But in his heart, Peter recognized the truth: they were now no longer two kids clinging together against the world. For with her ever increasing success, Liza now had business managers, press agents, and a whole entourage hovering around her constantly. At the time of their final separation, Peter tried to see her in her dressing room and interrupted her in the course of granting an audience to various members of her entourage. In an interview with Tom Burke of *Rolling Stone,* he complained, "She turned around, she was in makeup, the eyelashes, you know, like bugs, she looked . . . frightening, in these white lights, and frightened. I said, 'Now, damn-it, I'm still your husband, and I don't like having to make appointments to see you.' And she started to cry, the makeup ran, she kept saying over and over that she was at fault, that she was no good for me, that she had been a rotten wife. Which, of course, is nonsense. But it is what she felt at that moment. She is very much of the moment, isn't she?"

Peter had known her for all her adult life and was always a perceptive, deep-thinking man. His verdict on the woman he loved and lost is telling: "Liza was always jumping on people's laps and throwing her arms around their necks. People wanted to take care of her, and they did. She has the ability to totally believe in a situation in any given time, which is what Judy had too. She's incredibly smart and intuitive, but she never intellectualizes anything. She'll push down her natural intellect to work with her emotions every time. Liza's philosophy is to be a moving target, but if you keep moving, things still continue to pile up."

Peter moved to the Village, ended his partnership with Chris Bell, and came under the musical spell of Laura Nyro and Randy Newman. Emotionally, he felt like walking into

the river and disappearing forever, but professionally, his
career took flight. Comedian David Steinberg invited him to
open for him at the Bitter End and Peter debuted there in
June 1970. That night, Liza sent Peter a telegram which read,
"Dear Peter, All of my thoughts will be with you tonight. Be
marvelous as always. Love, Liza."

Peter and Liza remained friends but their official version
of the breakup was not the entire truth. Constitutionally
unable to be alone, five months before their official separation in April 1970, Liza had replaced Peter with a new love,
a man she had met and then selected in very much the same
way as Judy had once met and selected Peter for her in Hong
Kong.

One night in Houston, in November 1969, Liza, already
footloose and contemplating separation from Peter, met the
next man in her life. Musician Ray Rogers was the leader of
a group called Bojangles (which consisted of Gary Boggs,
Ozzie Heart, and Rex Kulbeth, who called himself Rex
Kramer). They were playing when Liza, accompanied by
drummer Jerry Fischer and conductor Jack French, walked
into Houston's La Bastille Club. Rogers says, "We played
such a variety, we did everything from rock and roll to Dixie-
land. We were feeling great, we were being promoted really
hot, and lo and behold, here's Liza Minnelli in person, standing there, watching our act."

Ray Rogers clearly remembers Liza's first words, words
that transformed the entire group's lives: "She said, 'You
guys are great. Would you have any interest in joining my
act?' We said of course, it would be wonderful. Then, almost
immediately, Liza flew us to New York to meet her agent,
Stevie Phillips, at ICM."

Just as Judy had once played Svengali to the Allen
Brothers, Liza now took it on herself to do the same with
Bojangles. She may indeed have genuinely been struck by
the talent of the group. After all, RCA had already discovered them, there had been talk of a contract, and they had
been compared favorably to Crosby, Stills, and Nash. They
were young, talented, enthusiastic, and the jewel in their

crown was Rex Kramer, an average guitar player, singer, and songwriter, a green-eyed twenty-one-year-old from Arkansas with boyish charm, an ingenuous smile, and an endearing manner.

Rex was married to a pretty young blond country girl named Peggy (whom he had wed in August 1967) and they had a baby son, Chad. But his domestic responsibilities, the dullness of his daily grind back in Houston—all that was fast discarded by Rex long before he and the band arrived in New York, primed to rehearse with Liza for their February opening at the Waldorf-Astoria.

Liza spent three weeks in intensive rehearsals, working night and day with the Bojangles, with Fred Ebb working on lyrics for them and a new edition to her team, choreographer Ron Lewis, designing a routine for them.

The Waldorf show marked the start of an invaluable collaboration for Liza. She had contacted Lewis at his base in Las Vegas, where he produced shows, and asked him to work with her, but he had refused. Lewis remembers, "I said no because I had seen Liza the previous year at the Sahara and I felt that she was overemotional and oversold and I wasn't impressed. But when I saw *Sterile Cuckoo*, I was so impressed that I contacted her again and we met.

"I spent one second with Liza and I felt I had known her all my life. She jumped all over me, kissing and hugging me. So I began working with her. And I loved it. She's a gypsy. She told me once that she wanted to be a dancer more than a singer and she is a top flight dancer.

"My only problem with her was that she would always come to rehearsals too early. She worked harder and sweated more and got on her knees more than the others. She loves music and she loves to dance, she loves the applause, and she loves to be around dancers. She loves what they talk about, that they work so hard."

At that stage, Peter Allen was still involved in the Waldorf-Astoria show with the Bojangles, and Ray Rogers says, "He was very nice. As a matter of fact, he put together one of the medleys that we did, and he worked with us on it.

But he was still sort of in Liza's shadow. And, from the start, we all understood that although Peter and Liza were married, they were married in name only. Peter would show up for things and his sister, Lynne, went everywhere with him and he made it obvious that he wasn't with Liza. Peter and Liza were really like brother and sister. Sometimes we would go to dinner after rehearsal (Liza always invited us everywhere she went) and Peter would be there, with his sister. Then, after dinner, Peter would go his own way, and Liza would go her own way.''

Liza received a standing ovation at the Waldorf on opening night. Wearing a long red sleeveless dress, she mixed contemporary songs like "Everyone's Gone to the Moon" with classics like "By the Light of the Silvery Moon." The *New York Times* described her as "glowing with bright ideas and vitality."

Ray Rogers and the rest of the band were also glowing with triumph, dazzled by the celebrity-studded evening. Ray says, "On opening night, my parents came up along with the other stars like Gina Lollobrigida and Ed McMahon. But when my parents arrived, she pulled them off to the side to make sure they were happy and treated them like royalty.

"We all had our own rooms at the Waldorf. And after everybody left after the first night, we all went up to Liza's suite. She was very nice to me and she just wanted to talk so we sat in the bathroom—which was as ornate as the Taj Mahal. We sat there and we talked and Rex was banging on the door, and I had a feeling then that something was going on. I kept saying, 'Liza, you know, Rex wants to come in.' She said, 'Don't worry about him.' We were talking and drinking and I remember thinking how great and what a friend Liza was. I was concerned though; I didn't know if Rex was making a move on her or what. I soon found out because, from that night on, Rex and Liza became inseparable."

After the Waldorf, Rex, Ray, and the Bojangles continued touring with Liza, appearing at the Concord Hotel in New York's Catskills Mountains, Constitution Hall in Washington, Hotel San Juan in Puerto Rico, and then the *Ed Sullivan Show.*

Ray Rogers watched Rex gradually insinuate himself further into Liza's heart and was dismayed. "Rex was a con artist—a hustler. Sometimes Liza would make funny little remarks about him to us when he wasn't there and we'd realize that she knew what he was about."

Up till now, Liza had been an old-fashioned daddy's girl, content to dream of love and romance as portrayed in lush MGM musicals. Sex hadn't played a part in Liza's relationship with Peter. Their marriage had always been one of companionship rather than sexual passion and possessiveness, as Peter followed his romantic inclinations and Liza followed hers.

At this stage in her life, Liza became a romantic extremist. Excessive in her appetites and emotions, her tastes in men suddenly began to career dramatically from one extreme to another. With Rex, she ripped away her inhibitions and became suddenly at one with her generation of free love and uninhibited sexuality. Ray Rogers said, "Rex was a superstud. And Liza made it very clear to us that he performed very well sexually and that that was what she wanted from him. She and Rex looked as if they were terribly infatuated and they were all over each other in public, kissing and hugging. At the Concord Hotel one night, all of us went to the bar and Jack French played the piano. All through it Liza and Rex were so physical in front of all the people watching them that we couldn't believe it."

Liza had fashioned for herself yet another version of *A Star Is Born* with a new and unusual twist. In this, her own creation, she was the star from the start. Rex was the newcomer whose ascent to fame and fortune she could facilitate. Not that Rex was waiting around for Liza to work her magic in his favor—taking matters firmly into his own hands, he had no qualms about asserting himself professionally, dominating the entire tour, and distancing himself as much as possible from Bojangles.

Eventually Rex's ambiguous role in the group created an

unbridgeable gap between him and the other Bojangles. "All of a sudden, Rex wanted nothing to do with us. He patronized us. All of a sudden he was telling us what to do," remembered Ray, with bitterness. "We were reminders of home, of a time in which he wasn't the king, when he wasn't all-important, the way Liza made him feel.

"One night at the Concord Hotel, Rex had the audacity to get up and demand to play bass with Jack French and Jerry playing on the drums. He was awful. Jack and Jerry were just looking at each other, like, 'Jesus!' Liza was sitting there looking at him like, 'Oh, isn't he wonderful!' " says Ray who, open-mouthed, watched the entire performance.

Mac Hayes, who played in the band American Sunshine (the successor to Bojangles in Liza's life) and traveled with Liza and Rex for a year, also witnessed similar scenes in which Liza and Rex publicly flaunted their passion for one another, and other moments in which Liza fortified the flames by catering to Rex's ego.

"Liza told me that she loved Rex, but in public she played a role with him. Rex was in a very defensive position. He had always been a ladies man and he was trying to pretend he was Liza's equal, but he wasn't secure. So, when she was with other people, Liza played subordinate to him. In rehearsals, Rex would take command, get a bright idea (which really was useless), then he would try to challenge Jerry Fischer and Jack French, who had been with Liza for years. Liza would sort of say, 'Yes, that's a great idea, Rex; let's try that.'

"But behind his back, she'd give us a look like, 'Please guys, go along with me on this, and then we'll do it the way we want later.' She told me later, in effect, that she appreciated the fact that we kind of went along with it. I saw a lot of tension between them, but Liza did her best to keep his ego fed. She is one of the nicest people in the world and she played the role of 'Oh, I need you, Rex,' to keep him happy."

In March 1970, Rex Kramer left his wife, Peggy. Aware that Rex had been unfaithful to her before, this time, Peggy, who still loved him, felt unable to compete with Liza Minnelli for her husband's affections and contacted a lawyer.

"Twenty years ago, when I first met her, Peggy Kulbeth was a quiet shy country girl who came to me to get a divorce," said her former lawyer, Donald R. Royall. "She loved Rex and he broke her heart. She told me he had run away with a musician and I asked the musician's name. She told me it was Liza Minnelli. Then I heard the full story. Rex was an aspiring musician, Liza Minnelli tore into town like a tornado, they met, and the rest is history."

Royall, the young Houston-based attorney to whom Peggy turned for help, specialized in family matters and was knowledgeable about the more obscure avenues of the law. The Kulbeth case was one of the most notorious of his career and he remembers the details with relish.

"In Texas, at that time, alienation of affection was still a viable course of action and, after three weeks, I realized that Peggy had a case against Liza. My theory was that Liza had used her power in the music world to literally entice Rex away from Peggy, hiring the entire band just to get him."

Liza was in Montreal touring with Rex when she heard the news: Margaret "Peggy" Kulbeth had filed a suit against her for $506,352 for the alienation of affections, in court papers alleging, "Shortly after they met, and with full knowledge that Rex Kulbeth was married to me, the defendant, by use of great power, wealth and influence, gained the affections of Rex Kulbeth and enticed him to abandon his wife."

Liza was petrified. For a time, she and Rex escaped to the relative safety of his grandparents' home in Warren, Arkansas. Then they carried on touring. In the meantime, back in New York, stung now that Liza's relationship with Rex had become public knowledge, Peter Allen uttered a few choice words about the man who had supplanted him in her affections.

To Tom Burke of *Rolling Stone,* he commented, "Rex's relatives live in Arkansas. She goes there with him to pick blackberries, or whatever they pick in Arkansas. Maybe she needs that. She never had any sort of childhood, you know, so maybe she's reverting. He's an incredibly noisy hick; maybe she needs that too. In Arkansas they don't care about Judy Garland."

In an interview with *Time,* Peter went on to say, "Rex was exactly opposite from me. He was a country boy who hated the city and loved girls. Liza enjoyed herself at first. She thought she was getting back to her roots, and after that she began talking about spending the rest of her life on his family's farm in Arkansas and eating black-eyed peas and grits."

Peter's candid but vitriolic comments carry with them an unerring ring of truth, both about himself and about Liza. Months afterward, while filming *Cabaret* in Berlin, Liza would elaborate on her Arkansas interludes to celebrated show-business writer Rex Reed, enthusing, "It's terrific. They're always saying they are poor people, but they've got land as far as you can see and rolling meadows, and grow their own vegetables and fruits, and put up their own canned goods and jellies. And Granny makes corn bread and black-eyed peas and the country tomatoes and that's what life is all about. They've got land, and that's all that's left. They call me Liza Mae, and nobody thinks of me as the daughter of Judy Garland. I don't have to prove anything."

All her life, Liza had lived a rarefied Hollywood existence and she would forever hunger for the innocence she had never known as a child and for the normalcy that she felt incapable of attaining. Continually searching for what she had always lacked, Liza would turn first to Arkansas musician Rex Kramer and then, twenty years later, to Texas musician Billy Stritch.

In May 1972, Margaret Kulbeth's case against Liza was settled out of court, but not before both sides took a series of depositions. Donald Royall, who took Liza's deposition, says, "She was really scared. This was pretty serious litigation. Really, she, Rex and Peggy were just three frightened kids."

Most of the court papers remain sealed in Fort Worth, Texas, but isolated excerpts cast an interesting light on the whole episode. The papers reveal that, for a time, Rex was torn between loyalty to Peggy and passion for Liza. "All I can say is, I don't know how I felt. It was very confusing. One day I felt I did, the next day I felt strongly for Liza." Rex stated that Liza called him many times and that he twice bought her plane tickets so that she could fly down to Houston to see the Bojangles open at La Bastille. Asked whether he knew that Liza was "a stepping stone in your career," with frankness Rex replied, "Businesswise, yes. Not personally."

Both Rex and Liza gave depositions regarding drug taking, but those depositions are not available to the public. However, Ray Rogers has a related comment. "Rex tried to get rid of us by telling Liza that David and I were doing drugs—which was the funniest thing. I think they were doing stronger stuff than grass." Asked whether Rex and Liza were using cocaine, Ray, who adores Liza, answered bluntly, "Yes," then hastily qualified his reply by withdrawing his first, spontaneous answer with "But I don't know for a fact."

Rex and Liza spent a year together, traveling all over America, living out their sizzling love affair. There were continuing problems with Rex feeling professionally undermined while Liza did her utmost to circumvent them by pandering to his ego. Ray Rogers explains, "If Liza found herself in an uncomfortable situation, she would never confront it. She would always rather walk away from reality than confront it. When Liza saw a problem coming, she knew she didn't have to stay to work it out. She totally walked away from it and went on to the next high. She is very insulated."

Mac Hayes, who stayed with Liza long after the end of Rex's reign, adds, "There is no two ways about it; Rex was an opportunist and he tried to make the most of his situation with Liza. I've known him for years and I know he used Liza. But I think Liza knew he was using her. She really loved him."

CHAPTER THIRTEEN

Her relationship with Rex was, in a way, a form of rebellion, a departure for her, one that was totally unrelated to her previous life, to her role as Hollywood's princess. But no matter how carefree her relationship with Rex, no matter how reckless her physical abandonment to him, she could never truly escape the sometimes sobering consequences of being Judy's daughter.

Ray Rogers remembers, "When we were appearing at the Waldorf, Johnny Ray came backstage to see Liza after the show. She had been a stupendous success, but all Johnny Ray could talk about was Judy. She had just finished giving a wonderful performance, then Johnny Ray walked into the dressing room and all he could talk about was her mother. The minute he did that, Liza just turned and walked away. She just didn't want people to talk about her mother all the time. It had nothing to do with her being jealous of her mother because she loved her mother more than anything in the world."

* * *

Just as Liza had campaigned to play Flora in *Flora, the Red Menace* and Pookie in *Sterile Cuckoo,* she threw her heart and soul into capturing the role of Sally Bowles in *Cabaret,* the Broadway musical based on Christopher Isherwood's *Good-bye to Berlin.* She auditioned an incredible fourteen times for producer Harold Prince. But despite Liza's determination, the part finally went to actress Jill Hayworth, who opened on Broadway in 1966 as Sally.

Still convinced that she was born to play Sally, Liza took to singing the song "Cabaret" at the finale of her nightclub act, usually bringing the house down with the sparkle and energy with which she attacked the song.

With her agent Stevie Phillips fighting hard for her, Liza's persistence ultimately paid off, and, to her stupendous joy, five years later she was signed to play Sally in the film version of *Cabaret,* directed by Bob Fosse with music by John Kander and lyrics by Fred Ebb.

Liza flew to Berlin with the blessings of everyone who loved her; Vincente advised her, "Listen to the director," and suggested that she use the actress Louise Brooks as the visual prototype for Sally Bowles. Gwen Verdon helped her pick out Sally's eccentric wardrobe in the Paris flea market, and Kander and Ebb contributed an additional song (written originally for Kay Thompson), which they then tailored specially for Liza, "Maybe This Time," a rousing anthem to hope and passion.

Rex and Ocho traveled to Berlin with her for moral support, although, as it transpired, Ocho ended up being far more important to the proceedings. Rex merely hung around the set, while Ocho upstaged him by playing Marisa Berenson's dog in the film.

Rex remained by her side all through the steamy summer of 1971, and it seemed that his grip on her affections and his place in her life had cemented. He gave her a ring and she, in return, gave him one. Rex had a badminton court set up and, during breaks in filming, he and Liza played together. And although Rex spent his days waiting around for Liza, he did all he could to further his career through her.

Whenever possible, he worked on a documentary of Liza dissecting her stardom. The film opened with a scene showing masses of flowers being delivered to her before a show and Liza in bewilderment, exclaiming, "It's funny. People send you things and you haven't done anything yet."

He also produced an album with her, *New Feelin'*, featuring a new style in which Liza sang standards like "Stormy Weather" in a softer, huskier voice. The album did not do well. "Rex conned her into letting him produce that album for her," says Ray Rogers, acidly adding, "He was way up over his head, but knowing Rex, he must have figured, 'I'm such a good con artist that I can pull the wool over everybody's eyes.' At the time, it may have seemed to him as if he was succeeding, but all those great people who worked with Liza like Jack French and Jerry Fischer, they hated Rex. They hated his guts. Perhaps they wouldn't have felt that way if Rex hadn't boasted about what a great musician he was. To my knowledge, Rex didn't even read music."

When asked in Berlin in July 1971 whether marriage was in the cards for her and Rex, despite Rex's all-embracing involvement in her life, Liza asserted to journalist William Hall, "It's not nice to be trapped, to run and leap into marriage."

Even if her relationship with Rex had approached perfection (and she knew it didn't), by now Liza had slaked her thirst for the conventional, had transcended her Arkansas period, eventually explaining, "First I thought, 'Oh farms are the good life, the simple life.' Only to discover that the good life ain't so simple. A month of it and you've to say, 'O.K, now out of the overalls, where's the action?' "

The answer was simple. The action was to be found with her *Cabaret* director, Bob Fosse. From the first moment that they met, Fosse would prove to be an electrifying element in Liza's life, both personally and professionally. Nearly twenty years older than Liza, he was born in Chicago and, riveted by the theater, trained as a dancer and began performing in vaudeville and burlesque when he was only thirteen years old. After dancing on Broadway, he relocated to Hollywood and appeared in MGM musicals, including *Kiss Me Kate*.

Fosse established himself as a choreographer whose touch was inspired and innovative. He moved on to Broadway to stage *How to Succeed in Business without Really Trying*, to codirect and choreograph *Little Me*, and to direct and choreograph *Sweet Charity*. But although the Broadway production of *Sweet Charity* was a triumph for both Fosse and Gwen Verdon (his second wife), the film, which Fosse also choreographed and directed, was a box office disappointment.

It was therefore imperative to Fosse's career that his next film erase the failure which threatened to blacken his previously flawless record.

Always a driven man, he had an attraction to the illicit, which, according to actress Jessica Lange (who worked with him and spoke about him in a 1991 *Vanity Fair* interview), included a taste for pornography. He was drawn toward the abyss and satisfied his need with a variety of drugs and women. He was immensely gifted and obsessively self-destructive and would be Liza's mentor (and, some say, her lover) until the day he died.

She was now intoxicated with the novel, flirting with the dangerous, skirting anything too conventional, traveling new and titillating avenues with Bob Fosse.

On a visit to Hamburg, she experienced the seamier side of life, later admitting to Rex Reed, "We went to the Dens of Sin on the Reeper Bahn, where they still have semblances of cabaret-going-lesbians fighting in mud puddles on stage, live pornographic sex shows that invite the audiences to participate."

Despite Fosse's influence on Liza, Rex was still in Berlin, increasingly dissatisfied with his role on the periphery of Liza's life. As *Cabaret* script supervisor Trude Von Trotha recalled, "We worked very, very hard on the film. Liza worked harder than anyone, but Rex would just come to the studio and sit around and do nothing. She got sick of him and fell out of love with him."

Liza ultimately decided to allow her head finally to rule her heart, eventually commenting, "I knew Rex was using me. I suspected that way back in Arkansas." Telling Rex that she had fallen in love with another man, despite his entreaties, she broke off the relationship and, in the words of a crew member, "She dumped him in Berlin."

Naturally, Rex, when interviewed by *Time* magazine in 1972, in the aftermath of their love affair, told quite another story. He complained, "The pace she sets for herself is simply terrific. But she just can't slow down. She would worry about not sleeping and would start taking downers to help herself." Rex told tales of tantrums—which closely resembled those described by Georgette Magnani-Minnelli, Liza's stepmother—tantrums after which, Rex insisted, Liza would "literally rave, then collapse." Liza denied that his allegations were true.

There is no concrete evidence that Liza's denials were false, although, having grown up with two parents who were the product of the MGM publicity mill (that factory of misinformation), she has never exhibited a burning obligation to tell the truth to the press. And other factors do suggest that Liza's mood during the *Cabaret* shoot was less than stable.

In June 1971, London *Observer* writer Marcelle Bernstein, who interviewed Liza in Berlin, reported, "When the nerves get really bad she's 'having a willie' and takes Dramamine air sickness pills to calm her down." However, it appears that Liza was also turning to a stronger substance as well. A confidential source who worked on *Cabaret* in Berlin confirmed in a taped interview that he had seen Liza and Bob Fosse snort cocaine during the making of the film, that when his supply of the drug ran out, Fosse became demanding and impossible to deal with, and that the ravages of cocaine also took their toll on Liza.

She was twenty-five when she gave her bravura performance as Sally Bowles. And twenty years later watching that performance—a tour de force in which Liza finally shook off the gilded shackles of the shimmering Garland mystique forever—the sureness of her touch, the radiant effervescence of her performance, are rendered even more miraculous when one considers that throughout much of *Cabaret* Liza was using cocaine.

Despite her subsequent openness about her substance abuse, with the exception of the source who witnessed Liza and Fosse snorting cocaine together in Berlin, the rest of the cast and crew of *Cabaret* maintain a protective silence about what really transpired during the film's shoot.

Script supervisor Trude Van Trotha says carefully, "Liza was a brilliant mimic. At the end of the day, she would ride in the car with me and she would imitate me. She was a marvelous sport. She and Fosse worked very well together. She listened to everything Bob said and followed his rules. If he wanted something, she did it. And she rehearsed everything until she had it. She was very good."

Production manager Pia Arnold worked very closely with Liza and paints an illuminating picture of her at that time.

"I made *Judgment at Nuremberg* with Judy Garland and, in my absolute naïveté, when I met Liza the first time, I said, 'How wonderful, I made a film with your mother.' And it took me weeks to overcome her horror at what I had said. Because, above all, she wanted to be her own person.

"She was generous and warmhearted and giving. We adored her and everybody paid homage, a homage that was due to her. The homage expressed itself with feeling. With admiration and with a special adoration that is reserved for someone exquisitely special, different and delicate.

"She made many friends among the cast and crew; she really did. I think she was young for her age. She was even spoiled, she was half spoiled child and half disillusioned child. She wasn't a trusting person, but she wasn't mistrustful either. She had been hurt so much, and in spite of that, she was outgoing.

"Her charm was (and she wouldn't like to hear this) an attempt to hide her vulnerability. That was the greatest charm she had. This lust for life, this touching way of hiding her vulnerability and outgoing generosity. That was her charm."

During the shoot, Vincente became ill and, although Liza couldn't leave the set, Pia flew to Los Angeles on her behalf and spent a few hours with him.

"I felt it was my duty to soothe Liza, pacify her, and reassure her. She was the star, and I liked her and I wanted to make her feel safe. So I went to see Vincente and sat with him and told him all about his daughter. He was strangely aloof and very gentle, although he was alert when it came to talking about Liza. But other than in those moments, it was as if he was already out of it all."

At that time, Liza was still involved with Rex, and Pia describes him as "her little cat, to feel warm with," observing, "When she was on the farm with him, it was her desperate attempt to feel normal.

"She is a born entertainer and once said, 'If I can't sing anymore, I want to die.' Singing is her life. She feels best when she is singing. She has more than ambition: she is consumed by energy, by drive."

Pia concedes that Fosse (who, at one point, asked Liza to do a nude scene, which she categorically refused) was a difficult and exacting director. "Fosse burned the candle at both ends. He was as ruthless with Liza as he was with any of the actors because he was a perfectionist. But he treated her well and she understood and labored and slaved because she didn't care about anything but the picture.

"She lived on Coca-Cola and potato chips. Everyone wondered, 'How can this beautiful girl live like this?' Because, of course, she had rashes on her skin through eating that kind of food. But even in her most rotten physical state, she was always warmhearted and generous.

"My crew started to complain about a few things but I took them aside and told them, 'Look, Liza is somebody who is so vulnerable and so talented that whatever happens, there will always be somebody who will give her whatever she wants just to exploit her talents. So be gentle to her; be kind to her. Understand the vulnerability and the dangerous situation in which a person like that can be in and forgive.' And it worked."

CHAPTER FOURTEEN

In *Cabaret* when Liza, all dewy-eyed hope-fulness, sings "Maybe This Time," the song encapsulates everything that is Liza: the self-doubt, the passion, the drama, the vibrancy, the innocence. And it was all these qualities that would captivate the next man in her life.

Originally Liza had expected Rex and American Sunshine to open for her at her upcoming concert at the Paris Olympia. But now, after their split, Rex had returned to Houston, where he played with various bands (according to his ex-wife, Peggy, today he teaches tennis in Arkansas). The Paris opening was a few weeks away, and for the first time in years she was alone. On a whim, she flew to Paris anyway and checked into the luxurious Plaza Athénée Hotel on the Avenue Montaigne. Scared thoroughly by her aloneness, she spent an hour biting her nails and shaking with anxiety. Then she made two phone calls. The first was to Kay Thompson, who advised her to run into the street, throw open her arms, and scream, "Paris, I love you." The second call was to actress Marisa Berenson.

Marisa, Liza's co-star in *Cabaret,* played Natalia Landau,

the aristocratic young German-Jewish girl whom Sally befriends. Just two years younger than Liza, Marisa was a princess of international society. Born the granddaughter of both Elsa Schiaparelli, the great fashion designer, and Bernard Berenson, the prestigious art critic, Marisa was also the niece of Robert Berenson, who was in shipping with Onassis.

Beautiful, sophisticated, educated, and multilingual, Marisa had modeled for Diana Vreeland in *Vogue,* was extremely stylish, and had high-level social connections to which Liza was not indifferent.

Both Liza's admirers and her detractors tend to characterize her as a wispy fairylike character, floating through life without direction or emotional control. There is no doubt that when transported by passion Liza is, indeed, sometimes rendered directionless and strung too highly for her own well-being. But it would be a mistake to ignore her capacity to calculate, to make the right moves at the right time, to do what is best for Liza.

Remembering that Marisa, of all those social connections, was in Paris, she contacted her, probably not bothering to hide the desperation in her voice. Marisa, reacting swiftly, promptly invited her to the Riviera, where she was a houseguest of the illustrious Rothschilds.

Although she was aware that her clothes might not be sufficiently chic, after biting her nails even harder, she mustered up her courage and accepted Marisa's invitation. On arrival at the Rothschilds' house, she quickly proved that she was a child of Hollywood. She knew that her hosts numbered among the wealthiest families in the world and, just as she knew (as surely as she knew her own name) that the bigger the Hollywood star, the more opulent the home, it followed that she expected the Rothschilds' home, in keeping with their fortune, to be the glitziest of the glitzy. Instead, she was surprised to find that by Hollywood standards, the Rothschild house was patently unpretentious.

Rallying, she resorted to playing the part of Hollywood ingenue, and when Guy de Rothschild asked her what she wanted to drink, artlessly answered, "Oh, just a bit of home brew." She had thought that she was being cute, beguiling, that her hosts would be charmed by her irreverence in labeling the fruits of the sacred Rothschild vineyards as "home brew." But the only person who laughed was Baron Alexis de Redé. After dinner he asked her out.

Although Liza painted herself as the gauche newcomer, she had, in fact, already been exposed to European aristocracy. Judy, a close friend of the duke and duchess of Windsor, had taken Liza to dinner with them in Paris. And Denise had already introduced her to the baron de Redé, when she invited him to the Persian Room opening.

At the time of their meeting on the Riviera, Alexis de Redé was forty-eight. Wealthy, charming, educated, and distinguished, he has been described as one of the great figures of international finance. He was about as far removed from Arkansas country boy Rex Kramer as the moon from the depth of a coal mine.

She had always been addicted to extremes, and the contrast between Rex and Alexis was monumental and exhilarating. For although Alexis de Redé was not destined to be the great love of her life, he introduced Liza to another theater—one through which she, to this day, moves with grace and self-confidence: Parisian high society.

Alexis invited her to Deauville, but after having sampled life with the Rothschilds, Liza was petrified that her clothes weren't equal to Deauville high society. She flew to New York and begged renown fashion designer Halston for help.

Liza had known Halston since the age of nineteen. She had never had any self-confidence, had always been diffident about her looks, and was insecure about her appearance. She once admitted: "I certainly don't think I'm stunning, but, listen, if I thought I was spectacular looking, maybe I wouldn't be able to act so well. I don't know. Momma didn't think she was attractive, you know. Perhaps because in those old MGM pictures, she was always playing the dumpy girl next door."

Halston reversed all that by reassuring her that she was beautiful. And from the time of their first meeting he did his best to influence her style. Liza later remembered, "Halston liked bosoms when bosoms weren't in. Everybody wanted to look like Twiggy and Halston looked at me and said, 'What are you doing? You've got a great bustline; you have to celebrate it.' And I said, 'What?' Nobody had ever talked to me as if I had any glamour or style or anything. And he really did give it to me, and he continued to give it to me.''

But it was only when she asked him to outfit her in her new persona as the baron's latest love and the toast of *le tout Paris* that Halston's quirky imagination truly caught fire and he finally established himself in Liza's life once and for all. Until then, despite the early blandishments of her stepmother, Denise, she had embraced a kooky beatnik style and never acquired any dress sense. She had always felt unappealing, and she approached her own body accordingly, disguising it, hiding it under as many folds of material as possible.

He instructed her to go to Louis Vuitton to buy some luggage, telling her to select only the number of pieces she could afford. Liza bought five matching pieces of luggage, had them sent to Halston's salon and, a few weeks later, found that Halston had designed an outfit for every occasion—for the races, for the casino, for lounging about at home. He gave her a style that she could call her very own, presenting her with a leather-bound notebook complete with sketches of all the outfits along with color-coded details of how to coordinate them. He also designed special shoes for her with five-inch heels that would show off her spectacular legs.

She enthused, "I love Halston's pants with his blouses with the padded shoulders. They're very, very feminine. They make me look like a female Fred Astaire. What I like best is that all his outfits are carefully planned, even to the hats, but they never look that way."

From that time on Halston became Liza's Pygmalion, guiding her from blue jeans and nebulous dresses to her elevated status as one of the ten best-dressed women in the world, feted by *Vogue* and *Women's Wear Daily*. Along the way, he would also become her best friend, her brother—and her partner in drug addiction.

Armed with Halston's wardrobe, she returned almost immediately to Europe. When she was once again with the baron, he presented her with a diamond ring. Friends and press whispered that an engagement was inevitable, but Liza demurred, "It's a friendship ring; we are just friends." Calling Alexis a great gentleman, she added, "Very serious, I'm always saying to him, 'Alexis, laugh.' And I, like, jab him in the ribs or sort of punch him, and he laughs."

Alexis and Liza laughed their way back to the Riviera again, where, on September 3, 1971, they attended the Raffles Red and White Ball at the Hotel Eden Roc, Cap d'Antibes. According to social columnist Suzy, "The Baron never left her side. The Baron, a prime mover in the international set, is celebrated and rightfully so, for his unerring taste." Liza wore a white jersey Halston outfit and the baron's ring, and danced the night away under a full moon.

In the second week of September, following Liza's grand triumph at the Olympia (where, at a $500 a person charity gala, the audience gave her a standing ovation lasting almost an hour), Alexis threw a party in Liza's honor at his seventeenth-century palace, the Hotel Lambert on the Isle St. Louis in the heart of Paris.

Liza made a memorable entrance down the palace's ornate staircase, lit by a hundred candles, while violins serenaded her in the background and the scent of a thousand hothouse orchids floated in the air. Later, Fred Ebb observed, "Liza was like Alice in Wonderland that night." Mac Hayes, then with American Sunshine and opening her Olympia show, also felt as if he had stepped through the universe's most precious looking glass and into a radiant dream.

He remembered, "That night in Paris was the ultimate experience. We traveled with Liza for a year and a half. She loves everyone she works with to be part of one big family and she treated us that way and invited us everywhere. Liza insisted on including American Sunshine in the most elegant of evenings—we were like her family.

"Liza was dating the baron, and the whole of international society seemed to be there that night, including Salvador Dali, Richard Burton, and Elizabeth Taylor. Just after her entrance, we tried to get a drink, when Richard Burton stopped and introduced himself to us. He said how much he enjoyed us in the show, then asked if we were from Texas, and laughingly said, 'Boy, you don't see this kind of crap in Texas, do you?' We mumbled something like 'No we don't.' And he said, 'Well, these people are all a bunch of stuffed shirts. Come on, I want you to meet the old lady.'

"He dragged us over to the table where Elizabeth Taylor was sitting. Burton walked right up to her and said, 'Fatty, I want you to meet the guys in the band.' Then he introduced us and Elizabeth insisted that they get us chairs so we could sit with them all evening. That was what our life with Liza was like on the road, because she was so goodhearted and included us in everything."

By the end of the month, Liza's spell as "La Petite Americaine" (as the bedazzled French called her) was over. She was back in America, first singing at the Greek Theater, then at the Riviera, Las Vegas, where she broke all existing box office records. For two performances a night, seven nights a week, four hundred and fifty people a show flocked to see her, with fans tipping maitre d's as much as $700 extra for a ringside seat.

As in Paris, in Las Vegas Liza was feted by ecstatic audiences every night. At the time, Eugenia Shepherd noted, "Standing ovations are no every night occurrence in a place where some of the world's top talent is entertaining its heart out to amuse moody and tired gamblers. Las Vegas has the reputation for being the world's coldest audience, but Liza Minnelli knows how to arouse it."

Eugenia queried Liza on the possibility that marriage to the baron was imminent. For a moment, she stalled, then eventually replied, "If I'm getting married, I don't know anything about it yet. I don't even know if I want to get married. It doesn't seem very necessary these days."

Speculation was rampant that a de Redé–Minnelli union was still likely, but Liza's intimates whispered that she found Alexis's sophisticated European way of life a trifle awesome.

Las Vegas, however, did not overwhelm her in the least. During her Riviera run, she stayed in a rented house on Rancho Circle, went to bed at 4:00 A.M., slept until 12:00, and spent her afternoons in the swimming pool.

Liza was alone, and alone had always been synonymous with lonely for her. Around the time of her Las Vegas appearance, a rare period in her life when she was free of romantic entanglements, Liza talked to Tina Nina about her inability to be alone. "She told me that she didn't sleep nights," Tina Nina remembered. "And she said, 'Sometimes, at three o'clock in the morning, I have to phone my friends and make sure nothing is going on without me, and only then can I fall asleep.' That impressed me so much because it showed me that Liza has an enormous, abnormal need not to waste any time. She doesn't want to miss anything. She's a wonderful person to be with and you always have a lot of fun with her.

"But she is not a normal person. There is nothing average about Liza. She is constantly looking for someone to love her, to make her feel worthwhile. She loves people and she loves to be loved."

Rex no longer figured in Liza's scheme of things and Alexis was six thousand miles away in Paris. She was only happy when she was in love, so she did what she had to and sought love from yet another source. In many ways, Desi Arnaz, Jr., and Liza Minnelli were made for each other. Far more of a show business baby than Peter Allen, and as boyishly charming as Rex, Desi, like Liza, was Hollywood aristocracy—as royal, in Hollywood terms, as Alexis de Redé was in his world.

Liza was six years old when Desi was born on January 19, 1953. The birth of the first child of Lucille Ball and Desi Arnaz, Sr., was an event hailed with such fanfare that it even upstaged Eisenhower's Inauguration in the headlines. As a baby, he appeared in *I Love Lucy;* when he grew up, he became a rock singer and musician, and he made his film debut in 1972 with *Red Sky at Morning.*

Their parents had been friends. However, Richard Heard, a childhood friend of Liza's who lived on the same Beverly Hills street as Lucy, claimed that she secretly despised Judy. "Lucy was a hard worker. Judy was boozed up, drugged up, but she had great talent and had the fans, so Lucy was vociferous in her dislike of Judy."

Nevertheless, Vincente had worked with Lucy and Desi; they were part of her childhood memories, adults who had been around for as long as she could remember. So when Desi Arnaz, Jr., materialized backstage at the Riviera Hotel on her closing night, Liza greeted him like a long-lost relative.

Desi had just seen a Tony Bennett concert and, afterward, had decided to go to the Riviera to pay his respects to Liza. He would always remember her, as he first saw her: "If it wasn't love at first sight, it was just instantaneous. I looked at this girl and thought, 'Well, I want to be with her forever.' Right then, there was no doubt in my mind that we were destined to be together for the rest of our lives. I never felt totally secure before, with anybody. I never felt so without fear. I could see that Liza could handle anything."

Peter Allen came from another world, miles from the country of Liza's birth; Alexis from another social stratum; and Rex from another universe. But Desi, almost literally, was just the boy next door, a family friend whose relatives worked in the same family business.

As Liza put it in a conversation with writer Guy Flatley, "If you've both been raised in show business, that eliminates a lot of opening questions like, where are you from? We had the same kind of life."

Desi proposed marriage to Liza just three weeks after their first meeting. At the time, they were both in Arizona, where Desi was playing in a tennis competition. Liza was there in a cheerleading capacity. Afterward, he disclosed, "I made it a definite proposition in a much more romantic place. At night. And she accepted right away. Liza is making me very happy and has brought out in me all the virtues. More tolerance. More love. More understanding."

Desi's version of his whirlwind romance makes it sound as if, from the first, his love affair with Liza progressed effortlessly. But that isn't the truth. Mac Hayes, who was in Las Vegas with Liza, says, "I remember Liza came to my room late one night and she told me that she and Desi had had an argument and that she just wanted to talk. She said that he had stormed out, or something like that, and then she started crying.

"She was unsure about whether or not she should be dating him, because he was so much younger than her. She was worried about Desi and worried if she was doing the right thing. But I never saw them fight.

"Desi was just a fun loving kid. He and Liza had a great physical attraction and they had a great rapport for each other from their childhood, and because of their families, they had a lot of things in common. Desi was really just a good-time guy."

As always with a new love, never one to hold back, Liza instantaneously gave herself up to Desi, making him the fulcrum of her existence and surrendering herself totally to him. "Desi and I are deeply in love," she proclaimed ardently, before settling down and attempting to analyze the attraction. "The great thing about him is, he's not only my beau, but my friend too. That's important. He's intelligent and considerate. He's not as wound up as the rest of his family. He's what I had in mind in my romantic fantasies of the true gent.

"Because of the way we were raised, always around show business people, Desi is much older than he is and I'm much older than my 26 years. Desi always puts me at ease. He's so understanding. He really has a much greater understanding of people than anyone I've ever met, perhaps, a psychiatrist or a psychologist. He studied psychology, you know. All aspects of people interest him. But don't get me wrong. He's not the kind of person who types you or gives you advice. He just listens. He's always helpful, besides being terrifically funny."

After Las Vegas, Liza played Tahoe, Toronto, and then the Olympia in Paris. Her French fans lived in hope that Liza would soon become the baroness de Redé. But by December 22, reports began to surface that Desi Arnaz was seen in Liza's dressing room at the Olympia. The de Redé interlude was definitely over.

CHAPTER FIFTEEN

Nineteen Seventy-two would be Liza's year. The excitement and energy of her performances, both live and on film, were at their peak. At the beginning of the year, just a short time before the *Cabaret* premiere, she opened at the Eden Roc in Miami. According to an eyewitness, her performance was so wholeheartedly physical that after just two numbers, her plum colored dress was spotted with sweat. Meanwhile, her dresser waited in the wings, prepared with oxygen, smelling salts, a towel, and another dress for when an exhausted Liza came offstage.

When her show closed in Miami, Liza was guest of honor at Diana Vreeland's party thrown for her at Al Mounia, feted by a group of assorted glitterati who were eminently worthy of her new high-society sophisticated image: Marisa Berenson, Kitty Carlisle Hart, Maxime de LaFlaise, Andy Warhol, Arlene Dahl, Lily Auchincloss, and Joel Grey.

Cabaret opened in New York on February 13, 1972. During filming, Liza had been insecure about her performance, calling Vincente innumerable times for advice. Invariably, he counseled her to listen to the director, and when he saw the rough cut of the film, he acknowledged that his advice had paid dividends.

The film that showcased Liza's talents so effectively was a complete anomaly. *Cabaret*'s backdrop of the perversion and decadence of Berlin in the jaded years between the two wars was diametrically opposed to the old MGM musicals that had made Judy Garland a star.

This was Liza's declaration of independence from the legacy of Judy, marking the transition from Liza the stray waif whom everyone wanted to adopt to Liza the vamp. As Sally Bowles, she is by turns wistful, brittle, optimistic, soulful, intense, childish, vampy, stagy, and romantic. Liza's Sally sparkles with desperation and glitters with all the possibilities of life.

Of Liza herself, her *Cabaret* co-star Joel Grey observed, "She has that personal magnetism. She is capable of making you care about her, making you want to protect her. Then you realize that she is perfectly capable of protecting herself. She's the best person to be around because she tends to get very calm in frazzled situations. She's a good anchor, a steady ship. She's had to be—considering plenty of people have tried to sink her."

When Liza makes her first entrance in *Cabaret*, the camera skims over her. She is thrown into relief by the contrast made by girls of the Berlin Kit Kat Club, who are world-weary black-stocking-clad robots. At this stage Liza is peripheral. It is the MC (played by Joel Grey), sinister, lascivious, who has the spotlight.

We only see her in close-up in the next scene, in which she welcomes the suave Michael York (who plays the English teacher Brian Roberts) to Berlin, struggling to express herself in German. She calls everyone "darling." Her face is unlined, her round eyes are fringed in acres of eyelashes, and she strains to be nonchalant.

In the next scene, Liza sings "Mein Herr" at the Kit Kat Club, and her revealing costume shows that she is plumper in *Cabaret* than in previous films. When she sings, wearing a bowler hat, black stockings, black calf boots, using the chair as a sexual prop, it is an act full of suggestiveness, one from which rock star Madonna would borrow nearly twenty years later.

Liza's fashions, redolent as they were of Marlene Dietrich in *The Blue Angel,* exuded tremendous style. As soon as the film was released, drag queens began sporting black stockings and bowler hats, and Liza's entire *Cabaret* look materialized in bars all over the world. With the advent of *Cabaret,* Liza, like her mother, had caught the imagination of female impersonators, who from that time forward would obsessively parody her.

Watching *Cabaret* again, in the light of the years that have passed since Liza made the film, it is almost eerie to realize not only how autobiographical but also how prophetic parts of the script have turned out to be.

Guided by the hand of Kander and Ebb, who were playing an increasingly large role in enhancing the mythology that was the bedrock of Liza's career, the reworked character of the cinematic Sally Bowles is also sometimes indistinguishable from that of Liza Minnelli herself.

Sally romanticizes her father, just as many people close to Liza believe that she has romanticized Vincente. Her relationship with Michael York's character, Brian, in many ways parallels her relationship with Peter Allen. Her relationship with the baron mirrors her next relationship, with Baron Alexis de Redé. And her line "I am going to be a great movie star if sex and booze don't get me first" would also prove to be chillingly prophetic.

The *New York Times* praised Liza's performance without reservation. "And when at certain moments that theater is occupied by only Liza Minnelli, working in a space defined only by her gestures and a few colored lights, it becomes by the simplest means, an evocation of both the power and the fragility of a movie performance so beautiful that I can think of nothing to do but give thanks. As for Miss Minnelli, she is sometimes wrong in the details of her role, but so magnificently right for the film as a whole that I should prefer not to imagine it without her. With her expressive face and her wonderful (and wonderfully costumed) body, she moves and sings with a strength, warmth, intelligence, and sensitivity to nuance that virtually transfixes the screen."

She made the covers of *Time* and *Newsweek* in the same week and afterward cracked, "Where can you go after that? Only down." She may have been joking at the time, but her remarks had been prompted by a deep and abiding insecurity that would never completely evaporate. For just as Judy had reached the pinnacle far too soon with *The Wizard of Oz*, so, it would transpire, did Liza with *Cabaret*.

Cabaret was an unqualified success, a sure-fire hit, which Liza promoted via a plethora of press interviews. Yet despite her triumph, despite the praise her performance as Sally Bowles was garnering, Liza was under a great deal of nervous strain, and her skin was marked with blemishes.

Cosmopolitan writer and editor Guy Flatley interviewed her in the aftermath of *Cabaret*. He recollected, "We were at the Plaza Hotel and she was accompanied by her publicist and seemed very exhausted. She almost fell asleep. She was not uncooperative, but not very forthcoming, either, so it wasn't much of an interview. I said, 'Well, I can see you're very tired and I've got enough here, so there's no sense in staying.' And she said, 'Hey Guybo, where are you going?'

"She was surprised that I was upset and she asked me to come to 'The Dick Cavett Show,' where she was guesting the next evening, and suggested we go back to her apartment afterwards. So I did. She was still living in the apartment she had shared with Peter Allen because although they were divorced, they were still friends.

"So, we all sat around waiting for her to finish the show, and then we went to the apartment. Desi Arnaz was there and was relatively unguarded, animated, laughing and joking. Somehow, the conversation got around to the child he had with Patty Duke. And I said, 'If you and Liza get married, what are you going to do with the baby?' Desi said, 'Which baby?' And I said, 'Well, it says right here that you fathered Patty Duke's baby.' He said, 'Oh yeah, that's right.'

And then Liza laughed. She thought that was pretty funny that he didn't know which baby.

"That second evening Liza looked terrific, but I think she even commented on her appearance and referred to it as 'Nothing so great, but what can I do about it?' I asked her the question 'Is it true, Miss Minnelli, you drink a bottle of Grand Marnier a day?' She got up, and I think she took a slug of scotch or something because she thought it was so silly that I asked her that. But I had the impression that she was a pretty big boozer at that point.

"I liked her. And she was fascinating, talented, gave me a lot of time, although she didn't have to. She seemed genuinely nice. The second night, I would say she was a super energetic, vibrant, warm personality. I felt that she was sincere."

After her success in *Cabaret,* Liza went on to triumph on television as well. Her television special, *Liza with a Z,* was taped in May at the New York Lyceum in front of a large audience which included Kay Thompson and Harold Arlen.

Liza wore a Batman-style white slack suit with a white fur wrapped around her neck and sang "Liza with a Z," a song written especially for her by Fred Ebb. The show in turn reflected each of Liza's chameleonlike images: the lost waif, the romantic dreamer, the clown, the sophisticated Parisian cabaret star. The audience at the Lyceum stood up and cheered as Liza sang "Cabaret."

Liza with a Z was aired on September 10, 1972. After-ward the respected *Daily News* critic Kay Gardella extolled her virtues: "Liza hit the home screen like a new life force, illuminating it with an electrifying brightness. She has the love of her profession and this comes through. She has the great talent inherited from her mother, Judy Garland, and this comes through. And she has something handed down from all the truly great performers from the past—her whole-hearted desire to entertain you and her determination to give all and then some. It's been a long time since we cried at the end of a television show. *Liza with a Z* was sensational with an *S*." Kay Gardella's review chimed with the opinion of Liza's peers, for she went on to win an Emmy for the show.

In the course of her press interviews she announced that she intended next to star as Zelda Fitzgerald, an interesting choice given that Zelda, like Judy, was an alcoholic who spent much of her life in institutions. But Liza, glossing over that aspect of Zelda's life, explained, "She had all those energy levels going for her. And nowhere to put them. I've got a lot of sympathy with energy levels."

She also planned, she said, that Vincente would direct the film. "Ever since I was five years old and first learned to tap dance, I wanted to work with my father. I've got to be terribly sophisticated in it, you know. You don't think that's really me? Well, Daddy made a lady out of Mom on the screen and I'm looking forward to him doing it for me."

Her mother remained very much alive in her heart and in her mind. In the spring of 1972, Jim Bailey, the actor-impersonator whom Judy had befriended, also became close to Liza. She had seen him perform as Judy and had swooned, "Oh, he is Momma; he even sings like her. I was totally speechless with admiration! He becomes Momma when he is performing. I even went backstage and congratulated him, and he was really super nice, and so I asked him over because I wanted to talk to him about how he does it; it's a mystery to me. When he's onstage, for me, it's like Momma is alive again."

Always *une excessive,* seeing Jim Bailey on stage as Judy wasn't sufficient for Liza—she had to be on stage *with* him.

Bailey remembers, "Liza approached me and asked how I felt about trying to re-create her Palladium appearance with Judy. She explained, 'We wouldn't be doing it for anyone else, just for ourselves.' "

Thrilled at the prospect, Bailey willingly agreed to appear with Liza in a special two-night show at the Flamingo, Las Vegas. "During rehearsals, Liza kept it light and was fun," remembered Bailey. "But before the show, when I was getting ready and was already in my makeup as Judy, my dresser told me that Liza had come to see me. I motioned her to bring her in. The door opened. And then I heard Liza say in a trembling voice, 'Momma, I have something for you.'

"All of a sudden, I realized that she was doing an improvisation and that, even though we were not on stage, she was already relating to me as her mother. It was most eerie for me because I had to get into the part even before I got on stage and this was as if I were already on stage. Only now there was no audience, just Liza and me.

"She sat down next to me. Then she said again, 'I have something for you, Momma.' And she handed me a small box. I opened it and inside was a ring—a ring that Judy had once owned. I looked at Liza and she said, 'It belongs to you, Momma. The ring belongs to you.' And then she started crying. She cried her eyes out, cried as if her heart was breaking. It was very emotional."

After Liza left the dressing room to repair her makeup, Bailey was called onstage and opened the show as Judy. Then he brought Liza out and, in a re-creation of Liza and Judy's first Palladium appearance, he introduced Liza by singing "Hello, Liza!" to the tune of "Hello, Dolly." Then they sang duets, joked, and did their utmost to duplicate Judy and Liza at the London Palladium.

The rest of the show consisted of a solo performance by Liza and then ended with a final song from Jim Bailey. "Liza introduced me to the audience," remembered Bailey, "then she said, 'Jim has the gift of the angels because, through him, I have been able to see my mother once more.' It was very moving and I understood. For those two nights, Liza was on stage with her mother and she had the chance to have what she really wanted: for an audience to see her working with Momma again. To the average person this may sound sick, but to Liza, I think it was a chance to relive the past."

During their time together, Bailey witnessed Liza's ambivalence toward Judy, as well as her flirtation with drugs. "At the time I was aware of the drugs," says Bailey, then he pauses and qualifies his statement. "I wasn't totally aware, but I saw her depressions and her insecurities. She's very hyper, and she is the kind of person that can't be alone. She

needed people around her constantly. She was very insecure. I would see her do an incredible show, and she'd come
off and say, 'Oh God, was I any good, was I really good?' And
I'd say, 'Oh Liza, yes, you were wonderful.'

"She was always striving to be her own self, as opposed
to being Judy Garland's daughter. But I don't think Liza will
ever get over her mother's death. There were a lot of things
that were left unsaid between her and Judy. Liza wanted to
almost lionize her mother. There were times when she said
that Mother was bad about this or that, but it was difficult for
her to talk about her mother in that way.

"Liza was hit with a lot of negative problems from her
mother, and she tried to clean them up. She paid off a lot of
Judy's debts. She didn't have to. She did it because she
wanted to preserve the memory of her mother."

In May 1972 Liza flew to London for the British premiere
of *Cabaret*. While she was there, she and Desi were separated for six weeks while he was making a film in Japan.
Impetuously, Desi confided, "It's the longest time we've
been apart and it's terrible without her. I can't get her out of
my mind. All we want to do is love, live and love together."

On May 21, 1972, Desi announced his engagement to Liza
with the words "I love Liza very, very much and we will
most likely be married within the next six months. The difference in our ages is no problem. That's not as important
when you are as much in love as we are."

Over in London, Liza didn't sound completely committed to the idea of becoming Mrs. Desi Arnaz, Jr., in her
characterization of the engagement: "The reason Desi announced it officially was because some people were trying to
make our friendship sound cheap. Desi wanted to make it
clear that I wasn't just a girlfriend—we are engaged." Then
she mused, "It is so nice that there is somebody left with
honorable intentions. I like Desi better than anybody else.
That's all I want to say."

She did finally elaborate in another interview with the
British press, during which, dressed all in black and wearing
no socks or shoes, she said, "My ugliness overwhelms me.

I'm really weird looking. Take your average standards of beauty and that ain't it." Then she reflected for a few minutes before adding, "I'm engaged to one of the great looking men of our time. So I can't be too unattractive. Can I?"

On May 23, 1972, after having turned down four previous invitations to appear in front of them, Liza gave her first performance for the British royal family, starring in the prestigious "Royal Variety Performance," a televised gala held that year to raise funds for the British Olympic Appeal. Dan Rowan and Dick Martin were compeers, and the show co-starred Roger Moore, Michael Caine, and the Osmond Brothers. At that stage, the Osmonds were at the height of their fame, mobbed before the show by adoring British fans. Nevertheless, Liza was indisputably the star of the whole event. As *Daily Telegraph* critic John Barber observed admiringly, "Surely no one ever took the stage of the London Palladium like Liza Minnelli."

Liza and Desi were reunited and, now formally engaged, returned to California and toured the States in Desi's Aston-Martin. This was Liza's first holiday in four years and she relished every second of her time with Desi.

In some ways, he was a combination of Peter and Rex, in that like Peter, he was a brother figure, and like Rex, a sexual partner. Desi also possessed another advantage—a family. Liza, who had divided her childhood between Judy and Vincente and their respective partners, had always longed for a conventional family and so had embraced life with the Kulbeth family wholeheartedly. In theory, the idea of becoming a Kulbeth of Warren, Arkansas, had been a seductive one for Liza. But now that the novelty of life down on the Kulbeth farm had worn off, the Arnaz family were an ideal substitute, eager and willing to welcome Liza—exactly what Liza yearned for.

In September of 1972, Liza and Desi were living at home with Lucy. The scenario might not have suited another twenty-six-year-old, set on independence. But Liza was different. Liza was searching for a family and yearned to belong. And, at that moment, the Arnaz family seemed to be tailor-made for her. As Liza said, "Lucy's a genius. I adore her. Wherever I am, she calls me up to see if I'm taking care of myself. For Desi's sake, especially, I'm glad we moved in with her."

When Liza played Las Vegas in October 1972, at the Riviera, Liza introduced Lucille Ball as "my future mother-in-law." Lucy, returning the compliment, said of Liza, "Yes, I love Liza. She is a wonderful girl. She has a mind like a trip hammer and a huge vitality. My husband and I just know that she and Desi are going to be great for one another."

Desi's sister, Lucie Arnaz, apparently was not so sure. A source close to Liza says, "Lucie was immensely jealous of Liza. Lucille Ball wanted Liza to marry Desi and mothered Liza. But Lucie Arnaz was jealous. On one Halloween, Liza was all dressed up for a costume party as an ice cream soda. She ran up to Lucie Arnaz and asked her, 'Guess what I am?' and Lucie snapped back, 'A sore throat.' Liza knew how jealous Lucie Arnaz was of her, so she just walked away. She knew exactly who she was dealing with."

She was still working with choreographer Ron Lewis, with whom she had first worked at the Waldorf. He remembers, "At one point Liza had the idea of doing an act with two girls. Fred Ebb and I and everybody else were really against it. Liza is not Christie Brinkley in the looks department. So we thought it wouldn't be a good idea to put two dancers (who were probably going to be younger and better looking and would probably dance better than her) on each side of her. And also, at the time she was fighting her weight. But Liza insisted on sticking to her concept, so we went with it.

"We held an audition for girls and a thousand girls turned up. Liza watched the audition and didn't say anything, until we got to the best last ten dancers. Then she picked the two best looking, best dancers there. We kept saying, 'Don't put that girl next to you.' But Liza did and it was a wonderful act.

"When Liza worked with me she was just like one of my dancers. When she was playing in Vegas and I was rehearsing one of my other shows—every morning at ten she would come to a warehouse and learn all the steps, dancing behind the kids. She wanted to learn everything. We were doing a cancan and Liza said, 'I've always wanted to do a cancan.' So there she was—after doing two shows at the Riviera—dancing behind these chorus girls, trying to learn the cancan number because she had never done one. She was a big star, but she still did everything she could to learn."

In October 1972, Liza went to see Lorna Luft, who was appearing at the St. Regis Maisonette. Since her late teens, Lorna had desperately craved singing success, but it had somehow eluded her. Her inheritance compelled her to suffer comparison with both Judy and Liza, and it was inevitable that she would be found wanting. Always feisty, Lorna insisted, "People say to me: do I identify with Mama or with Liza? And I tell them the only person I identify with is myself. I may be the daughter of Judy Garland and the sister of Liza Minnelli, but I also happen to be a performer in my own right."

From her father, Sid Luft, Lorna had inherited a relentless determination to succeed, and she had done her utmost to carve out a niche for herself in England. There she attempted to storm the London Palladium, causing *Daily Express* critic David Wigg to comment, "In time, this bubbly blonde should blossom into a stylish cabaret singer. But first she should find herself and forget her family."

For the time being, however, Lorna's family did all they could to support her show business career. That night at the St. Regis, Liza joined her in a duet of a Judy favorite, "You Made Me Love You," which Liza called "a family song, no matter which of us sings it—and someone will always sing it." Peter Allen, ever loyal and loving to Liza, was there that night too, and in a moment of nostalgia perhaps contrived for the photographers present, he and Liza danced together. Two months later, in December 1972, their divorce became final. Liza was now free to marry Desi and to take her place in the Arnaz family.

* * *

On March 22, 1973, Desi was by Liza's side as he, Vincente, Lee, and Liza attended the Academy Awards. She had
been nominated as Best Actress for her performance as Sally
Bowles, and before the ceremony an intrepid reporter rashly
suggested to Liza that Judy's ghost would be hovering over
the proceedings. A startled and discomfited Liza laughed her
edgy laugh, then with presence of mind reasoned, "Perhaps
it's no bad thing. Maybe it's a kind of proof of eternity. That
something remains, and goes on and on."

Liza wore yellow—her father's favorite color—to the ceremony and, as the names of the other nominees were called
out, held on tight to Vincente and Desi's hands. When Rock
Hudson read out Liza's name, he said, "This is a horse race
and bloodlines count. Liza's got the bloodlines." She was not
amused, but all that was forgotten when presenter Gene
Hackman announced that she had won and she and Vincente
and Desi all let out almighty shrieks. Her acceptance speech
was simple: "Thank you for giving me this award. You've
made me very happy."

Vincente's instinctive reaction was to think how much
Judy would love to be there to see this moment. Although
she had won a 1939 Special Oscar for "her outstanding performance as a screen juvenile, during the past year," Judy
had never won the Best Actress Oscar and had always re-
gretted it. In his heart Vincente knew that although Judy the
mother would have been proud, Judy the actress might well
have been jealous that her daughter had surpassed her.

CHAPTER
SIXTEEN

After the Academy Awards, Liza said, a trifle wistfully, "When you have a great success early on in your career, as I did in *Cabaret,* that first rush of success becomes related to a character who is extroverted and kind of racy. That image of you will continue when it never really had anything to do with the way you felt inside."

There are those who believe that Liza, despite her protests, had in her intensity assumed Sally Bowles's personality. And, just as Sally was addicted to adventure, to drama, to serial relationships, so, it seems, was Liza.

In May 1973, exactly a year after Desi had first announced their engagement, she was in London giving three performances of *Liza with a Z,* the first at the London Palladium, the second at the Royal Festival Hall, and the third at the Rainbow Theater, Finsbury Park.

She and Desi, separated again through work, were talking to each other on a twice-daily basis. Nevertheless, here was Liza, in London, the toast of the town, without Desi, but with Kay Thompson by her side.

Her first night, at the London Palladium, was ultra-star-studded, with Michael Caine, Bianca Jagger, Jack Jones, and Susan George in the audience applauding her admiringly. With them was British comedian Peter Sellers, who, after the show, went backstage and congratulated her.

When they met, he was already an international star, celebrated for his role as Inspector Clouseau in *The Pink Panther* series. Privately, he was also known as an inveterate womanizer. Married in 1951 to Anne Howe, he left her after falling passionately in love with Sophia Loren. His son, Michael, recalls, "The singer Dorothy Squires, a friend of his, talked to him about Sophia Loren and asked him, 'Peter, what do you want to mess your life up for?' He thought for a minute and then shrugged and said, 'Luv, I just can't help it.' When he got the 'scent' he just couldn't help himself."

Passionate and impulsive, he fell in love with the stunning blonde Swedish starlet Britt Ekland in 1964 and married her just eleven days after they met. At the time of his initial meeting with Liza, he was on the verge of divorcing his third wife, British aristocrat Miranda Quarry, and as Michael Sellers puts it, "He was looking out for wife number four." Setting eyes on Liza Minnelli for the very first time in his life, Peter Sellers was convinced that she fit the bill.

"It was like an express train bearing down on me and I simply could not resist her," recalled Peter, sometime before his death in 1980. "Liza was performing in London and she used to insist that I sit in the front row of every one of her performances, and she would sing just to me. It was an incredible experience."

Peter believed in astrology, clairvoyance, yoga, reincarnation, and all manner of psychic phenomena. He was a child of the cinema, an incurable dreamer who admitted, "With women I was always romantic and expected the best, and if they were mistakes they didn't seem like mistakes at the beginning." Liza was no exception. To Peter, she seemed ideal, and he raved to Michael, "Mike, have you seen Liza's eyes? They're like big brown saucers. How can any man escape when she turns them on you in the way she did to me?"

Far from trying to escape, Peter flung himself into wooing Liza, an easy task given that she had always been a fan. She was staying at the Savoy in her usual eighth floor suite, and for about ten days they kept their romance secret from the ever-watchful British press.

Ostensibly he was a father figure in the Aznavour mold, a diminutive dark-haired older man with a unique talent and an impeccable show business pedigree. Like Liza, he worked in the music halls as a child, appearing with his parents, who were both music hall artists.

According to Peter, one night, after they had spent hours together, at three in the morning Liza suddenly wanted to go out. In Peter's latest film, *The Optimists*, he had played a music hall artist whose performing dog Bella died, and Liza announced that she really wanted to see Bella's grave.

Eager to oblige her, Peter took Liza to a little cemetery near a park keeper's hut in Hyde Park. There, as he recounted the story, "We climbed over into the cemetery, and all the time Liza was calling out, 'Where is it? Where is the place that Bella is supposed to be buried?' Then we hid while some fellow went past. It must have been four o'clock. Very dark. No sound other than the popping of the bubbly cork.

"We were searching again for the grave when a park keeper loomed up and said, 'Now then, what are you doing down there?' I stood up and said, 'Excuse me, this is Miss Liza Minnelli.' You'll appreciate that the fellow appeared baffled. I told him, 'You see we felt like having a drink in the park.' He considered for a minute and said, 'Well, there are some seats over there, instead of sitting here on the ground.' So we sat and talked and finished the champagne."

As Sellers told it, Liza was deeply moved by Sam, the character he played, and dissolved into floods of tears when she saw the film. For, as Sellers tenderly deduced, "You see, she is the same kind of professional as that old music hall man. Liza was involved with the same kind of theatrical background through her mom, touring around and mixing with artists."

* * *

Still friendly with his ex-wife, Anne Howe, the mother of his children, Sarah and Michael, Sellers was in the habit of introducing new girlfriends to her so Anne could vet them. And Liza, superstar or not, was no exception.

Michael Sellers was with his mother on the night that Peter took Liza round to her house in Hampstead for her approval. "They came over for cocktails. Liza wore a plum colored track suit and she and my father were like two teenagers in love for the very first time. When my mother was making cocktails in the kitchen, my father followed her in. My mother whispered to him that she liked Liza and my father replied, 'Yes, well, I did love her mother's old films.' "

Anthony Haas, one of Michael's friends, who became Peter's protégé and is now a producer and making two films about him, reinforces Michael's view that Peter was dazzled by Liza's professional identity, "Peter could be a little star struck. When he was in his early thirties in Hollywood, he used to go around with an autograph book. He only stopped when his agent cautioned, 'You can't do that, you're a star.' He told me that Liza was very exciting as a person. He loved her shows and he loved her music. And the relationship soon became very sexual and passionate."

Michael Sellers, who was nineteen when his father was involved with Liza, remembers, "He liked her setting the pace with all her vivaciousness. He never liked people who were quiet and reserved and slightly gloomy. Liza was very friendly. We got on very well. We had a great time. She was very bubbly.

"We went to see *Liza with a Z* and Marlene Dietrich was in the audience, and she came on and took a bow with Liza. Afterward Liza came off stage and whispered to me, 'My God, she's held together by a rubber band!' Apparently, when Marlene bowed, on the back of her neck she had a vertical and a horizontal rubber band, which sort of hooked together and held her face in place."

Eventually, Liza and Peter went public with their romance, dining together on May 21 at the Trattoo Restaurant

in Kensington. After dinner, Liza and Peter put on an impromptu cabaret and sang "Tenement Symphony" together.
And then Liza leaned against a piano and sang, "Can't Help
Loving That Man," her luminous eyes never leaving Peter's
love-struck face. The evening ended in the small hours of the
morning with Peter and Liza singing practically every
Gershwin tune and old music hall song ever composed.

By now Desi, six thousand miles away in Los Angeles,
had heard gossip about Liza's new infatuation. His voice
shaking with hurt and bewilderment, he said, "Something
has gone wrong, that's for sure. And it all turned sour since
Liza went to England. When I drove her to the airport, we
kissed and she said she would hurry back. But when I
phoned her in London, her attitude had changed. In the past
week, she hasn't called me at all. I can't understand how we
can both be in love one day and out of love the next."

Desi didn't realize it at the time, but Liza, free and single,
believed that she had found the man she wanted to marry,
the man she wanted to make her second husband.

On May 22, Liza, dressed in a black trouser suit, clutching nervously at a pendant around her neck, gave a three-
minute press conference at the Savoy Hotel, where she said,
"My engagement to Desi Arnaz—well, the relationship has
been deteriorating for some time. There is no engagement.
Since arriving in London, I have had a marvelous time. I also
met a man called Peter Sellers and fell in love with him. The
marvelous thing is that he is in love with me." Asked
whether marriage was on the agenda, Sellers snapped,
"That's private. That is bloody private."

The following day, the normally reticent Peter revealed,
"I'm going to marry Liza. We fell in love when we first saw
each other. In the meantime, we would just like to get on
with being together. I think Liza is a fantastic actress and
singer. I went to see all three of her concerts in London last
week—I think they were the best three nights in my life. We
weren't particularly surprised when news of it leaked out.
Liza has a most fantastic personality and she is an incredible
person to be with."

The next day, Liza sped off from the Savoy in her red Mercedes and drove to Shepperton Studios to watch the filming of the new Boulting Brothers comedy *Soft Beds and Hard Battles,* in which Sellers played six characters. Set in a French brothel during the Second World War, Sellers appears as a French general, a British Intelligence officer, a Gestapo chief, and Hitler, among others. At the studio, Liza watched Sellers and, transfixed by his comic talent, bubbled, "It's terrific to find yourself in love with a genius."

During a break in filming, Peter and Liza strolled through the park surrounding the studios, hugging and kissing. Peter said, "We are terribly happy. And we are just going to get on with being together. What attracted me to her? She's a fantastic personality, an incredible person to be with and a marvelous performer. We met and fell in love when we first saw each other."

Liza interjected, "We were going to be terribly dignified about all this and I'm with my fella. I've been a fan of his for years. I'm in love with him. I'm in love with a genius."

The avalanche of publicity surrounding their relationship caused cynical observers to wonder whether or not the Sellers-Minnelli romance was merely a publicity stunt concocted by both parties. But Michael Sellers and Anthony Haas are adamant that for a heady few weeks Peter and Liza were definitely infatuated with one another.

They exchanged engagement rings and Michael verifies, "He was serious about marrying her. There was a real attraction there. Her look was extraordinary. And she is such a bubbly person, which was a major part for him. When my father wanted something, there was nothing that got in his way. He was living off her bubbliness and was showering her with gifts and taking her everywhere. Both of them were able to sort of cancel out their stardom, as it were."

Anthony Haas, who was on very close terms with Peter and became close to Liza, added, "Liza said it was a relationship that meant a great deal to her romantically. And she said that she loved Peter."

* * *

Liza moved into Peter's house in London's Belgravia, and the two continued to be the talk of London. Then, on May 29, Liza flew back to America to fulfill a previous singing engagement. The world press was at hand, eagerly noting that when Liza sang "Maybe This Time," it was blazingly obvious that she was singing to Peter Sellers.

But the May madness of their brief engagement ended as abruptly as it had begun. Suddenly, torn with doubts about Peter and the marriage, Liza turned to a psychic for advice. Astrologer-psychic Frederick Davies had predicted on the BBC radio program *Today* that Liza and Peter would never marry. His predictions made headlines, and soon afterward he received a call from Liza.

"Liza came to my home in mid-June. We talked a little and then I read the Tarot cards for her," recalled Frederick. "I told her that the romance was ill-fated. She became slightly emotional. Then she dabbed her eyes and confessed that she was thinking about breaking off the romance. All I could tell her was that it seemed to be the right course for her."

The cards had confirmed Liza's worst fears. That night she and Peter had an argument that became so heated that even the neighbors complained. The British press were alerted and arrived in time to see Liza's piano being moved out of Peter's house en route to her eighth floor suite at the Savoy Hotel.

That same night, a distraught Peter went to see his son Michael. "He was devastated and with tears in his eyes said, 'I loved her, Mike, and I love her now; I really do; it hurts so much.' Part of the reason why they'd had the fight was because my father had his own favorite psychics in whom he deeply believed and consulted on a regular basis and he was furious that Liza hadn't contacted any of them.

"Really, though, he initiated the breakup himself. He told me that he couldn't stand Liza's entourage and the fact that she always had to have someone around her at all times. Kay Thompson was with them constantly. My father liked her, but he said he never got any peace and quiet or privacy.

Kay was always present and Liza was determined not to give her up. My father begged her to get rid of Kay and the rest of the entourage, but she flatly refused and told him, 'Get rid of them? These are my friends, Peter; they're always going to be my friends. I just can't cut them off dead. If we're going to marry, then you are going to have to accept them.'

"Liza liked her life-style the way that it was. But I think that at some point my father suddenly saw his private life looming as large as his public life. He used to say he didn't even know who he was. He liked his celebrity, but I think he saw his whole life becoming the property of the media. He was serious about marrying Liza, but then when he weighed it up, he thought, 'Well, I'm going to be marrying her and X amount of other people.'

"So there was an argument between them about the fact of him not wanting loads of people around. At that point, I think they decided the marriage would never work. They were both excitable and not easy to live with, and they decided the marriage didn't have much of a chance."

Costume designer Theadora Van Runkle, who went on to design costumes for Liza in *New York, New York,* was also a close friend of Peter Sellers. Theadora visited him in a Geneva hospital before he died in 1980, and she offers another version of why he and Liza broke up.

"Peter was mad about Liza," she says. "He told me she was really sexy. But he got really angry with her one night at dinner because she crept up behind him and pulled off his toupee. He was livid with her and that was the end of the relationship."

Whatever the grounds for their breakup, on June 19, six weeks after their fling had first begun, Liza flew out of London dressed in black and made an announcement that the romance was over.

Without a tremor in her voice, she declared, "Yes, it is over. No, I have no regrets. How can I regret anything that was so happy. Peter is marvelous and we had some wonderful times. Honestly, there never was a row or split-up. Our relationship was great. Peter's a lovely, lovely man.

"My departure today has nothing to do with the breakup.

I was going anyway because I have to do concerts in Baltimore and Cleveland. I'm a working girl, and I have to keep working. Peter is the same so perhaps marriage was never in the cards anyway. We were really pushed into making an engagement announcement. You might say we were pushed out of it as well. We are still good friends and I think Peter is a wonderful man."

Her ex-husband, Peter Allen, put the entire Sellers debacle into perspective when he wryly commented, "Dear silly Liza. One week she holds a press conference to announce she is in love and the next complains that the press have broken up her romance."

As a child, she had been the epitome of good sense and seriousness. Now Liza was acting like a giddy teenager. She immediately directed her considerable energy toward recapturing Desi. She launched her campaign by sending him peace offerings ranging from boxes of chocolates to an expensive silver cross, all of which Desi duly returned.

Indignantly, he stormed, "Frankly, I can't trust her or believe anything she says. She kept telling me how much she loved me, and all the time she was secretly going out with Peter. I vividly remember how she called me from London before I learned at the same time as the rest of the world did that she was going with Sellers. I think Liza realized how much she loved me after her affair with Peter. But it's a little too late. I could never take her back."

Instead of reconciling with Desi, Liza ended up in Italy with yet another man. On July 7, 1973, it was reported that Liza was going out with 32-year-old producer-actor Dyson Lovell. The couple met at the beginning of July in Positano, Italy, and had a vacation together at director Franco Zeffirelli's home in Italy. It was sixteen days since her breakup from Sellers.

CHAPTER SEVENTEEN

In October 1973, Liza was invited to sing on Alice Cooper's *Muscle of Love* album, which was to be recorded in New York at the Record Plant on West 44th Street. Press and photographers were on hand to cover the session.

Actor Eddie Albert, Jr., accompanied Liza to the studio. She had met Albert earlier that year at the Golden Globe Awards, where he had won the Most Promising Newcomer award for his role in *Butterflies Are Free*. He was five years younger than Liza, professed to like older women, and dated her sporadically during 1973.

Ronnie Spector and the Pointer Sisters were also singing back-up on the album with Liza, but according to eyewitnesses, Liza didn't appear to want to be there at all, chain smoking and coughing. It took ten minutes for her to loosen up, smile, and promise, "Whatever they want me to sing, I will sing with vigor."

Ronnie Spector remembers, "The press posed the three of us together at the microphone, but I don't think Liza was too happy about having to share the spotlight with me. I was so happy for all the attention that I let loose with a few 'ooohs' and 'aaahs,' and the reporters got a kick out of that and started applauding. And that really got Liza steamed up. She couldn't figure out why this girl with the weird voice was getting all the laughs, so she just stood there snuffing out cigarettes and glaring at me while I put on my little show for the photographers.

"She was going out with Edward Albert, Jr., at the time, and he came over to the studio that day. The instant he walked in, Liza grabbed him and spun him around so that his back was toward me the whole time. I guess she was being protective of her man.

"She was sort of conceited, you know, she knows she's Liza Minnelli, the daughter of—she didn't like me that much. I met Peter Allen sometime later and he told me she had a terrible ego. He said that when they were married, he babied her, and he adored her, like he adored her mother."

Soon after Liza's recording with Alice Cooper, she traveled with Marvin Hamlisch to London and, on October 17, 1973, taped *Love from A to Z* at the Rainbow Theater with Charles Aznavour. The show later aired in America in the spring of 1974. The *New York Times* critic said, "The teaming of Charles Aznavour and Liza Minnelli was delightful."

Liza originally planned to fly to Israel from London and entertain the troops stationed on the Syrian and Sinai fronts. Then, on October 21, it was reported that she had to call off the trip because she had bronchitis and her doctor had ordered her to stay in bed for at least three days.

When she recovered, Liza flew to Paris; on November 28, 1973, she starred in the event of the international season, a Franco-American charity fashion show at the Marie Antoinette Theater at the Palace of Versailles.

Halston's publicist, Eleanor Lambert, and Marc Bohan of Christian Dior had created the show highlighting the best of French and American designers, featuring the collections of Hubert de Givenchy, Christian Dior, Pierre Cardin, Emanuel Ungaro, Yves St. Laurent, Bill Blass, Stephen Burrows, Anne Klein, Oscar de la Renta, and, of course, Halston. The baroness de Rothschild was president of the committee,

Princess Grace of Monaco was guest of honor, and all 720 seats in the theater were sold out at $235 each. Liza's segment of the show, in which she was slated to wear Halston's designs, was directed and choreographed by Kay Thompson, also a Halston customer.

During rehearsals, Halston exploded in a tantrum because too much attention was being paid to Anne Klein; he flounced out of the palace and locked himself in his limousine. Liza followed him, banged on the limousine door, and stamped her foot to no avail. Whereupon she appealed to the models: "Listen, kids, we've got a show to do, so don't start this. You're in show business and the show must go on. Cut all this out and let's go rehearse." Eventually Halston went back into rehearsals but pouted the entire time.

There were, however, extenuating circumstances for Halston's petulance. Publicist Eleanor Lambert explained, "Everybody was scared to death. They were all on edge. Here we were in Paris trying to outdo—not outdo—but equal the glamour of French couturiers and it was awesome."

The tense mood of the evening was infectious and, before the show, a terrified Liza paced up and down in the wings and kept repeating, "I don't know about this; I don't know about this." But once she made her entrance, clad in gray cashmere Halston pants, an off-white Halston turtleneck, a matching hat, and Elsa Peretti silver bracelets, singing "Bon Jour, Paris," Liza was home and the audience loved her, going so wild and applauding so rapturously that they even threw their $27 programs at her feet.

Liza repeated and eclipsed her Versailles triumph when, for the first time in nine years, she opened on Broadway, starring in her one-woman show, *Liza at the Winter Garden*. The limited three-week run was a sell-out, and black market tickets soared to $200 each.

When the show opened on Sunday, January 6, 1974, Vincente flew in for the opening and was in the audience along with Halston, Diane Von Furstenberg, Lorna Luft, and Neil Simon. After the show, they all went to a party at the Rainbow Grill, where an Italian buffet was served.

Liza's performance at the Winter Garden was not only a spectacular hit (subsequently recorded in a top-selling album) but also won her her second Tony Award. At the time, Clive Barnes wrote of her Winter Garden performance, "She has urchin hair, big Gypsy eyes, good legs, lovely expressive hands, and a voice that can purr, whisper, snarl and drool. She's also very sexy in an old-fashioned way that I was beginning to think went out of style." Barnes's valentine to Liza was the first of many and he was to become one of her staunchest supporters in the media.

During the Winter Garden run, Liza remarked that she was terrified of missing a performance and was proud that she never had. All that lay ahead of her—missed performances, illnesses, disaster. Yet even in those days, she was already haunted by scandals, the latest linking her to black entertainer Ben Vereen, whom she had first met on May 30, 1972, after seeing his much praised performance as Judas in *Jesus Christ Superstar*.

And however much Liza might deny the romance—even insisting to Earl Wilson, "That's such an exaggeration. Ben and I are very dear friends. We should be. We're both protégés of Bob Fosse's. When we go to shows together, it is to take notes"—she and Ben, even to this day, remain extremely close.

Known for his vibrant energy as an all-around entertainer, an original, Ben Vereen was born in Miami, won early success in *Hair* and *Sweet Charity*, and was awarded a Tony for his performance in *Pippin*. At the time that he was first linked to Liza, Ben was married to his second wife, dancer Nancy Brunner.

Although, like Liza, he had been enrolled in the High School of Performing Arts, Ben, the son of a Baptist minister, was torn between the theater and the church, and eventually studied at Manhattan's Pentecostal Theological Seminary. Six months later, Ben went back to show business and went on to appear in *All That Jazz* and *Roots*.

When Ben and Nancy were married in 1967, they made a vow not to disclose their marriage to the press. Ben said, "Our secrecy pact had nothing to do with the fact that

Nancy's white. My wife is just anxious to keep my show business life separate from our family life."

Initially, Ben and Liza did nothing to hide their relationship. On January 21, they left the theater together and drove off in her limousine, in full view of a hundred fans as well as members of the press, who scrambled to report their departure together. Ben and Liza attended parties, spending the evening huddled close together, dancing cheek to cheek, and, in general, acting like young lovers. Consequently, by the spring of 1974, it was common currency on Broadway that Liza Minnelli and Ben Vereen were having an affair.

They added fuel to the flames by posing together topless for a widely published Scavullo photograph. Predictably, bigots, both black and white, sent Vereen poison pen letters. Ben said, "At the time, I kept thinking the Liza connection was going to ruin my career. It was a friendship that almost broke up my family. I was getting blind threats because of it."

Liza, too, received hate letters regarding her relationship with Ben. But, ignoring the pressure, she remained loyal to him. Ben's first wife, Andrea Vereen, who is the mother of two of his children, Ivy and Benjie, says, "I don't know if they were having an affair. I know they are still close. They have always been very good friends. It could probably have been true that they had an affair, but at the time it didn't interest me."

Years after the rumors of their interracial love affair threatened to tarnish their careers, Liza was instrumental in persuading Ben to go for treatment for his drug problem. Afterward, she and Ben joined forces with other celebrities and founded Celebrities for a Drug Free America.

Approached after his one-man show at the Jupiter Theater in Florida, Ben fielded a question that began, "Ben, I'd like to ask you about you and Liza founding—" by quickly saying, "Oh, we are just good friends," and walking away.

Liza weathered the storm surrounding her relationship with Ben Vereen, only to be confronted by yet another scandal in February 1974, when a British columnist alleged

that during their romance, Peter Sellers had taken siz-
zlingly explicit nude pictures of her. Sellers indignantly
protested, "I categorically deny ever having taken pictures
of Liza Minnelli in the nude or near nude ever. I don't have
any pictures of her in the nude, so I can't possibly return
anything I don't have."

But Michael Sellers contradicts, "My father took lots of
pictures of Liza. He was a camera nut and routinely took
pictures of all of his girlfriends. He had nude snaps of most of
them and he showed me some of the pictures, but he never
showed me any of Liza. It is conceivable that he did have
nude pictures of her, though. But before he died, my father
burned all his photographs."

Professionally, 1974 was proving to be one of the most
hectic years ever for Liza. Her schedule for just the first half
of the year alone read, the Winter Garden, New York, followed by the Riviera, Las Vegas, the Nacional in Rio. Then
San Juan, Puerto Rico, the Diplomat, Florida, a benefit in
Los Angeles, then the Riviera again. Next she opened the
Academy Awards show.

In Rio, at the end of February, Liza had a fling with a
young Brazilian, Pedro Aquinaga, a rich playboy who showered her with flowers daily and joined her in the revels celebrating the Carnival in Rio.

Liza celebrated her twenty-eighth birthday in Puerto
Rico, still with Pedro. But by April 14, she was back with
Desi again. Triumphantly, he declared, "Liza and I are still
very, very much in love. But now we have a new understanding for which we probably have to thank Peter Sellers.
Our agreement is that if either of us wants to date somebody
else, this must be accepted without resentment or jealousy.
The only stipulation is that our dates must be temporary and
never reach the heart."

It seemed that Desi's mother, the formidable Lucille
Ball, had played a part in their reconciliation, advising her
son to lower his expectations. "If you think that Liza is going
to turn into a little woman waiting in the kitchen for you to

come home, you're mistaken. Liza is a superstar—no little girl next door."

Not that Desi had lingered long after Liza left him for Peter Sellers. He consoled himself with beautiful actress Victoria Principal, who went on to find fame and fortune playing Pamela Ewing in *Dallas*.

In the ten months since Liza first strayed from Desi to Peter Sellers's side, she had shifted into faster gear. She had been involved with Dyson Lovell, Eddie Albert, Jr., Ben Vereen, Pedro Aquinaga, and now she was back with Desi again. With no more Peter Allen to protect her, no more stable brother figure to make sure that she stayed on the straight and narrow, Liza began the downward slide.

On April 16, she collapsed before a performance at Harrah's Club. Harrah's issued a statement saying that Liza had not appeared because she was suffering from symptoms of flu and an upset stomach, thus marking the first recorded missed performance of Liza's career.

During her year apart from Desi, Liza had worked as narrator on *That's Entertainment,* a tribute to MGM's great musicals written, directed, and produced by Jack Haley, Jr. She and Jack had first met at one of George Hamilton's birthday parties when Liza was only fourteen. Thirteen years older than Liza at the time of their first meeting, Jack was already in the air force but, impressed by her maturity, he spent the entire party talking to her.

In Hollywood terms, they were related. Jack's father had played the Tin Man in *The Wizard of Oz,* and, like Liza, he was purebred show business. His mother, Florence Haley, was a former Ziegfeld girl, his godparents were Fred Allen and Portland Allen; his father had taken him onto the set of *The Wizard of Oz* when young Jack was only six.

But although he studied cinema arts at the University of Southern California and the University of California, Los Angeles, Jack devoted his entire professional life to television rather than films, winning several Emmy nominations, eighty-six television awards and co-producing many of

David Wolper's productions. Jack was a walking encyclope-
dia of knowledge of every facet of show business trivia. A
genius at visual reconstruction, eternally obsessed with the
cinema, he was also involved in *Life Goes to the Movies;* and,
later in his career, became president of Twentieth Century–
Fox Television and executive producer of "Entertainment
Tonight."

That's Entertainment was a natural progression in a career that had been devoted to the magic of the movies. Nar-
rated by eleven stars, including Elizabeth Taylor, Frank
Sinatra, and Gene Kelly, Jack Haley, Jr.'s, script was witty
and nostalgic without being cloyingly sentimental.

Liza, however, was overcome by emotion when Jack
invited her to help him with film clips of Judy for her seg-
ment of *That's Entertainment.* She had, of course, seen many
of them before, but viewing them all together, she started
crying helplessly.

"There was so much of my life and my parents up there,"
recalled Liza. "There was a scene from *An American in
Paris,* which my father directed and in which Gene Kelly
starred, where I was up in the rafter of the studio with Gene's
daughter, throwing confetti down on everyone. It brought all
that back.

"It was like watching my parents' lives go by up there on
the screen. I'd never seen my mother singing with her sisters
before and then there was all my dad's work and at the end,
me as a baby. I couldn't handle it at first. It just broke me up.
I cried and cried."

Jack did his best to comfort her, finally taking her outside in the fresh air. Then the children of Dorothy and the
Tin Man walked arm in arm around MGM's backlot, where
their parents had once been stars.

Jack Haley, Jr., was the perfect successor to Aznavour,
Sellers and Fosse, an ideal father figure who had once been
engaged to Nancy Sinatra and was completely unfazed about
tangling with a Hollywood princess, confidently claiming,
"Liza and I both have success. We share the same roots, the
same interests, and we've discussed all the various pres-

sures. I think we've got a marvelous chance of making it work together."

By the time *That's Entertainment* opened on May 29, 1974, Jack and Liza were seriously involved. Liza said of Jack, "He's so strong, totally male and always has been. Jack is very big—he's like a corner I hide in." She also enthused, "He's a marvelous man. When we met he said, 'You've got a pretty hot reputation, haven't you?' So I looked right back at him and said 'So have you.' He'd always been seen around with blondes with marvelous figures, you see."

And Tina Nina, who spent time with Liza and Jack, observed, "He was very loving and he was protective of her and he would take care of her. He was somebody that you could seek anything with. He was very understanding; he was like Liza's father. He was very calm, and he would tell Liza what to do. Jack was very protective."

However protective and fatherly Jack may have been, discerning onlookers believed that he hadn't quite managed to exorcise all of Liza's demons. Interviewing her in mid-1974 for an article that appeared in *Cosmopolitan* in November, writer Charles Michener was disturbed by Liza. He wrote, "I wonder about all that glowing self-knowingness, that bright-eyed air of togetherness, that boundless drive to rise to every occasion."

He went on to term her "dazzling, reassuring, but also perhaps a little too disarming?" In the same interview, Liza also conceded, "I never get mad; I'll chew Valium rather than throw a scene."

On June 22, 1974, Liza was in Monaco with Jack Haley for a charity event thrown by Princess Grace. And on August 9, she announced that she was going to marry Jack.

Before the wedding, she and Jack were together in New York, where Jack bought her a five-carat emerald surrounded by diamonds. Then, on September 12, she attended the showing of Halston's collection, wearing dark glasses, a pink ultra-suede jacket, and Elsa Peretti's diamonds by the yard. She sat in the front row, looking relaxed and happy, smiling her glittering smile, and spent $25,000 on her trousseau, which included a brilliant chrome yellow silk jersey pant suit for her to wear at the wedding ceremony.

The world press were ecstatic at the prospect of Liza and Jack's marriage, and the bridal pair did nothing to diffuse the rarefied Hollywood atmosphere swirling around their impending nuptials.

The wedding ceremony was held on September 15 at El Montecito Presbyterian Church in front of only nine guests. The ceremony was conducted by Judge John Griffin of Beverly Hills. Beforehand, Jack presented Liza with a gold bracelet set with diamonds inscribed with the words "I offer you all my worldly goods, my name and my heart."

The best man was Sammy Davis, Jr. (also a close friend of Haley's), and Sammy's wife, Altovise, was matron of honor. Then there was a small champagne buffet at Jack Haley, Sr.'s, house.

The big event, however, the wedding reception, was slated for the following evening, at Ciro's on Sunset Boulevard. Liza declared of the reception, "It will be a real star party. They are going to make Ciro's look as much as possible the way it did in the 30s."

Seven hundred guests attended the party, including Elizabeth Taylor, Rock Hudson, George Hamilton, Jack Benny, Milton Berle, Yul Brynner, Ann-Margret, Raquel Welch, Johnny Carson, Vincente, Shirley MacLaine, Goldie Hawn, Gene Kelly, and Fred Astaire. Liza wore a long black velvet Halston gown with red shoes—a replica of those Judy had worn in *The Wizard of Oz*. The shoes struck a slightly eerie note, given Liza's previously defensive attitude about Judy. But perhaps by marrying Jack, she was finally embracing the past completely. And as the wedding guests cheered the new Mr. and Mrs. Jack Haley, Jr., it appeared that Liza was home at last.

CHAPTER EIGHTEEN

Jack and Liza spent their honeymoon in London. Liza gushed, "The sun seemed to follow us at first. But we spent an awful lot of time splashing through puddles when we were walking. London loved my mother. And she, too, had a great and deep attachment for it. I guess I have inherited that attachment. Jack and I have both got lots of friends in London and we're both confirmed Anglophiles."

Once the honeymoon was over, they flew back to California and Liza moved into Jack's house, high on a hill in West Los Angeles. Furnished in Spanish style, the home included a mock-Tudor four-poster bed. A few months after their marriage, she confided to *McCall's* writer Barbara Grizzuti Harrison, "When I wake up alone in a strange city and Jack's not in bed to hold on to, I get terrified. I'm frozen when I'm not with somebody I know and love."

Barbara Grizzuti Harrison's interview is illuminating, shedding light as it does on Liza during the early days of her marriage to Jack. Confiding that whenever she was on a plane, she looked at the other passengers to see whether

they had the air of people facing impending death, Liza also
made an attempt to counteract rumors of her drug dependency, protesting indignantly, "I've heard all the rumors. I
know they say I'm shooting up, pills, the whole works. How
dare they? I wouldn't go near anything hallucinatory."

During the Harrison interview, Liza used the word *fag-
got* twice and Barbara perceived that her attitudes toward
homosexuals and homosexuality were not uncomplicated.
Attacking bisexuality, she said, "There are just certain
things that I don't think are right. Bisexuality is one of them.
It takes away intimacy."

Grizzuti Harrison went on to note that many people
around that time were saying that Liza's marriage to Jack
was a marriage of convenience. And in the hour and a half
that Barbara Grizzuti Harrison spent with Liza and Jack,
Liza called Jack "Daddy" twice and called him "Vincente"
once.

Liza had turned down more than four hundred scripts
after *Cabaret,* but three years later she settled on the part of
Claire, a gun runner's moll in *Lucky Lady,* a comedy adventure about three misfits who become successful bootleggers
during Prohibition. "I love the part," she said. "It's the best
script I've read since *Cabaret.* She's a tough red-headed
cookie who gets caught in the dream of money, money,
money."

In the spring of 1975, Liza traveled to Guaymas, Mexico
(a port off the west coast of Mexico where *Catch-22* had been
filmed), and spent six months there making *Lucky Lady.*
But from the first, filming did not go smoothly. Director
Stanley Donen had imported a largely British crew, and the
town felt that they were very austere and didn't spend
enough money in the local community. As a result, there was
little love lost between the Mexicans and the despised crew
members. And although Liza's co-star, Burt Reynolds, was
popular, the other co-star, Gene Hackman, was not, because
he insisted on privacy and had a private plane standing by at
all times to whisk him away from Guaymas.

Half the film's action took place on the small sixty foot

racing sloop, *The Lucky Lady*. Because of the size of the vessel, fifty people and several thousand pounds of equipment were crammed onto a boat designed for a small racing crew. Even Liza, normally Pollyannaish, moaned, "It was murder to make. I mean fifty-five people packed aboard a boat designed for six! I seemed to spend most of my time lying on top of Burt with Gene Hackman's head in my lap."

She was next scheduled to play a fictional forties big band singer, Francine Evans, in the film *New York, New York*, and spent some of her stay in Mexico preparing for the part by studying 1940s movie magazines she had taken with her.

Most of the time, though, she was exhausted by her rigorous *Lucky Lady* schedule. In the film, she wore a wig and had to be up every morning at 6:00 A.M. to have it carefully fitted and secured. Long after filming was over, she shuddered, "Guaymas was not sort of dreadful. It was truly dreadful. There's nothing to do. It's very difficult to keep your energy level up every day from 6:00 in the morning until 6:00 at night."

Lorna visited the set and had a romance with Burt Reynolds. For a while they were inseparable, until Burt, still involved with Dinah Shore, defected from Lorna and spent a week with Dinah at her beach house in Malibu. Lorna was disturbed by Burt's rejection. Her career had not taken off, as reviewers continued to draw unfavorable comparisons between Lorna and Judy or Lorna and Liza. Yet she struggled gamely along, appearing with Eddie Fisher at the London Palladium. In America, however, her career prospects seemed decidedly limited and she remarked that she longed to find a husband like Jack.

Jack visited Liza in Mexico every weekend and, as there was no television, erected a bed sheet as a screen and bought a sixteen millimeter projector so they could all watch films.

Tina Nina also visited Liza and spent time in Guaymas with her and Jack. She remembers, "I was with them every day, and we became very close. We talked about Daddy a great deal and Liza told me that he had a lot of financial problems because he couldn't work. She explained to me that it was hard for Daddy to understand that they weren't making films anymore like in the old days. He was used to working with choreographers, writers, and costumers, but not to working with the money men—which is how they made movies now. He was very frustrated. He also chain-smoked and he had cancer.

"He would always send me some money each month. But Liza said, 'Listen, call Daddy and tell him not to send you money anymore. I'll send you some money instead of Daddy.' It was very hard for me because I really needed the money. I knew Liza wouldn't send me any and she didn't."

Events suggest that Liza was determined that Tina Nina's allowance be terminated and, with that end in mind, she also appealed separately to Tina Nina's mother. Georgette says, "When Liza was in Mexico, she told me that I should write and tell Vincente not to send any money to Tina Nina. The law didn't dictate that he still contribute financially to Tina Nina, but as he still sent her money, I told Liza I thought it must make him happy. The money was a great help to Tina Nina so I didn't write to him."

Liza's attempts to convince Georgette and Tina Nina to ask Vincente not to send any more money failed. Aware of that, she obviously decided to take matters into her own hands, for, just a few weeks after Liza left Mexico City, Vincente himself talked to Tina Nina, who remembers, "Daddy told me, 'You know I'm not doing very well, I'm not going to be able to send you the same amount of money, I'm going to send you a little less.' Then he just stopped. I never said anything to him."

Although they believed that Liza had willfully tried to deprive Tina Nina of the allowance Vincente was sending her, Tina Nina and Georgette continued to approach her with love. Says Georgette, "We felt sorry for her during that time in Mexico. We could all see that people were after Liza for money. We invited her to stay, to be in a family, so we could give her love. When you are with Liza, she makes you feel you are so important to her; you believe it, then, the very next day, there is nothing."

* * *

Back in America, Kander and Ebb's latest musical, *Chicago*, directed by Bob Fosse, opened on Tuesday, July 1, 1975, at the 46th Street Theater in New York. The following month, the star, Gwen Verdon, suffering from a throat ailment, took five weeks off and Liza agreed to replace her temporarily. Although she said at the time, "I haven't done Broadway in ten years because I don't like being pinned down to any one spot for too long, and if you're in a hit, it means at least a year in one place," she was exhilarated at the prospect of her short Broadway interlude.

She took over Gwen's part of Roxie Hart on August 8, 1975. Clive Barnes, noting that Liza was doing the show as a favor to Kander and Ebb, wrote, "As a performer, Miss Minnelli is larger than life and twice as beautiful. She has a monumental show business personality, but a certain gamin quality that suggests the soul and heart of a Piaf."

But with only a week in which to rehearse, Liza's subsequent performance was less than flawless. *New York Post* critic Martin Gottfried berated her, "She was frankly amateurish, even allowing for a brief rehearsal time." His carping engendered an avalanche of letters in defense of Liza. Some came from the cast and background people working on *Chicago,* and, according to Gottfried, "The emphasis was really on her personal decency, her generosity, her help to *Chicago,* and her audience popularity."

Liza's generosity was evident at the end of her *Chicago* run when she threw a closing party at the St. Regis Hotel costing an estimated $15,000. Mayor Beame presented her with the keys to the city and the cast gave her a silver onyx triangle necklace with "Love From Chicago" on it. And a grateful Fred Ebb gave her a solid gold charm in the shape of a Lifesaver.

During her 1975 *Chicago* run, Liza became reacquainted with New York and discovered a city that had changed since her early days there as a struggling young actress dreaming of making it on Broadway. She enthused, "I love New York so; luckily so does Jack. He's a New York man. Never stops. He's filled with energy, and he's got that New York humor—fast. New Yorkers are at 78 rpm's and Los Angelinos are at

33⅓. Things are happening there now that remind me of the way it must have been in the early thirties, when people like Dorothy Parker and my dad moved there—new energy, new brainwaves, new people. The parties are getting better, there's an onslaught of glamour and there are more new faces from Europe. Things are just starting to happen again."

They certainly were. The sexual revolution was at its peak, and disco was about to burst onto the New York scene, along with a chic new club called Studio 54 and a drug with which Liza was intimately familiar: cocaine.

Halston remained one of the most important male figures in Liza's life. Although it is undeniable that Liza lent Halston cachet by wearing his clothes and that he enhanced her self-confidence and gave her an aura of glamour, there was a less positive facet to their relationship.

There was no limit to their friendship, no boundaries restricting their affection, and it appears that Halston was consistently ready and willing to accommodate any and all of Liza's appetites, some of which he shared. Halston intimate Robert Jon Cohen told Halston's biographer, Steven Gaines, "Liza and Halston were really cocaine buddies. Once Halston had bought an ounce of cocaine. It was in a plastic baggy and Halston put it in a Gucci binocular case and gave it to Robert Jon to carry over to Liza's place."

In 1979, she went to spend the weekend with Halston at his house in Montauk. That weekend, drink and drugs took their toll on Liza, and in an attack of drug-induced paranoia, she became convinced that the satellite *Skylab* was about to fall down on her. Aware of her state, Halston attempted to pacify her by telling her that *Skylab* was targeted to land thousands of miles away in the middle of the Indian Ocean, but Liza refused to be mollified, convinced beyond a shadow of a doubt that it was about to crash onto her head.

Tenderly, Halston took her by the hand, led her to the porch, pointed at the lawn, and said, "Look, that's where *Skylab* is really going to fall. And wouldn't that be fabulous? And you and I are going to pull up a couple of chairs and wait for it." He cooked them both a wonderful meal while they both waited and watched. Later that night, *Skylab* fell into the Indian Ocean as scheduled. And it was only when she heard the news that Liza was able at last to fall asleep.

In his biography, *Simply Halston,* Gaines gives further insight on other aspects of Halston's role in Liza's life at that time. "To see Liza and Halston in a room together was to know just how much they loved each other. They were like young lovers, hugging and touching and sometimes Liza would sit cuddled in the same chair as Halston as he whispered bon mots in her ear. Although they would be photographed together on endless nights on the town, at stellar publicity events and parties, the best moments of their friendship were spent in Halston's kitchen on nights when just the two of them were together, telling each other the story of their lives while Halston cooked pot roast for dinner. They drank wine and giggled and Halston listened and advised Liza on her complicated love affairs, unrequited crushes and unfulfilling marriages."

Halston's lover for sixteen years, Victor Hugo, recalled, "I met Liza with Halston around 1970. Liza was like the girl next door and Halston was society's darling. She would come and spend a week with us at Montauk. She was like family, a kid sister. I remember once, on the anniversary of her mother's death, she asked me to go out and buy a Bible. Then she read Corinthians, chapter 32, to us. She read so beautifully that we were very moved.

"She always consulted Halston about her entire wardrobe. She believed in him. They had ups and downs in their relationship, but they were far too sophisticated to fight. He used to get upset because sometimes Liza would get a dressmaker to make cheap copies of his designs, but he never said anything to her."

Aside from her intermittent defections, Liza was always eager to return Halston's friendship and to support him in every way possible. In 1977, when *People* magazine prepared a cover story on him for their June 20 edition, Liza immediately agreed to participate, as did Elizabeth Taylor. Photographer Harry Benson was hired to take the pictures of

Halston, Liza, and Liz. The location was Wolf Trap, the concert area outside Washington, D.C.

People journalist Lee Wohlfert, who worked on the story, remembers, "Everything was set up at the location and Elizabeth Taylor arrived promptly, in time for the photo session. Halston was already there, but Elizabeth looked around and suddenly realized that Liza hadn't arrived.

"Aware that she was now in the position of waiting for Liza Minnelli, Elizabeth exclaimed, 'Oh, my lipstick' and then turned around and went back into her dressing room. We had a very short time in which to have the pictures taken and we knew Liza was arriving any second, so I went chasing after Elizabeth. Well, she found her little bag with her lipstick in it, and then came back.

"By the time Elizabeth got back to the location, Liza was sitting there already waiting and seemed extremely miffed and annoyed. She was not very warm in her greeting and she and Elizabeth didn't exchange one word with one another. There was no warmth between them. I had thought they would at least exchange some wisecracks or witticisms with one another, but they didn't."

Liza's next film, *A Matter of Time,* was her gift to Vincente. Tina Nina knew how much the project meant to her father and remembered, "Daddy had so many ideas about the movie, he had me read the book, we talked about it, he didn't have anything else on his mind. He and Liza exchanged wonderful ideas about the movie too. It was important to both of them."

A Matter of Time was based on a French novel, published in 1954, called *La Voulte d'être.* Liza's role was of an impoverished peasant called Nina, who in 1949 goes to Rome to work as a chambermaid for a contessa (played by Ingrid Bergman). In her youth, the contessa was loved by kings, and in an old hotel in Rome she teaches her amorous arts to Nina. Nina's impressionable mind and imagination are so stirred by the old lady that she fantasizes about having lived the contessa's life and undergoes a metamorphosis.

Vincente and Liza stayed at the Ambasciatori Palace

Hotel in Rome and shooting took place at the Piazza Navona and at the Roman Forum, where Liza played a scene over-looking the site of Julius Caesar's assassination.

On the set, a blissfully happy Vincente said, "One day I knew I would make a film with my little daughter. It was only a matter of time. I've wanted to do a film with her much sooner than this. But maybe this is the one waiting for her. It's really the perfect part for her. Legends? Yes, they both are. Just look at Liza. She is as big a star today as Judy was and yet she can go much further—if that's possible. Yet somehow, I don't think the surface of Liza's talent has been scratched. There's much more to come out. It's so hard to compare them. Liza is great—just like her mother. But she is great in different ways. In fact, I find less and less of Judy in our daughter. Liza has got her mother's sense of humor but little else."

John Gideon Bachmann reported in *The Guardian:* "There is no doubt that this is a couple in love, and there's no doubt that they are not afraid of the shadow of Judy. I have watched them shoot and I have watched them rehearse and eat lunch and wait for Geoffrey Unsworth lighting set-ups, and I have watched them watch the result of their labors in a screening room and with well-placed radio microphones, have listened in upon their intimate exchanges, and have found no chink in their oedophile armor.

"The best shots in the rushes we are watching, according to her, are the ones where her father has succeeded in mak-ing her look like her mother. No wonder they both tell me, independently in conversation, that they have waited to work together until 'the perfect story came along.' In as much as this one tells the tale of a young woman taking the place of an old one in the affections of a father figure that people it, this is the perfect story."

Apparently after every scene, Liza eagerly asked Vin-cente, "Was I all right?" Naturally, Vincente adored Liza's performance and loved every minute of directing her; and he said with pride, "When I directed her, I treated her just like I treated her mother—as a fine actress, a marvelous come-dian, and a great tragedian."

* * *

Vincente hadn't made a film for six years, since *On a Clear Day,* which had not been his greatest musical success. During *A Matter of Time* it was patently obvious that he found it difficult to cope with a new order of independent movie packaging, which involved him, in an expanded role, finding the financing and controlling the script as well as all aspects of the production. The shooting was supposed to last just three months but took five months, and delays were blamed on Vincente.

The crew found it difficult to work with him as he was accustomed to crews at MGM who instinctively understood his every need, even if he didn't explain his instructions in detail. Liza did her utmost to help Vincente in every way, but in December she was contracted to fly to Los Angeles for the opening and promotion of *Lucky Lady*.

She flew via London and there talked to journalist William Hall, who broached the subject of recent rumors (fueled by the smocks she was then wearing) that she was pregnant. Emphatically denying them, Liza said, "Pregnant? Oh, my Lord, that's all I need! I'm booked solid for the next year, and if I were pregnant now, it would be a million dollar baby! That's not to say I don't want a baby. I'd adore one, but not now. Maybe in two or three years. We'll be so happy when we can finally announce that I'm expecting. We'll shout it from the rooftops. But for now I wish everyone would stop talking about it."

On her arrival in Los Angeles, Liza was invited to an advance screening of *Lucky Lady* and hated the entire film. She was so outraged that she went as far as to make her feelings known to the press, spilling over with indignation, telling journalists at a conference on the *Queen Mary* in Long Beach, "It was a total shock to me. I'm upset and stunned by the picture. It's not the film I signed up to do. It's the difference between a work of art and a commercial movie."

Gene Hackman and Burt Reynolds agreed with her and director Stanley Donen, who had directed *Singin' in the Rain* and *Seven Brides for Seven Brothers,* retaliated: "I find it sad that they can't accept that there's only one guy who takes the rap—me."

By the time *Lucky Lady* was released on Christmas Day 1975, it had been previewed with two different endings, one of which was rejected by the audience as being too sad; the other was voted down by Liza herself.

The film was not critically well received and some of the barbed reviews were directed at Liza. Vincent Canby of the *New York Times* wrote, "Liza was neither funny nor sad, but an actress trying like hell to convince you that she is. The more she tries, the worse she gets." And Frank Rich acidly observed, "At times, Minnelli's cuteness also makes her seem like the oldest child actor in show business."

Doing her best to ignore all the negative reviews of *Lucky Lady,* Liza flew back to Italy and carried on filming *A Matter of Time* in Rome and in Venice.

Lorna visited her in Rome and the two sisters were escorted by men about town, Fabio Testi and Egon Von Furstenburg. By February 3, gossip was yet again rampant that Liza was pregnant and an insider on the film set was quoted as saying, "The wardrobe people on the film set are on standby to alter her clothing."

Lorna may have been painting the town with Liza, but she didn't succumb to the wiles of the Roman charmers courting her. Filming of *A Matter of Time* ended in April 1976, and that summer Lorna met her present husband, New Yorker Jake Hooker, the 26-year-old lead guitarist of the rock group the Arrows, and the couple settled in London. Eventually they would marry and live together happily. But they were short of money and Liza's friends have alleged that she has financed many areas of her sister's life. Lorna herself has gratefully acknowledged that Liza paid for her six-month drama course at the Herbert Berghof Studios in Manhattan. And Georgette Magnani Minnelli remembers visiting Lorna's home and hearing her and Liza discussing Lorna's new furniture, when Lorna wryly admitted, "After all, you were the one who paid for it."

Lorna had found happiness in love and marriage, but her

career still appeared to be doomed. On stage she was lively, nervy, bubbling over with energy as she belted out song after song, but somehow she lacked Judy and Liza's charisma. Always known as "Judy Garland's other daughter," Lorna struggled valiantly to establish herself. In an attempt to carve out new territory, she subsequently hosted a British television show. Yet large-scale professional success continued to elude her.

Liza, too, at that point, was floundering. After the failure of *Lucky Lady* and the predictions of doom and gloom emanating from the grapevine about the upcoming *A Matter of Time*, industry gossip about Liza's alleged drug usage was running wild. She did all she could to counteract it. In a July 1976 article published in *Ladies Home Journal*, Kathleen D. Fury wrote, "Liza once worked with a performer who had a well-known heroin addiction, and she was willing to discuss that, as long as the actress wasn't named. 'I have no sympathy for anybody like that,' she said of this co-worker whose arms were covered with needle marks. 'I just wanted to smack her. If you get close to somebody like that, they drag you down. If you're going to commit suicide, don't do it in front of me. You know, if I survived all that happened to me and I'm O.K., I have no sympathy for somebody who went through less and turned into a mess.' "

A Matter of Time opened at Radio City on October 7, 1976, to the accompaniment of boos from the audience. Before releasing the film, the president of AIP (the company that had produced the film) reworked it to such an extent that Martin Scorsese organized a petition, which many major directors signed, protesting the way in which Vincente Minnelli had been treated.

Despite the petition, the film was a disaster for both Vincente and Liza. Rex Reed commented, "She should call it What I Did for Love. How else can you explain this brainless gumbo of incompetence? Liza obviously did it to help out Daddy, who hasn't been getting too many jobs lately as a director."

Vincent Canby of the *New York Times* was similarly unimpressed by the film and said of Liza, "She has talent of her own, but it comes to us through the remembered presence of others."

The failure of *A Matter of Time* was a bitter blow to Liza, coming as it did after the *Lucky Lady* disaster. But for Vincente, it was a tragedy. He had always dreamed of making a film with Liza and his dream had at last come true. But the results were now being ridiculed, and he would never be given the opportunity to make another film. *A Matter of Time* would be the final epitaph for Vincente Minnelli, who had once been one of Hollywood's most revered directors.

CHAPTER NINETEEN

In the summer of 1976, Liza was deeply involved in her current project, *New York, New York,* which was scheduled to take twenty-two weeks to shoot. At the outset, it appeared that for Liza, at least, all the omens were favorable. Budgeted at eight and a half million dollars, the film co-starred Robert De Niro and was directed by Martin Scorsese, who had already won countless accolades for his *Taxi Driver* and *Mean Streets.*

For the first time in her career, Liza was working at MGM, the studio over which her mother had once reigned supreme. She was allocated Judy's old dressing room, and, poignantly, her hairdresser for *New York, New York* was Sidney Guilaroff, the legendary hair stylist who had cut Judy's hair for *The Wizard of Oz.*

Links with Liza's childhood pervaded the production, as Jack Haley, Sr., played a cameo role in the film and Vincente visited the set. Scorsese, a great film historian, had always venerated Vincente above all directors and the two formed an instant rapport that would be sustained through the years. During the romantically staged ballroom scene when Liza, De Niro, and five hundred extras celebrated VJ Day, seeing Liza with her forties hairdo, Vincente was overcome with emotion. His voice shaking, he said to Scorsese, "Gosh, you know, she looks so much like Judy."

Vincente's visit to the set was overlaid with sentimentality, particularly as the film was being shot at the studio where he had created his legendary triumphs, *Meet Me in St. Louis* and *Gigi*. And individual scenes were also shot on Stage 29, the very stage where Vincente had made *An American in Paris*.

Then there was the nostalgic plot of *New York, New York,* an updated *A Star Is Born* scenario, which opens during the midforties—the years of Judy's heyday. Liza, her hair short, 1940s style, looking like a cross between Betty Boop and Judy, plays Francine Evans, a big band singer who loves, marries, and leaves saxophone player Jimmy Doyle, played by Robert De Niro. When Francine's career skyrockets, Jimmy's sinks into obscurity, but they reunite briefly when Jimmy, now a nightclub owner, writes a song for Francine, "New York, New York."

Liza's part as Francine is dramatic, tragic, gilded with an old-fashioned glamour as she sings lush period songs like "Once in a While" and "You Are My Lucky Star." The role combines drama and romance, and at the time appeared to be a god-given opportunity for Liza to refurbish her *Cabaret* crown, which, after the disasters of her subsequent two films, had been sadly tarnished.

Everyone involved in the project, especially Liza, believed that *New York, New York* was virtually guaranteed to be a gigantic success, winning Liza her second Academy Award along the way. Shooting began amid an upbeat atmosphere of intense optimism.

Although, by rights, the making of *New York, New York* should have been suffused with bittersweet memories for Liza, the many sentimental undercurrents at MGM only contributed to her happiness at working there. The princess had returned to her childhood domain. Forever the director's daughter, she was working on her father's home ground, where he was often on hand to bless her with his approval and encouragement.

This time, though, Liza wasn't merely the director's daughter: she was also the director's girlfriend. Martin Scorsese, then married to an extremely pregnant Julia Cameron (who had written the *New York, New York* script and was on set throughout the filming), fell passionately in love with Liza and she with him.

There was no question whatsoever that Scorsese—a director like Vincente, Italian, slight, with bushy eyebrows like Vincente—belonged in the father figure category of Liza's men. Like Vincente, he had a raging temper, sometimes in the throes of an outburst flinging around telephones and chairs. One of the most gifted directors of his generation, as Vincente had been of his, Scorsese was wild and flamboyant but also a deep-thinking man whose spirituality had once led him to consider becoming a priest.

Initially inspired by John Cassavetes, he became camera assistant for John Avildsen and taught film at New York University. His realistically gritty films, among them *Taxi Driver* and *Mean Streets,* consistently won critical acclaim. An extraordinary man, Scorsese was a volatile firebrand and talented visionary whose effect on Liza would be profound and enduring.

"Even today, people still sit around in the early hours of the morning and tell horror stories about *New York, New York.* We would get our morning call at 7:00 A.M. and they wouldn't get their first shot until three the next morning!" says costume designer Theadora Van Runkle, who has worked on more than forty films, including *Bonnie and Clyde* and *Heaven Can Wait,* but has nothing but unhappy memories of the twenty-two-week *New York, New York* shoot.

"Liza was on cocaine and so was Martin. The crew felt completely victimized. They were treated like peasants and they hated it—which is why they still talk about it."

Liza may have gushed to a journalist during the shooting, "We're so invigorated, we keep right on going, even if it's 1:00 A.M.," but Thea Van Runkle tells quite a different story, one corroborated by other sources and subsequent events.

"The crew would spend the entire day and evening waiting around. All that time, Liza and Marty would be closeted in his trailer. Going over the script, presumably.

"Julia Cameron, Marty's wife, was nine months pregnant and was always on the set. She was cold to everyone, but she had every reason to be an iceberg. Before she was very much into her power of being with Marty. But now, given what was going on between Marty and Liza (who just left her to wonder what was going on), she was in agony and she took it out on other people, making snotty comments and taking advantage of people who couldn't talk back."

Although New York, New York was not Liza's most shining hour, Thea Van Runkle says she still liked her a great deal. "She has the most extraordinary, hysterical sense of humor. She would tell funny stories about predicaments she and Judy had been in. And I loved her looks. Without makeup, Liza looks beautiful, innocent and lovely. She has translucent skin, snow white, pure and flawless. For one scene, we dressed her up as Marilyn Monroe. They cut it out, but she looked beautiful. Towards the end of shooting, though, she did get a bit pudgy and couldn't fit into her gown."

Added to Liza's weight problems was the fact that, as a result of special lifts created for her (very similar to the ones Marlene Dietrich used years ago when Liza saw her perform in Europe), she began to suffer blindingly painful headaches.

In the wake of two failures, Liza did her best to remain optimistic while waiting for the release of New York, New York. In the middle of November, she was in New York at the off-Broadway Village Gate, energetically applauding Kander and Ebb's musical Two by Four. Wearing a green blouse, black pants, and an antique necklace, she jumped on stage after the show and sang "New York, New York."

On November 21, she appeared in Gala, Gala, the Inter-

national Circus of the Stars, alongside Charles Aznavour, Paul Newman, Raquel Welch, and Joanne Woodward. The show was extremely chaotic, and Liza stopped the cameras in the middle because her dress had come apart and she was left standing virtually stark naked.

The show was normally taped in Paris, but this particular year it was filmed in Los Angeles. Taping took more than five hours, in the course of which an exasperated Paul Newman, Christopher Lee, and Raquel Welch walked out. Interviewed afterward, doing her best to strike a positive note, Liza declared, "It may look a little chaotic now, but when it's edited it will look marvelous."

By the time *New York, New York* had its world premiere at Alice Tully Hall on June 21, 1977, gossip about on-set cocaine use had leaked into the press and the glowing promise that had initially surrounded the production had faded considerably. The critics, who were not enamored of the film, accused Scorsese of drawing a Judy impersonation out of Liza in some of the scenes.

He had, in fact, told her to tone herself down during shooting, and later he moaned, "You put a wig on her and she looks like her mother. What can I tell you?"—overlooking the point that he had directed Liza to wear the wig in the first place.

In *New York* magazine, critic John Simon launched a searing attack on Liza, blasting her performance. "The only other idea—if you can call it that—was to encourage Liza Minnelli as Francine to act and sing as much as possible like her mother, which she usually does anyway. The result is rather like urging someone who has been spontaneously walking to walk consciously, which leads, of course, to paralysis or falling on one's face.

"In any case, the big difference between Garland and Minnelli is that Garland, though less than comely, was not (until near the end) grotesque and goony; that Garland, even if overacting, did so in her own style at least; and that though one sometimes refused to cry with Garland, with Minnelli one can never help giggling."

Rex Reed clearly loved her performance, writing of Liza's "wide eyed appeal and a comic sensibility that is awkward, crazy and totally touching," but few other critics agreed. *New York, New York* did not become a box office smash, and as Liza said with a brief, bitter smile, "In Hollywood you're not allowed three bad pictures in a row."

Long before the release of *New York, New York*, Scorsese had already gambled that the film would be a success. He was so passionately in love with Liza that he began rehearsing her in a new show a month before the film opened. *In Person* was a Broadway musical with a Kander and Ebb score in which Liza starred as Michelle Craig, an ex-movie queen turned nightclub performer. Michelle, as created by writer George Furth, is a pastiche of Judy Garland and Debbie Reynolds, with an overriding resemblance to Francine Evans, Liza's character in *New York, New York*. But the similarities between Michelle and Judy were manifold: for example, Michelle is married to a film producer and her daughter wants to be a singer like her mother.

Months before the show opened, Liza emphasized, "This character is not Momma. She was in go-go movies, graduated to dramatic films, then got kicked out because she's ruthless. She's tough, she's ruthless, she'd sell her folks for a job. Okay, one thing is that I understand some of what this character is going through because of what I've seen."

The two-and-a-half-hour musical called for Liza to sing twelve numbers and to stay on stage for all but four minutes of the entire show. It opened in Chicago in the summer, after George Furth had written twelve drafts of the book, switching the title from *In Person* to *Shine It On* to the final title, *The Act*. Scorsese had never directed a musical before. Moreover, as he boasted to Betsy Haug, assistant choreographer to Ron Lewis, "He was proud he had never even seen a Broadway show before. I think he was detrimental to the show and made it very difficult. But Liza really believed in Scorsese's talent."

Dancer Roger Minami, who appeared in *The Act*, recalls, "I think Martin was out of his element. He was famous for doing movies and he kept looking at the stage through a viewfinder."

Another production head said, "Now most everyone thinks having him around is a good thing—it works better because of their relationship. It's like she's out there working for him. The only problem is she's excessively loyal to her men. She loves, perhaps, too blind and that's where she comes close to the story of the show."

There were also other factors at work which seemed to distort reality for both Liza and Scorsese. On July 10, Julia Cameron went to Elaine's with Andy Warhol. In his *Diaries*, Warhol recalled, "She said that Marty has coke problems and he now takes medicine to clean himself out."

Despite Scorsese's quest to break his cocaine habit, the drug inevitably had repercussions on his relationship with Liza, which was often stormy. Kander and Ebb wrote the song "Please Sir" for Liza; its sadomasochistic overtones were rumored to be partly inspired by the nature of their relationship. But before the show opened on Broadway, the song, considered too obscure for the audience, was cut.

It would be fair to say that their relationship wasn't solely sustained by drugs and sex (although Liza loved Marty's virile Latin passion), but by their mutual self-interest as well. Scorsese's cocaine habit required endless supplies of money, now provided by the producers of *The Act*. And he was not indifferent to the advantages of being professionally linked with a major box-office draw like Liza. Liza, for her part, believed that Scorsese was a genius heaven sent to direct her career so she could once again shine as she had in *Cabaret*.

Throughout all the well-publicized drama of Liza's affair with Scorsese, Jack Haley receded into the background while all three parties denied that anything illicit whatsoever was going on. Although reports surfaced during the San Francisco run of *The Act* that Marty and Liza stole away to a little restaurant in Berkeley, where they held hands over a romantic dinner, and that they had adjoining suites throughout the tour, Liza, Jack, and Scorsese continued to deny that there was any truth in any of the rumors.

It was reported that every time an item appeared in the columns about their alleged split, Haley sent Liza a present, including a broad-tail coat and a diamond pendant. But it was highly likely that either Liza or Jack, in quest of an image of renewed marital bliss, leaked the story to the press. Not only that, Liza, Marty, and Jack posed together for a photograph. According to one of her closest confidantes during *The Act,* when that picture of Liza, posed between her husband and her lover, splashed on the front page of the *New York Post,* she was thrilled. The idea of having two men both in love with her at the same time fulfilled her all-consuming need for love and attention.

If Jack was content to play the silent cuckold, the spirited and much abused Julia Cameron Scorsese definitely was not. On August 28, she filed for divorce from Martin Scorsese. Those divorce papers are not a matter of public record, but in October 1983, in court papers related to her bid to increase alimony payments from Martin, Julia stated, "In 1977, my former husband became seriously involved with cocaine and began spending enormous amounts of money on the drug. In addition, I discovered he was having an affair with Liza Minnelli, among others. In fact I will never forget the day when he gave her a gold medallion, which was mine."

Liza and Martin were in Los Angeles when news broke that Julia had filed for divorce. Ironically, on the very same day, they were confronted with another stark reality: the powerful *Los Angeles Times* critic Dan Sullivan, echoing the distaste of Chicago critics before him, sniped that *The Act* was "the dumbest backstage musical ever, to the point when you figure they've got to be kidding."

Countless changes had already been made in the show, as *A Chorus Line* creator Michael Bennett had come to the rescue to advise the producers on relevant alterations and cast changes. Thea Van Runkle, who had been initially hired to design Liza's costumes, had also departed.

Van Runkle says, *"The Act* is a sad and painful memory for me. I did the show out of loyalty to Liza and I had to design eight costumes for her. But the choreographer decreed that Liza had to have all her changes at one time and not go off stage to change costumes. So it was up to me to create eight changes for her to wear at once and not look fat or weird.

"She was at least twenty pounds overweight to begin with. She was inclined to retain water and maybe she was drinking. And I had a terrible time piling all the costumes on top of each other.

"Marty was adorable and always lovely to me. He really enjoyed my drawings of the costumes, but in many ways he was bored by the show.

"Then Liza went to Halston, and he said, 'Well, Theadora is a great designer for film, but obviously can't do theater.' He took over."

Thea Van Runkle wasn't the only person associated with the production who allegedly didn't seem able to make the transition from film to theater. Three weeks after Julia Cameron filed for divorce, Martin Scorsese left *The Act*.

Liza's contract allowed her full creative control, and during the shambles of the fifteen-week sold-out Broadway tour, many of the cast clamored for Scorsese to be replaced as director. At the beginning, Liza recoiled from firing Scorsese and instead watched in silence as he proceeded to flounder around attempting to direct his first Broadway musical.

Bill Thomas, who was involved in every aspect of the show, working closely with Liza's then-manager, Deanna Wemble, remembers, "Liza had the most incredible instincts and knew she couldn't go into New York with a turkey. She took drastic measures and replaced Martin with Gower Champion.

"I'm sure the producers arranged the situation with Martin, but they wouldn't do it without discussing it with Liza first. And she did what she had to do for self-preservation."

Roger Minami adds, "I think Liza wanted it all to work with Martin, but it just wasn't happening and the reviews were bad and the reaction wasn't all that good for the show. Gower did come in, everyone fell in love with his background; he just pulled it together to make it work.

Liza in her Oscar-winning performance as Sally Bowles in *Cabaret*. © *Photofest*

Judy and Vincente at Liza's christening. © *Photofest*

Liza with her baby sister, Tina Nina. © *Georgette Magnani Minnelli de Ramirez*

Liza in one of the costumes Vincente had made for her. © *Georgette Magnani Minnelli de Ramirez*

(left to right) Vincente, Georgette, Tina Nina, and Liza. © *Georgette Magnani Minnelli de Ramirez*

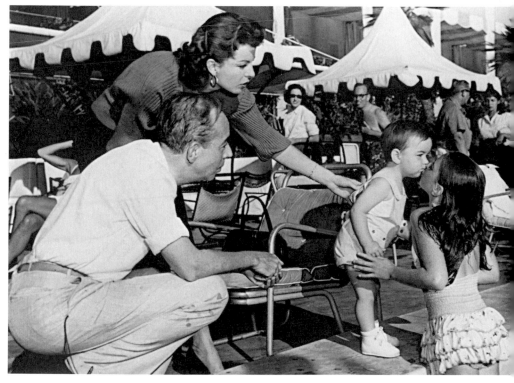

Liza arrives in New York with Lorna, Joey, and Judy
in March 1958. © *Photofest*

Traveling with George
Hamilton and his mother,
Ann. © *Ann Hamilton*

Liza and Judy's first
professional appearance
together, on Judy's 1963
TV show. © *Photofest*

A portrait of the third Mrs. Vincente Minnelli, Denise Hale.

© Russ Fischella

With Albert Finney in
1968's *Charlie Bubbles*.
© *Photofest*

Dancing with first
husband Peter Allen.
© *Oscar Abolafia*

Partying with
Desi Arnaz, Jr.
© Oscar Abolafia

Publicity photo of
Liza posing with Ed
Sullivan and the
group Bojangles.
Rex Kramer is
far right.

In London with
Peter Sellers in 1973.
© *Photofest*

With second husband
Jack Haley, Jr.
© *Oscar Abolafia*

On the set of *A Matter of Time* with Vincente in 1976. © *Photofest*

With longtime friend Ben Vereen. © *Oscar Abolafia*

As Francine Evans in *New York, New York.* © *Photofest*

At *New York, New York* premiere party, with co-star Robert DeNiro *(left)* and Martin Scorsese.
© *Oscar Abolafia*

A Studio 54 party with *(left to right)* Bianca Jagger, Halston, and Jack Haley, Jr. © *Oscar Abolafia*

With Baryshnikov.
© Oscar Abolafia

Unwinding on the
Studio 54 dance floor.
© Oscar Abolafia

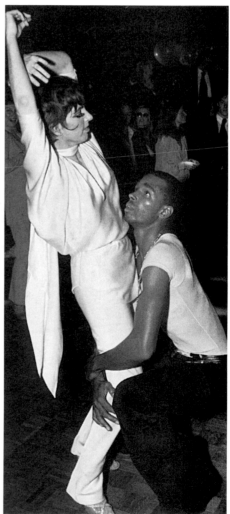

Vincente with his
grandchildren, shortly
before his death.
© *Georgette Magnani*
Minnelli de Ramirez

Tina Nina Minnelli.
© *Georgette Magnani*
Minnelli de Ramirez

With Peter Allen
in February 1992,
four months before
his death.
© *Albert Ferreira/DMI*

With third husband,
Mark Gero, and
Elizabeth Taylor.
© *Osca Abolafia*

As Mavis Turner
in *Stepping Out*
© Photofest

"And it did work. Liza had boundless energy. But *The Act* was a really hard show for her. She was never offstage and if she was, it was a really quick change. We in the cast felt like we had to give her the support we could. She was definitely killing herself.

"The same vulnerability that makes Liza so spectacular on stage is something that you feel offstage as well, so when you know her, you want to help her and give her support. You don't want to let her down."

Scorsese apparently wanted *The Act* to be a musical drama, while many others who worked on the project wanted it to be a nightclub revue. Furthermore there was conflict between Scorsese, who is heterosexual, and the homosexual men around Liza—many of whom were devoted old friends—who were used to exercising a certain amount of control over her career. As was her wont, Liza did her utmost to avoid taking responsibility or initiating any direct confrontations. She was often heard by all and sundry to call herself "the Director's Daughter" and to say, "The director is everything, and I am just the hired girl."

Scorsese was continually forced to grapple with situations that undermined his machismo. Overshadowed by Liza, he was forced by financial pressures to maintain the charade of posing with Liza for the benefit of the press, and dancing attendance to her on opening night.

Even on the road, Liza was strained to breaking point doing eight grueling performances a week, becoming so exhausted that after many shows she had to be literally carried off stage and into the wings. Friends worried that she was heading for a nervous breakdown, and she herself was terrified that the back-breaking schedule would ultimately hurt her voice.

In San Francisco, doing one of the show's most difficult numbers, Liza suddenly sat down. She made a brief attempt to begin dancing again but then staggered into the wings. There, she clutched at a lighting boom, struggling desperately to support herself. In horror, she realized that she was starting to crumble, was on the verge of collapse. Two stagehands rushed to catch her. Her arms and legs were dangling loosely as if she were a puppet with severed strings. When she had recovered, a shocked Liza confided, "I thought the stage was trembling, I thought it was an earthquake. That's when I sat down. But when I got up to dance, my feet wouldn't support me. Everything was shaking." Nevertheless, she regained her equilibrium and, in true show business tradition, went on with the show.

CHAPTER TWENTY

The Act opened at the Majestic Theater in New York on October 29, 1977. Liz Taylor, Halston, and Sammy and Altovise Davis gave Liza a standing ovation. After the show, six hundred guests celebrated at Tavern on the Green. There, Jack Haley presented Liza with a fourteen-karat gold Valium. As the evening went on, in the hope of scotching gossip, Liza and Jack gravitated toward Scorsese's table, joining him and his family.

The guests at the party included Bob Fosse, who had remained close to Liza (and, at the time of *The Act,* according to an eyewitness, was still using cocaine with her). His verdict on the show was "I'm such a pushover for Liza that I can't be objective. But there are things in the show I didn't like—but they're not her fault. Whatever the faults and failures, people are seeing a superstar, and they don't often get the chance to do that."

The critics, however, were not as kind: *Newsweek* critic Jack Kroll characterized the dialogue as something that "would even curdle the sour cream in the Borscht circuit."

The Act was torn apart: it was described as structureless, implausible, derivative; the costumes were ugly; and the entire show hollow. Notwithstanding, the majority of critics agreed that Liza's performance was tornadolike in its energy and passion. In the *Wall Street Journal,* critic Edwin Wilson wrote, "Miss Minnelli dances with style and élan, and as a singer she can caress a song softly or build it to a big finish. She can also act, as she proved in the film *The Sterile Cuckoo,* but there's little chance of that here. Let us hope that some-day she will appear in a Broadway show worthy of the full range of her talents. Then not only will her fans be at her feet, but those who love good theater as well."

John Simon, the critic who had never been a rabid Min-nelli fan, launched into a vitriolic diatribe against her in *New York* magazine, hitting out with, "I always thought Miss Minnelli's face deserving—of first prize in the beagle cate-gory. Less aphoristically speaking, it is a face going off in three directions simultaneously; the nose always en route to becoming a trunk, blubber lips unable to resist the pull of gravity, and a chin trying its damnedest to withdraw into the neck, apparently to avoid responsibility for what goes on above it. It is, like any face, one that could be redeemed by genuine talent, but Miss Minnelli has only brashness, pathos and energy."

A storm of controversy ensued as a result of Simon's barbed remarks, but whatever her innermost feelings about the personal nature of Simon's comments (comments that in a subsequent article he defended as being part of his function as a critic), Liza's only recorded comment on the review was that Ron Lewis hadn't been given sufficient credit for his work in choreographing *The Act.*

Despite horrendous reviews and top ticket prices, Liza's star power insured that *The Act* continued to sell out. Throughout the show's run, a steady procession of Holly-wood stars and high-society luminaries saw the show and paid homage to Liza afterward.

Bill Thomas remembers, "Jackie Onassis came back-stage to congratulate her one evening. Then, another time, the king of Saudi Arabia came backstage to see her and Liza yelled, 'Oh King, honey, thanks for coming to see me.'

"No one had ever called him 'King, honey' before, and he sent her the most incredible diamond, onyx, and gold necklace. Liza showed it to me, laughed and said, 'Can you believe this?'

"Another night, Marlene Dietrich sat in the front row. She was wearing a long turtle-neck gown. Everyone stared at her throughout the show. At the end, Liza bent over and took her hand to kiss, but just as she was about to, realized that the woman wasn't Marlene Dietrich at all, but a New York psychiatrist who is always being mistaken for Marlene. Liza was so shocked that instead of kissing the woman's hand, she ended up jamming one of her fingers up her nose. Liza was hysterical—tears were running down her face!

"But the pressure on her during *The Act* was incredible. When the show closed, they tried to find someone to replace her, and every female actress who saw the show said, 'No way! I wouldn't go in and try to replace Liza Minnelli.' She was that phenomenal. I worked with Liza long after *The Act* and also did *Liza in Concert* with her. She's the most fascinating, kind woman who ever walked the face of the earth.

"Every time she came off the stage, there were people waiting to carry her into the dressing room. We traveled with her, I sat through thousands of shows, and I never saw her do a performance that was even slightly off.

" 'Mark' in show business means you do a half-assed job. But Liza doesn't even know the meaning of the word. She comes out, full energy, full-tilt every night because she is the ultimate, professional performer. Whatever Judy's problems, as a performer, she was highly responsible. She never marked a song. She sang the hell out of the song. Judy never went out on the stage and did a half-assed performance. And Liza is the same. Listen, there have been times when Liza missed shows too, but when she's out there, the audience gets every nickel they paid for.

"People expect Liza to be normal—that's a mistake. Why would she be normal? She didn't grow up under normal circumstances. She's never seen normalcy as far as the white picket fence and four or five kids. She grew up under phenomenal circumstances, with phenomenal talent."

Suzanne Soboloff, the widow of Arnold Soboloff (Liza's highly acclaimed co-star in *The Act*), remembers, "Arnold used to say that Liza just reinvented herself every night. He said that he had to keep on his toes because he could never really rely totally on his own technique when he was working with her. She was vulnerable and fresh and she always did something new. And he had to renew his own performance and reinvent himself as he went along in order to respond to her. Liza is vulnerable and her emotions are close to the surface.

"But it was a happy show with a happy cast. Liza invigorated them. She excited them every night. She is an exciting person and she lends that aura of excitement to the show. Not only did she bring her own characterization to the show, but also her vulnerability, and she actually cried real tears on stage.

"I was friendly with Lorna Luft as well, and the devotion that she and Liza had to their mother was extraordinary. Whenever they spoke about her, it was with such a deep feeling and such a sense of caring. When Arnold died in 1979, Liza said, 'Arnold is up there with Momma now, and they're just waiting for Ray Bolger and they're gonna put on a show!' "

In November, not long after the show first opened, her friend the critic Rex Reed observed, *"The Act* is such a step backward it's stupefying. But Liza Minnelli is no joke. She is as real as breathing. Nobody the right age will be able to carry this show off. No fading star who might have made more sense playing a fading star will be able to make it work. If Liza ever runs out of energy or catches the flu, there goes the ballgame."

Either Rex Reed was clairvoyant or, alternatively, Liza had already, this early in the run of the show, begun her destructive descent into drugs and disco darkness and Rex was aware of it. Whatever the truth, it was clear that by December 1977, instead of pacing herself and resting in-between shows, Liza was partying until dawn at a club called Studio 54.

Much has been written about "Studio," as the cognoscenti labeled it. The phenomenon of Studio 54, of nights when the well dressed and the well known jostled on the pavement along with drug dealers and social climbers desperate to gain admission to its hallowed portals, is linked inextricably to New York of the late seventies.

Newly rescued from economic disaster, New York was then attracting a combination of Euro-trash (tempted to the pulsating city through films like Woody Allen's elegy *Manhattan* and Paul Mazursky's equally romantic *An Unmarried Woman*) and Americans who had been seduced into town by the "I Love New York" advertising campaign. Consequently, New York not only became the scene of a thousand parties but also the palpitating heart of the sexual revolution, with Plato's Retreat, the swinger's haven, and other, sleazier clubs like the Mineshaft catering to homosexual sadomasochism. And in clubs all over town, sexually related or otherwise, the sound of disco filled the amyl nitrate scented air, along with the message that everything was possible, the wilder the better, the more excessive, the more seventies.

Studio 54 swiftly became a monument to all that was wild, excessive, and seventies; a Mecca for the young and the carefree, the famous and the infamous, drunk with power, thirsty for yet more experience, hungry for more sex, more drugs, more wildness.

During her unique childhood, Liza had been prematurely forced into maturity and had never been allowed to romp carefree without troubling about the adult world. She had missed her childhood, but now, soon after her thirtieth birthday, she suddenly found the freedom to be young, to be irresponsible, self-indulgent, careless; to forget about work, about marriage, about who she was, about who her parents were and just throw herself into every excess Studio 54 offered.

Cocaine was ubiquitous at Studio, along with amyl nitrate sniffed out of small bottles, still sold legally on street corners in New York, providing an intense rush especially when inhaled at the moment of orgasm. Drugs were so prevalent at Studio 54 that at midnight every night, a sparkling image of a man in the moon snorting coke from a silver spoon was lowered onto the dance floor as the coke-elated crowd cheered conspiratorially and Studio's red, green, and yellow strobe lights glittered up and down phallically in the foreground.

The basement of Studio 54 was out of bounds for the average mortal but on most nights it was populated by VIPs in search of every type of sensation possible. A source who spent many nights in the basement says, "Every variety of sex under the sun went on in the Studio 54 basement, along with every kind of drug. Steve Rubell's high was ludes and Coca-Cola. In the basement, we all took drugs openly and indulged in every type of sex act. Halston and Liza were there practically every night."

Halston biographer Steven Gaines wrote a roman à clef, *The Club* (published in 1980 by William Morrow), revealing the secrets of life in Studio 54. When *The Club* was first published, Liza and Halston announced via Liz Smith's column that they both intended to sue Gaines. He says, "I stripped Liza bare in public. The information in *The Club* came from Robert Jon Cohen, who worked there as a bartender and witnessed everything that went on. So everything in *The Club* is true."

Gaines's central character is a world-famous entertainer named Jacky—"with a Y"—who is having an affair with an Italian film director, who, for the first time in his life, is directing a stage musical. Jacky, the daughter of a legendary singer who since her death has become an icon, is starring in the musical but jeopardizes her entire career by spending night after night at the Club, drinking, dancing, and snorting coke with her best friend, the world's most famous fashion designer, Ellison, who has a big cocaine habit as well.

Liza's wild nights at Studio were supplemented with evenings at a rival club, Limelight. Publicist John Carmen recalls, "She also went out with a Vice President of the Hells Angels called Richard. She came to the Limelight with him all the time."

Liza spent even wilder nights at another club, The Flamingo, where caged naked men were readily available for sex. Truman Capote went there with Liza and Steve Rubell, afterward telling every detail to Andy Warhol.

Steven Gaines confirms, "Liza used to come to The Flamingo. Flamingo was a huge gay dance club in a huge loft, on the second floor of a building on Broadway, near Houston Street. It was all men, and in order for you to be a member, you had to go up one day during daylight hours and audition. You went in wearing a tight T-shirt or something that looked really good and the owner asked you what your sign was or some such question and if you passed the test, you would be allowed in.

"At four o'clock in the morning, on a Saturday night after Studio 54 had closed, all the gorgeous boys would go to Flamingo and dance in tight jeans with their shirts off. Some nights there were around two thousand writhing bodies. I was a member and Liza came in. What I kept hearing was that she liked all the sleaze, the wild sex, the anonymous sex."

Whatever the truth about Liza's sexual appetites and drug habit, a disturbing sequence of events ensued which may well have been drug-related. On the morning of December 8, 1977, the drapes in Liza's Central Park South penthouse apartment caught fire. After reportedly suffering from smoke inhalation, Liza canceled that night's performance.

Then, on December 21, she suddenly ran a temperature of 104, was diagnosed as having a viral infection, and left the show for one week. Theater press spokesperson Merle Debuskey claimed, "She was crying because she couldn't make it. She was too weak to go on."

She was back again after a week, but on January 14 missed two more performances, again citing flu as the cause. On January 18, she was rushed to New York Hospital with a worried Jack Haley, Jr., by her side. As press photographers and reporters jostled her wheelchair, hiding her face in her hands, her eyes shielded by dark glasses, Liza sobbed, "I'm scared. They think I've got pneumonia!" Her publicist, Lois Smith, begged, "For heaven's sake, let her through. Can't you see she's desperately ill! She's sick!" Finally, Jack made it through the crowds with a trembling Liza cowering in her wheelchair, moaning, "Oh, God! oh, God!" over and over. The picture of Liza, huddled in her wheelchair, her face pale and drawn, her eyes more enormous than ever, was flashed around the world, along with much macabre reporting by the press, as droves of journalists wrote that now, at last, as prophesied, Liza Minnelli was following in her mother's tragic footsteps.

The Act closed for two weeks while Liza recuperated. She spent part of that time in Texas, at the prestigious Greenhouse health resort, and lost twelve pounds there. When she returned to the show on January 30, Halston was compelled to alter her entire wardrobe.

There were constant reports of her various absences during the run (twenty-eight missed performances by March), which cost the show's producers $331,000 in ticket sales. Yet Liza continued her Studio 54 dawn forays. Even after her two-week absence from the show, she still continued to manifest the consequences of a life-style she apparently refused to relinquish. During one matinee intermission, Liza turned white, started trembling, and looked as if she were running a high fever. Shaking with nerves, she confided to a stage manager, "I don't know exactly how I'm going to get through the next act."

Her nightly Studio 54 exploits, coupled with the strain of her marathon performance in The Act, were further complicated by a new love affair. She was now enmeshed in yet another extramarital relationship, this time with the charismatic Russian ballet dancer Mikhail Baryshnikov. Misha, as his close friends called him, was hypnotically attractive and dramatically talented, and projected a rampant masculinity. For Liza, who had never been convinced of her own attractiveness, her conquest of Misha, pursued as he was by countless lovelorn ladies, was living proof of her own desirability.

Still involved with Scorsese, she was disappointed that he refused to be caught up in the lure of Studio 54 and instead recruited Baryshnikov, who was far more receptive to dancing the nights away there. Liza's relationship with Baryshnikov, which began when Scorsese left *The Act,* was obvious to everyone in the show. Even Suzanne Soboloff, who prefers to draw a veil over anything negative related to *The Act,* remembers, "Misha was around a lot backstage. We saw them together a great deal."

Once again, Liza was juggling her men. Still married to Jack and involved in an extramarital fling with Martin Scorsese, she was also dallying with Baryshnikov in a very public way. In his *Diaries,* Andy Warhol noted that, on January 3, 1978, Halston told him of a confrontation in which Scorsese—right in front of Jack Haley, Jr.—questioned Liza point-blank about her affair with Baryshnikov.

Baryshnikov's notoriety as a womanizer and his reputation as the most legendary dancer of his era encouraged Liza to live out her exhibitionism. A source on *The Act* says that Liza and Mikhail began having sex extremely openly backstage. Another source, one who has been Liza's confidant for many years, adds bluntly, "Liza and Baryshnikov had sex everywhere. They would have had it in a broom closet!"

Steven Gaines says, *"The Club* tells about a night based on an incident which Robert Jon Cohen told me about when Liza gave Baryshnikov a blow job in the basement of Studio 54 and Halston joked that she left with semen on her lips." Publicist John Carmen says, "At Studio, she and Baryshnikov were all over each other in public. She was wild and I also heard the blow job story."

Despite his knowledge of Liza's infidelity, Scorsese continued his affair with her, while Halston watched from the sidelines, reveling in the intrigue. And it is indisputably clear that Liza's relationship with Halston, like those with Baryshnikov and Scorsese, was fueled by cocaine.

In his *Diaries,* Warhol, on January 3, 1978, reports a conversation with Halston. "Liza said to Halston, 'Give me every drug you've got.' So he gave her a bottle of coke, a few sticks of marijuana, a Valium, four Quaaludes, and they were all wrapped in a tiny box, and then a little figure in a white hat came up on the stoop and kissed Halston, and it was Marty Scorsese, he'd been hiding around the corner, and then he and Liza went off to have their affair on all the drugs."

Just three weeks later, as Warhol noted, a similar scenario took place, this time with Baryshnikov. On January 28, he recalled a visit to Halston's Olympic Towers apartment during which Liza asked the designer whether she and Baryshnikov could use the apartment. "And Liza and Baryshnikov were taking so much cocaine, I didn't know they took so much, just shoving it in, and it was so exciting to see two really famous people right there in front of you taking drugs, about to go to make it with each other."

Halston's relationship with Liza helped him immensely professionally, and he was quick to capitalize on it and introduce her to other associates who could also benefit from her fame and generosity. In February 1978, at Halston's suggestion she commissioned Andy Warhol to do her portrait.

"When I first discussed it with her, on the dance floor at Regines, Liza wanted a full length portrait," remembers Bob Colacello in his book *Holy Terror: Andy Warhol Close Up*. But he also illustrates Liza's practice of not confronting problems directly. "She said I should tell Andy that I envisioned her that way and not to tell him that she told me to say that." Halston convinced her she was wrong and Liza sat for four Polaroids, and Andy then produced four portraits in his trademark red, white, and black.

Colacello recalled that when the pictures were finished, "Liza arrived with her English secretary, Diana Wemble, carrying a little gray French poodle. She looked more frazzled than the day she had posed at the Factory, shakier, paler, down. But she came to life when she saw the portraits, which made her look happy, healthy, strong and sexy. 'I love them,' she screeched. She turned them sideways and upside down and said she loved them that way too. That night,

Andy and I had dinner with Lorna Luft. She was really worried about Liza, she said." The paintings cost $70,000 and Liza paid at once. The Warhol paintings, it would transpire, were worth far, far more to Liza: A Minnelli intimate recalled, "During Liza's worst times, she would look at Andy's portraits of her and feel so much better because, in them, at least, she looked fantastic."

Liza may have been living out all her wildness in the New York dawn, but during the day, before the curtain rose on *The Act,* she continued to fulfill her normal social obligations. As Halston's number one celebrity client, she attended the opening of his Olympic Towers showroom, along with Elizabeth Taylor and Bianca Jagger. Liza ended the show with "New York, New York," before handing Elizabeth Taylor a red rose.

Jack Haley was rarely present at any of Liza's official engagements. On February 26, 1978, a lawyer for Liza and Jack said that the couple had consented to a separation and that they had agreed to "live separately and apart," adding that Jack and Liza "hoped the separation was temporary."

They continued to live separate lives until, in December 1978, Liza announced their divorce, declaring that she would never get married again because "I never in my life again want to put someone in the position of being called Mr. Minnelli except my father." A short while later, Jack Haley filed for divorce in Santa Monica, citing "irreconcilable differences." The marriage of Dorothy's daughter and the Tin Man's son had been a romantic dream, doomed to plummet to reality and end in disillusionment.

CHAPTER
TWENTY-ONE

Each night, Liza was on stage performing nonstop for two-and-a-half hours. Then when the curtain fell, a limousine spirited her to Studio 54. On a typical evening, February 25, 1978, a witness saw Liza at the club with Halston. The time was 2:00 A.M., and she was dressed in tight white pants and a red turtleneck sweater, sitting beside the dance floor and drinking champagne. At 3:30 A.M. she looked really tired, disappeared, then came back at 4:00 A.M. and, full of energy though her eyes were glazed, began dancing wildly with dancer Sterling Saint Jacques.

At her thirty-second birthday party, thrown by Halston at Olympic Towers, she was feted by Andy Warhol, Carol Channing, Eartha Kitt, Melba Moore, Jane Holzer, Martha Graham, Diana Vreeland, Truman Capote, Al Pacino, Robert De Niro, Ken Harrison, Bianca Jagger, Steve Rubell, and Scorsese. But although she gushed afterward, "This is the happiest birthday I've ever had," she secretly admitted that she was very lonely and that the pressure of the show was unbelievable.

Halston's other close female friend, Bianca Jagger, enthused of her: "She's a very vulnerable person. When you see her, you want to give her a hug. And when you give her a hug, you feel she needs it. Like many people who've been robbed of their childhood in a way, who grew up too fast, Liza retained something very childish, very sweet. And she always tries to lift your morale. She'll tell you how wonderful you look, and you know she really means it. As a woman, you never feel in competition."

The reality was quite different. "Bianca and Liza didn't get on well. Bianca is pompous with airs and graces. Liza is more real. Liza is very nice. Bianca was arrogant to Liza, but Liza didn't take any notice," observed eyewitness Victor Hugo, who spent a great deal of time with Bianca and Liza.

Baryshnikov was besieged by women longing to sample his fabled charms, and surrounded by so much intriguing potential, he had not been faithful to Liza. Liza was disillusioned and disheartened by his infidelity, her relationship with him quickly disintegrated, and she started to drift back to Scorsese. Simultaneously there were also reports, never confirmed, of romances with David Bowie, Al Pacino, and John Travolta.

Around this time, too, Liza engaged in an edgy flirtation with television journalist Geraldo Rivera. Although the flirtation was never consummated, Geraldo's recollections, published in his autobiography, *Exposing Myself,* shed a certain amount of light on Liza's state of mind during her wild Studio days.

At the time of their first meeting, Liza was still married to Jack but thriving on wild nights at Studio 54. According to Geraldo, "She was going about a million miles an hour, energized by the frenzy of the place and numbed by whatever she had spent the evening ingesting." As always, the room was crowded, the music loud and throbbing, but amid the tornado of dancing and drug-taking, Liza and Geraldo exchanged glances, magnetized one another and, he says, "We briefly embraced, and then she grabbed my hand and pulled me through the crowd to the ladies room." There, "She

pulled me into a stall, and we enjoyed a hot grope and grind
that was made all the more exciting by time and place."
Suddenly, and abruptly, Liza walked away, leaving Geraldo
abandoned but definitely not seduced.

The way he tells it in his memoirs, many years of smoul-
dering but unconsummated passion ensued, with Geraldo
cast in the role of pursuer and Liza, his "wounded bird" who
persisted in teasing him, yet never succumbing to his ad-
vances.

At one point, they met at a party during which Liza
proceeded to spend the evening clinging to Geraldo, punc-
tuated by whispers of "I've got to get out of here" or "Take
me away from all this. This sucks." Yet when Geraldo suggested they leave, Liza insisted on staying. The portrait
Geraldo paints of Liza is of a frightened, confused tease, who,
during the lowest point of her life, was drug-driven and ca-
reening from man to man without truly being able to commit
herself to anyone.

Halston remained the most constant man in her life. On
April 26, at Studio 54's birthday party, after singing "Happy
Birthday" to Steve Rubell, Liza sang a tribute to Halston,
"I'm Always True to You, Darling, in My Fashion."

On June 4, 1978, beating Eartha Kitt for *Timbuktu* and
Madeline Kahn for *On the Twentieth Century*, Liza won her
third Tony. Journalist Sally Ogle Davis observed, "At the
Tony Awards, Broadway's biggest, most public night of the
year, she was a whirling dervish with a high manic cackle
and what looked like an extremely bad dose of St. Vitus'
Dance."

She was a party girl par excellence, a single girl about
town who also happened to be Broadway's number one star,
appearing nightly in a musical that was the show business
equivalent of a marathon. With Halston as the most important man in her life, Liza, forever riding recklessly on the
Studio 54 carousel of drugs, sex, and disco, had concocted a
recipe for disaster.

On June 26, she debuted at the Metropolitan Opera in
Martha Graham's *The Owl and the Pussycat*, in a perfor-

mance that she was to reprise in London. *The Act* closed on July 16, 1978, and, in an attempt to find stability, she made a date with Mark Gero, six years her junior, the show's stage manager. Six foot four, Italian, strong, silent, with a reputation for being a stud, Gero was a Robert De Niro lookalike. In fact, at their first meeting during the pre–*New York, New York* days, Liza had asked Mark whether he'd like to be De Niro's stand-in.

The son of Frank Gero, a stage manager who had worked on *Flora, the Red Menace,* Mark had first tried to date Liza during the San Francisco run of *The Act.* He made a few shy attempts to invite her to dinner after rehearsals but always met with the same excuse that she was too tired. And for a long time Mark subsisted on the cherished memory of the one evening in which he had managed to attract her attention long enough to have sandwiches with her in her suite in the San Francisco Hilton Hotel.

"Liza is the first girl I ever waited that long to go out with. She's the most vulnerable girl I ever met!" said an infatuated Mark. "We were walking in midtown last week and there was a pet shop with puppies in the window. Liza wanted to buy the whole litter of them, seven of them, and give them to friends for presents. I talked her out of it, telling her people might not find it convenient to keep the dogs. She cried like a baby."

As their romance progressed, Mark remarked proudly that often when they were out together he was mistaken for her bodyguard. He was tall and strapping, exuded an air of calm self-certainty, and was content to remain a quiet onlooker as Liza whirled all over town with what Gero with disbelief was to describe as "a thousand close friends." But despite her myriad so-called close friends, Mark was secure in the knowledge that Liza really cared about him. And, in return—for now, at least—she, too, was secure in his love. He reassured her constantly, enthusing to the media, "I'm crazy about her. I loved her from the very beginning, and she knows it. I'm beginning to think it's working now, because she had a long time to get to know me and to know I had good intentions."

Long after first witnessing the blossoming romance between Liza and Mark, Bill Thomas remembered, "It was always a well known fact that Liza had trouble finding someone that she really wanted to stay with. At the time, everyone believed Mark was the one. But Liza is too phenomenal and individual. She's going to eat every man up alive. Even the energy around her would wear a man out. I love her to death, but I don't think I could live with her. How could you ever be anything but Mr. Minnelli? How would you?"

Now that *The Act* had finally closed, in September Liza went on the road again, opening her American-European tour at the Saratoga Performing Arts Center in Saratoga Springs, New York, where her appearance was greeted with an ear-splitting ovation.

By November, though, she was involved in a new and painful controversy. On November 27, her mother's third husband, Sid Luft, held a sale of Judy's personal effects at the Beverly Wilshire Hotel. Sid's children, Lorna and Joey, tried to avoid becoming caught up in the resultant turmoil. Joey, in particular, had always assiduously avoided the limelight, first trying his luck as a drummer, then working for a pharmaceutical company, and, it was rumored, sometimes driving a limousine. But in this instance, Joey was so hurt by the painful wrangling over his mother's estate that he made a rare public statement, saying sadly, "I just wish the whole thing were over. It breaks up the family."

Outraged by Sid's plans to hold a glorified garage sale of possessions purported by him to have been among Judy's most cherished, Liza tried to have an injunction issued against the sale. The attempt failed and although Liza's lawyers appealed and won a new hearing, it was not scheduled to take place till the following year and the sale went ahead notwithstanding.

Repressing her fury and momentarily admitting defeat, Liza still couldn't endure the thought of her mother's dressing table and a small wooden statue of Mother and Child that she'd always loved belonging to strangers, so she put in a bid and bought them at the auction. Liza's purchases were authentic Garland possessions, but others cast aspersions on the authenticity of some of the items. Sid Luft, conceding that financial pressures had compelled him to hold the sale, sold Judy's Rolls for $60,000. At that juncture both Mark Herron and Judy's former housekeeper both alleged that Judy had never owned the car.

Sid Luft went on to raise $250,000 from the sale of supposed Garland memorabilia, including her reading glasses, which were sold for $300, and her false eyelashes, which were sold for $125. On January 7, 1979, it was reported that Liza had sued Sid Luft for the proceeds of the sale, believing they should go to the estate. Again she failed, but in August 1981 Liza went back to court in a bid to recover some of the money as well as other items from Judy's estate, including the sheet music of "Melancholy Baby" and the script of *Judgment at Nuremberg*.

Sid and Liza eventually reconciled and he has never discussed his attitude to her with a writer (other than Gerold Frank) except to say, "She is a lost soul." In the seventies, though, Patricia Seaton Lawford, then married to actor Peter Lawford (who had dated Judy), spent many hours with Peter at Sid's house in Los Angeles.

"Sid's conversations with Peter were sort of hateful. Sid's comments were in the vein that Liza had talent but was a cheapened version of her mother. That she wanted to be Judy. But that she wasn't the real thing."

In November 1978, Liza was in London, appearing at the Palladium. Mark, who was also managing her new stage show, stayed with her at the Savoy. During a conversation in the first week of December at the hotel with journalist David Wigg, she confided that she was in love with Mark and pleaded, "Please say it's nice and calm because it is. And what's more, the love is returned."

Wigg went on to write, "Liza sipped a glass of champagne in her suite at the Savoy Hotel. 'What am I doing? I mustn't drink when I've got a show tonight,' she suddenly remembered, immediately putting down the glass."

When asked in London about her tumultuous party-going life, she protested, "When I go to a party, it's a good one and that's the one everyone is watching. People think that because I played the messed-up Sally Bowles, then that's how I must be in real life. I don't take my life to the limit. I enjoy my life and I value it."

Mark and Liza spent Christmas in Paris, then traveled back to New York, where Liza was scheduled to open at the Promenade Theater in the off-Broadway production of *Are You Now or Have You Ever Been?* Her role in Eric Bently's dramatization of the House of Representatives Committee on Un-American Activities investigation required her to read Lillian Hellman's celebrated letter.

On February 5, after a dinner with Halston, Elizabeth Taylor, and Dolly Parton, Liza invited Andy Warhol back to her apartment to view Mark's sculpture. It was clear that Liza, always generous to all her friends, was now directing her energy toward promoting Mark's career and helping him gain professional status so that she wouldn't overshadow him totally. But when Andy arrived, Mark, an inveterate gambler, was out playing poker. However, undiscouraged, Liza asked Andy to look at his work anyway and afterward begged him to leave Mark a note saying that he would do his utmost to arrange a show for him.

By now, Liza had moved out of the apartment that she had shared with Jack at 40 Central Park South and had bought a house in Murray Hill. Halston, in Andy's words, was "trying to give her taste." He then observed, "I think all she really cares about is working; she doesn't care about decorating."

Still on tour, in the middle of February 1979, Liza traveled to Rio with Gero in tow. On opening night, however, events threatened to shatter Mark's romance with Liza. Brazilian composer Edu Lobo was in the audience with his wife, singer Wanda de Sa, and after the performance, the four of them—Wanda, Edu, Liza and Mark—went to Rio's hottest club, the Hippopotamus.

According to a writer who was in the club that evening, "Liza and Edu were in a corridor of the nightclub throughout the evening singing together." The attraction was instant and, with conflicting emotions, Mark flew back to New York, leaving Liza in Rio with Edu.

Shortly after Mark's departure, Zozimr Barroso Do Amaral, columnist for the magazine *Jornal Do Brazil,* revealed, "I think it's evident to anyone who has seen them together that they're very much in love. They're not making a secret of it. They've been seen in Rio restaurants and clubs and at a beach resort."

Around the same time, Edu left his wife and two children and moved out of their home into a Rio hotel. Soon afterward, Liza flew back to London for yet another appearance. But, as soon as she arrived there, a source claimed that Liza was calling Edu four times a day from England and had sent him hundreds of roses and a diamond wristwatch.

For a while, right through May, the couple was so deeply involved that Liza twice flew back from London to Rio to see him. A tortured Edu revealed, "I can't hide anymore. I care about her. She's a fantastic person. She is a marvelous human being." Back in New York, though, Mark was waiting patiently for Liza to come home to him, and finally she did, proclaiming, "The reports of all my different lovers are absolute nonsense. I'm still going out with Mark Gero, I'm still in love with him, and we're still living together."

Edu had been a brief, glamorous diversion and once again, she recommenced her quest for commitment and normalcy. But while Mark still seemed to be her best chance of a happily ever after, drugs continued to be a driving force in her life. In May, Halston became the recipient of the third Martha Graham Award. The award ceremony took place at Studio 54. The club was so full that former First Lady Betty Ford sat on Liza's knee. When, at one in the morning, Liza presented Halston with his award, according to an eyewitness, she and Halston were both incoherent.

Halston himself would eventually talk about Liza during her drug-ridden years, saying, "Liza is a national treasure but often when she would come to see me she would crawl up like a little kitten and sleep. That's all she wanted to do."

Once, in the late seventies, she was staying with friends at a private house on Fire Island. A fellow houseguest recalled, "Liza looked horrible and she was on cocaine for four days. They had a barbecue and the only thing Liza touched for the entire time was hot dogs and champagne and tons of coke."

Everyone who loved Liza hoped fervently that Mark would prove to be a stabilizing influence on her. But Mark, too, had his own demons, his own excesses. On one occasion, both Liza and Mark went to spend the weekend with Henry and Kathy Ford. Afterward, another attendee confided to a source, "It was a nightmare because Liza and Mark were so coked up that they didn't make any sense at the dinner table. They just kept jumping up and going to the bathroom. Making no sense and being the worst possible houseguests."

Although Mark purportedly sometimes used cocaine, Halston remained her prime cocaine playmate, her best friend whom she idolized and whose every venture she wholeheartedly supported. On July 20, 1979, Liza and Halston took the Concorde to London, where Liza was due to appear in Martha Graham's *The Owl and the Pussycat,* with costumes by Halston.

The Covent Garden opening on July 23 was studded with social stars, including England's Princess Margaret and her then-escort Roddy Llewellyn, Andy Warhol, Steve Rubell, Texas socialite Lynne Wyatt, and Halston with his friend Victor Hugo.

Martha Graham was in London for the opening. In her memoirs afterward she recorded that when she and Liza arrived at Covent Garden, Liza was mobbed by autograph seekers clamoring for her signature. No one, however, took any notice of Martha. But in a flash, all that changed and she, Martha, was suddenly mobbed by autograph seekers as well. Later, she learned that Liza had whispered to the autograph hunters that they were missing the valuable chance to get the autograph of a far greater star than Liza Minnelli or Judy Garland—Martha Graham.

After the show, Halston gave a private party at the

Savoy Hotel, attended by Princess Margaret. Liza, in a semi-see-through dress, her hair brushed back in a style her mother had once worn, was excited about meeting the Princess, especially here, at the Savoy. The venerable hotel, overlooking the majestic Thames, was redolent of poignant memories for her. Judy had always stayed there in splendor, and Liza had been there first with Peter and then on her honeymoon with Jack.

The setting was ideal, the occasion—the night of her Covent Garden debut—divine, and, for Liza, the prospect of meeting Princess Margaret at the Savoy must have seemed full of promise. She felt exhilarated, elated, but, as Victor Hugo remembers, that night Liza became the victim of her own effervescence. "You are not supposed to address royalty until you are spoken to. But Liza ignored protocol, rushed up to Princess Margaret and shrieked, 'Did you see my show? Did you see my show?' Princess Margaret looked outraged, turned to her lady-in-waiting, and in a very stern voice said, 'Can you believe *her*!' Liza ran upstairs in floods of tears. Halston wasn't that sympathetic. He told me, 'It was all Liza's own fault.' "

From September 4 to 14, 1979, Liza appeared in Carnegie Hall in her sell-out show, *Liza in Concert*. In the *New York Times*, critic John Wilson raved, "In *Liza in Concert*, Miss Minnelli has made that rare quantum leap from a status as an exciting performer who may not always sustain her apparent potential, to the fully controlled realization of her very impressive talent as an entertainer."

After the Carnegie Hall opening, there was a late supper dance at Studio 54, thrown by Halston. Vincente Minnelli and Lee Anderson had flown in from California and dined on lobster, along with Truman Capote, Andy Warhol, Diana Vreeland, Victor Hugo, Baby Jane Holzer, Anita Loos, Margaux Hemingway, and Diane Von Furstenberg.

On September 10, 1979, in the *New York Times*, John Rockwell wrote an article analyzing the phenomenon of the superstar who attracts mass adulation. Interviewed by him in the Russian Tea Room, Liza said, "I really like people;

otherwise it would scare me to death. You walk out and people roar at you."

Liza, asked by Rockwell why she thought she generated so much hysteria, answered, "Someone said to me after opening night, 'I think I know what it is. You give everybody hope.' It's everything positive that people want to hear. Momma and Piaf were very fragile and vulnerable. With me, it's like, 'Come on, let's go!' I think everybody likes to see people who enjoy what they're doing."

On December 4, 1979, Liza married Mark in a candlelit evening ceremony at St. Bartholomew's Episcopalian Church in Manhattan. She wore a Boise-rose chiffon Halston gown, Vincente gave her away, and Liza cried throughout the entire ceremony. She was marrying the man of her dreams and, what's more, she was also pregnant by him.

The deliriously happy couple exchanged rings in front of a congregation that included Elizabeth Taylor, Andy Warhol, Martha Graham, Ron Protas, Steve Rubell, Fred Ebb, and Halston; Mark's grandmother, Mrs. Antonio Gerolino; his father, Frank; his mother, Dolores; Mark's three brothers; and Lorna, the bridesmaid.

The ceremony was overlaid with memories, conducted as it was by the Reverend Peter Delaney, who had officiated at Judy's funeral. Monsignor Emerson Moore, who taught Mark to be an altar boy, blessed the marriage, and singer and poet Rod McKuen read a love poem he had written in the couple's honor. When Liza threw her bouquet, it was caught by Lee Anderson.

After the ceremony, Halston hosted a black tie reception for Liza and Mark, attended by, among others, Faye Dunaway and Fred Ebb. Liza said, "I'm a very happy woman. My father told me to marry Mark. I was proud of my mother, but I was really a daddy's girl. How did I ever find a man to match him? Well, it took three tries. I only married Mark because he told me to."

Of Mark she said rapturously, "He's very quiet. He's lovely, tall and very quiet, especially when he first meets you. He's completely dedicated to whatever he's doing."

The couple had decided that Mark would henceforth concentrate on his art and give up working in the theater. Liza clarified the situation by saying, "When I met him he was a stage manager, from a show business family. But it was too stupid, too incestuous, annoying and competitive."

From that time on, Mark became a full-time sculptor and, later, also a painter. Paul Steiner, a writer for *Art Speak/Art Liaison* magazine, who interviewed Mark about art, says, "As a sculptor, Mark is somewhat derivative, but what he does, he is skilled at. He cuts direct from stone which is unusual. He picks something like a bird in flight, but it's still abstract. But it's physical labor and he can only show six or eight pieces."

Just six days after the wedding, Liza suffered intense pains and, on December 10, she was rushed from her Central Park apartment to New York Hospital, Cornell Medical Center, where she miscarried. Sources claimed that she had been two months pregnant.

Having a child had been her most cherished wish. Her relationship with her mother had been so painfully close, yet she longed to re-create that very closeness. She had hoped that the child would be a girl and had planned to call her Judy. But, squaring her shoulders, Liza bravely declared, "We were both heartbroken, and it's a big setback. But it's not a disaster because I'm fine." Apparently, her doctor had assured her that she was able to try again, and Liza reaffirmed that she and Mark were very much in love and longed desperately to have a child together.

Later she elaborated, "My God, you know how lucky I am. That child could have been very sick. I've seen children who were born to people on drugs. Even though you stop taking everything when you're pregnant, the stuff stays in your system. So now that's one of my hopes for the future. Especially knowing that I'm O.K. and that I won't hurt a little baby."

Liza's comments, made much later when she had come to terms with the possible consequences of her own drug addiction, inevitably raise the question of Judy and of how much "stuff" had stayed in her system. Vincente had made it plain that she had given up drugs when she became pregnant with Liza, but Liza's remarks indicate her own fears of having inherited her mother's propensities when she was still in the womb.

Halston cast another light on Liza's first pregnancy and miscarriage: "She never thought she could have a child. She had been told by some doctors that she couldn't. It's the one thing that Liza wants and needs more than anything, a really strong home and family."

CHAPTER TWENTY-TWO

Work remained her most rewarding outlet and in the new year she was back on tour. Bill Thomas, who toured with her, recalls that time:

"Everything was first-class travel. It was sensational. Because it was a small cast on the road, we were invited to all kinds of places and wonderful things that I would have never gotten to go to. We went to dinner at the Rothschilds' in Paris. We went down to Rio and stayed on the plastic surgeon Ivo Pitanguay's yacht and went water skiing.

"Liza is impressed by celebrities. In Germany, Audrey Hepburn came backstage during intermission. She was with Ben Gazzara; they were doing a film at the time, and I think they were having a little romance. I was desperate to meet Audrey and, knowing how kind Liza always was, approached her and begged, 'Liza, I would kill to meet Audrey Hepburn,' so she introduced me. Audrey was dressed in a black turtleneck and black slacks and she looked incredible. In contrast, Liza had been sweating, and she looked like she had been through a war.

"Audrey left, Liza changed and when she was ready, I

walked towards the stage with her. Suddenly, she stopped, turned to me and said admiringly, 'That Audrey bitch was so fat!' We laughed, and then she said, 'Have you ever seen anyone thinner, or more gorgeous? I felt like the ugliest stepsister in the world!' She was awestruck by Audrey's beauty.

"Liza earns every iota of applause. She goes out on stage with a sense of awe and never expects the applause. She has the attitude, 'I will get them' Not, 'I've got them.' She tells herself, 'They paid a lot of money to see me. I will get this audience.' I don't think she ever really knew how good she was.

"When we were appearing in Munich, Germany, we didn't think the Germans would be all that enthusiastic about the show. Before the performance began, Liza swore, 'I'm going to go out there and get them!' At the end of the show, they started applauding and they didn't stop. Even after we had got dressed and were on the bus heading back to the hotel, we could still hear them. It was forty-five minutes later, and the audience were still yelling, 'Liza, Liza, Liza!' We were flabbergasted.

"People were paying $200–$300 per ticket. And they screamed the same way in Amsterdam and at the London Palladium, where the response was frightening. In Brazil, Liza's dresser and I kept pushing people off the stage. In the end, we had band people, everyone, trying to keep crowds away from her but Liza just kept on performing. After the show, she always falls apart physically because she is exhausted, but she is also elated."

Back in New York, writer Beverly Williston met Liza at a Studio 54 party for Bianca Jagger. She recalls, "At that point, I guess they were all pretty high. David Macmillan the trainer and I came to the party and brought a black panther. During the evening someone disobeyed instructions, switched the lights on, and the panther attacked David.

"Liza came back as she was so upset because David had been attacked. She sat and patted the panther for a long time and was very interested. She asked a lot of questions about exotic animals. I was surprised because she was not in the least bit afraid."

On February 19, 1980, CBS aired *Goldie and Liza Together*. Liza and Goldie Hawn had become great friends during the making of the special in October 1979, and Goldie had encouraged Liza to have a child, promising to be the child's godmother. She said, "I told Liza having children was beautiful, the most important thing you can do in your life." After the miscarriage, Goldie did her utmost to help Liza over her depression.

At the time of the special, Liza proclaimed that she was incapable of being depressed for more than two days. Of the miscarriage she said, "As they say in show business, I'm going to keep trying until I get it right! I always said I didn't want to grow up with my children. I wanted to grow up, then have my children."

She loved working with Goldie, paying her tribute with the words "My greatest talent is being able to find people who are better than I am to guide me. I want to learn."

Around the same time, she met famed actor Laurence Olivier at Sardi's. A beaming Olivier announced that seeing Liza had made his day. Afterward, almost speechless with wonder, Liza swooned, "He was so happy to see me! How about that! Laurence Olivier recognizing me!"

On April 20, 1980, the Sunday magazine of the New York *Daily News* published a less-than-flattering profile of Liza, one which focused on the possibility that all her disarming bubbliness, her verve, enthusiasm, and aching sincerity, were merely show business ploys. Written by journalist Joyce Wadler, the article revolved around a phenomenon that Wadler dubbed M.E.G.O.—My Eyes Glazed Over—a state which, according to Joyce, was induced by interviewing uninspiring celebrities.

During her interview with Wadler, Liza refuted the suggestion that she spent many an evening at Studio 54, in a denial causing the skeptical Joyce to comment, "The pictures of her partying night after night at Studio 54? A mirage." Liza valiantly attempted to paint a portrait of marital bliss, characterizing her day as beginning at nine thirty when she and Mark got up, followed by dance classes and rehearsal, ending with Liza's cooking dinner and their watching television together.

Joyce Wadler's interview was witty and bitchy and struck right at the heart of Liza's facade. She had wanted to talk to Liza at home, but excuses were made, culminating in the decision that Liza's publicist definitely would not permit her to be interviewed alone.

When it came to arranging Liza's photo session, to her consternation Wadler discovered that Liza's publicist insisted that it was mandatory that she engage a dresser, makeup man, and hairdresser. The hairdresser's bill was for $600, a sum which, Wadler acidly observed, "wouldn't be so hard to take if Liza hadn't been wearing a wig."

Liza arrived an hour late for the interview, and, according to Wadler, the entire process then slid downhill. Today Joyce Wadler recalls, "The main thing that I remember was that interviewing Liza was a disappointment because I had expected her to be fascinating. My main memory of Liza was that she was trembling and chain smoking and was one of the most nervous creatures I had ever seen in my life.

"I was with her about an hour-and-a-half. She was very fearful, and I remember I got nothing from her except the standard show-biz rubbish. So, it was just a frustrating experience, which was a pity, because she could be pretty funny. At one point, I was talking about the gay following that her mother had and having lived a long time on Christopher Street, and hearing people always singing "Over the Rainbow" at three in the morning. And Liza quipped, 'I wonder what they thought they'd find there?'

"She was so dry and her timing was so good. I felt that she could be fun but that she was so protected by her entourage. Afterwards, someone I knew saw Liza at a party. She was alone in another room, just listening to one of her mother's records. Just sitting there listening to it over and over again."

* * *

On April 24, 1980, *Baryshnikov on Broadway,* in which Liza and Baryshnikov sang and danced together to some of the great showstoppers, was aired on ABC-TV. Her romance with Baryshnikov had long since ended, and she was exhilarated by his praise that she had "crossed over" from pop artist to classical performer.

Liza's heart was still set on achieving cinematic success and reliving her *Cabaret* glory days. And when she was offered a relatively minor part in a new comedy, *Arthur,* she eagerly accepted. In June, she started shooting *Arthur* at the Astoria Film Studios. She co-starred with Sir John Gielgud and Dudley Moore (who was to become a close friend), but drugs and alcohol had had their effect and she was constantly tired throughout the shoot. Nevertheless, she delighted in calling director Steve Gordon "Boss" and remained gracious to her fans.

According to a member of the production, "John Gielgud liked Liza very much. And she was quite taken with Dudley Moore. But Steve Gordon had never directed a film before. We knew all about the booze and drugs from reliable sources. I felt sorry for her because I don't think she ever grew up, she just acted grown up. She moved into a new apartment and didn't know how to decorate it. Halston did everything for her; he designed her life, her apartment, her clothes, because she didn't know how to pick clothes. And she couldn't even cook an egg or lay a table."

During filming, London *Daily Mail* writer Jack Tinker was present during a scene shot in a church. "At the end of the service, Liza stood drinking coffee in the church hall while parishioners crowded round. A tiny old lady, bent double with arthritis, exclaimed: 'Judy!' Everyone in earshot held their breath waiting for the star's reaction. 'I've seen all your movies. Is it really you?' 'No,' said Liza softly, 'my name's Liza and I'm Judy's daughter. But I want you to know that's the nicest thing anyone has ever said to me.' "

By the fall of 1980, Liza and Mark had moved into the penthouse on the twenty-first floor of a modern high rise in

Manhattan's East Sixties, where Liza still lives today. Her neighbors were riveted by her arrival, but according to the late Doris Lilly, who lived in the same building, Liza wasn't the least bit stand-offish.

"Liza goes out of her way to be nice, to be neighborly. She is very friendly and always admires your dog and smiles her big, pretty, sugar-plum smile."

On moving day, she was so overcome with emotion that after Mark had carried her over the threshold, she asked Halston, who was with her, to leave them together for a while because, she explained apologetically, "It was such a personal and private moment."

The apartment consists of six rooms, furnished in art deco style, with marble floors, glass tables, and a black dining room table. Liza's collection of Lucite cigarette holders are on show everywhere throughout the apartment. Warhol's four silk-screen portraits of Liza command the entrance hall, while his pictures of Judy hang in the dining room.

Social columnist Suzy described Mark and Liza's apartment as "one of the most dramatic far flung apartments in New York, a sort of white marble, ultra-modern fantasy with touches of black and white and silver and crimson."

The apartment was decorated by interior designer Timothy MacDonald, whom Liza had hired after Halston introduced him to her. She had never thought much about design but was determined to have the apartment decorated in a style that she liked. MacDonald was very patient with her, listening to her ideas without offering up too much opposition, even when she announced dramatically, "I want something out of the Belle Époque."

Observing, "I've always been surrounded by sets," Liza decreed that, in homage to Vincente's style, the master bedroom was to be decorated rather like the *Gigi* set. In contrast, Mark's Poker Room, as Liza called it, boasted a contemporary bar and was decorated in red. The taste may have been highly questionable, but both Mark and Liza were content, and Mark sighed, "Liza and I have been much more relaxed since we've been here."

On Mark's thirtieth birthday, he and Liza held their first

party at the new apartment. Guests included Gregory Peck, Al Pacino, Ryan O'Neal, Farrah Fawcett, Bianca Jagger, Marisa Berenson, Vincente and Lee Anderson. An exuberant Liza looked radiant in a black wool Halston pant suit and served guests pasta followed by roast beef.

The apartment symbolized a new beginning for Mark and Liza and, on October 7, 1980, it was announced that Liza was pregnant again. But that same week, while appearing in a nightclub act in Framingham, Massachusetts, with Joel Grey, she was rushed from her Boston hotel to Massachusetts General Hospital suffering from severe abdominal pains.

A source close to Liza at the time said, "When she was brought to the hospital, she had all the symptoms of a miscarriage. But doctors now say that Liza and the baby are O.K. However, she needs complete rest. Both she and Mark want this baby very much. She is very happy to be pregnant again. We are praying that everything will be O.K."

The baby was due in April and, on doctor's orders, Liza canceled projected concert engagements in Denver, Columbus, New Orleans, Atlanta, Nashville, Houston, and Las Vegas and moved to a second home, a retreat that she and Mark had bought in Lake Tahoe.

As Lee Minnelli later explained, "She was working in Boston like a fiend, doing a concert, when she collapsed backstage. So the doctor said she'd have to take it easy, which she did, but despite her care, after five months she lost the second child." On December 31, at the Washoe Medical Center in Reno, she miscarried for the second time. Her spokesperson said, "According to Dr. Robert Stitt, a sudden turn of events proved it impossible for Miss Minnelli to keep the child. Dr. Stitt said there was no reason to assume she cannot conceive and have a successful pregnancy."

Later, her stepmother Lee tearfully confirmed, "It was such a blow to Liza. She was just having her new penthouse apartment redecorated and furnished. And she was having a nursery decorated. It just broke her heart. Liza wants a baby more than anything else in the world. She's lost two and it was a terrible blow to her."

Rallying and brightly insisting that she intended to have six children, Liza made the best of the situation. Hundreds and hundreds of women had written to her, sympathizing with her plight, detailing their own sorry sagas of babies conceived, then lost, and for a time Liza no longer felt so alone. She was heartened by some of the letters, like the one from a woman who had conceived but miscarried many times over eleven years, but after all that time she eventually gave birth to seven children. Taking comfort, Liza said, "It was so nice to hear, to get all that hope and encouragement."

As always, she recognized that working would distract her, would dull the pain of her loss. So, on March 16, she relaunched her national tour in Philadelphia. But, despite her indomitable will to survive, stress and unhappiness sometimes still overwhelmed her. On April 22, 1981, she was admitted to St. Joseph's Infirmary in Atlanta, looking pale as a ghost.

July, however, proved to be a happier month for her professionally. Her album, *Liza in Concert,* recorded at a live performance in New Orleans, was released to critical acclaim. And on July 6, *Arthur* was screened for an appreciative audience. Vincent Canby wrote in the *New York Times* of her role as the waitress who falls in love with Arthur, "Her performance is so richly comic and assured that the film is one of those unusual comedies in which you come to believe that the romantic leads were actually made for each other."

It seemed that she had broken the string of flops, and for the first time since *Cabaret,* her film career held promise. It also pleased her that Peter Allen had co-written the film's theme song and later won an Oscar for it.

Her social life, at first glance, seemed to be relatively conventional and no longer obsessively revolved around Manhattan's wild night life. On July 20, 1981, she and Mark Gero went to dinner with Kate Jackson and Rock Brynner at Mildred Pierce. According to eyewitnesses, Liza was shy, wasn't wearing makeup, and didn't want her photograph to be taken.

During the same week, Liza and Mark attended a party at Hisae for the opening of *Endless Love,* which was graced by a resplendent Elizabeth Taylor, dressed in red chiffon, sporting a blaze of diamonds, protected by six bodyguards.

Later that summer she went to a party at Halston's Olympic Towers apartment along with Andy, Hope Lange, John Springer, Lauren Bacall, Robert De Niro, Martin Scorsese, and Isabella Rossellini.

Around that time, Liza confided wistfully, "We're still trying to have a baby. They figured out what was wrong and can fix it. From the experience of two miscarriages, it should be easy the next time. I'm so well rehearsed."

She spent the rest of the year touring, spending time with Halston, encouraging Mark with his artwork, and also made sure she still found time for charity work, visiting sick children in Harlem. But she still wasn't healthy; drugs and alcohol still played a strong part in her life and there was no sign of a third pregnancy.

Meanwhile Lorna, now twenty-nine and managed by her husband, Jake Hooker, thirty-one, was making an attempt to break into films, appearing in *Grease II* in the part of Paulette Rebchuck. Still professionally unlucky, Lorna's role did not garner her much attention. She went on to make *Where the Boys Are '84*—but again failed to make an impact.

Ever the jet-set butterfly, in April 1982, Liza flew to Malibu from New York with Mark just to celebrate at a party with Alana Hamilton, Rod Stewart, Ryan O'Neal, Tatum O'Neal, Dudley Moore, and Joan Collins.

By June 1982, Liza was thirty-six and growing disillusioned with her marriage to Mark. He seemed, at times, to be far more wedded to the poker table than to her. And, as a result, Liza began to search for attention from other quarters.

In London in June 1982, she met the controversial singer Adam Ant. Adam (whose real name was Stuart Goddard), four years Liza's junior, was a superstar survivor of the punk era, notorious for the tattoo "PURE SEX" that he bore on his arm. At the time of his first meeting with Liza, Adam was in the process of getting a divorce. According to sources, Adam was besotted by Liza. A close friend explained, "They have nothing but admiration for each other. Adam went to see her in concert in Sydney last October and met her at a reception afterwards. Then they met up again later in her tour in Perth, and then again in Japan. Liza is such a radiant, charismatic lady that Adam was totally knocked out.

"They wrote to each other and then met again in London and had lunch together at Langan's Brasserie. They genuinely enjoy each other's company and have a great deal to talk about." Whether or not Liza's dalliance with Adam Ant progressed beyond conversation is not on record.

On October 9, Liza was in Sun City, Bophuthatswana, where she had been booked for eleven shows in front of a crowd of six thousand people at a time. As soon as tickets went on sale, crowds streamed over the South African border by the thousands. Sinatra had sold out in Sun City fourteen months before, and Liza's opening night was also SRO.

Liza had flown into Johannesburg with an entourage of twenty-five, including twelve musicians and two male dancers. She followed Shirley Bassey, Olivia Newton-John, Cher, the Osmonds, and Paul Anka in appearing at Sun City. But although she was playing in front of a mixed race audience, only two hundred black people had been able to afford the price of a ticket.

When she was challenged at a Johannesburg press conference with a political question relating to the explosive racial tensions sweeping South Africa, Liza defended her decision to play Sun City by saying that it had evolved out of her family history because Vincente's first film had been an all-black musical, *Cabin in the Sky*. She went on to vow that she would never appear in front of an audience that was segregated.

Afterward the *New York Times* observed, "The paradox is that the audience could be far more multi-racial if a star like Miss Minnelli consented to perform in Johannesburg, but such is the stigma against performing in South Africa, that stars who are tempted by the kind of money that Southern Suns is ready to pay are relieved that Bophuthatswana is someplace else."

However, Liza skillfully managed to avoid the burgeoning controversy and, as usual, on opening night was showered with applause and accolades.

She and Mark spent Christmas in Gstaad with Roger Moore, Julie Andrews, Richard Burton, and Elizabeth Taylor, before flying to Vienna (where Liza was booked to appear in a New Year's concert) via Paris, where they attended a black-tie dinner hosted by the baron and baroness de Rothschild.

At the end of January, Vincente was fitted with a pacemaker and Liza rushed to his side. He withstood the operation well and on February 19, a retrospective of his films was held at the Palm Springs Desert Museum.

Liza was scheduled to sing at the retrospective and, knowing that this was her father's night, rehearsed for the evening diligently. As always, she checked with Vincente at every stage, eternally eager for his approval. And naturally he unstintingly gave her his praise and his encouragement.

Before dinner in the museum's gallery (which had been decorated in Vincente's honor to resemble Maxim's), Liza performed at the Annenberg Theater for an audience of four hundred and fifty. Among the celebrated group, who'd paid $1,000 a plate, were Kirk Douglas, Frank and Barbara Sinatra, Gregory and Veronique Peck, Lucille Ball, the Louis Jourdans, and Eva Gabor.

Many of them had known Liza since she was born, and they applauded rapturously as she sang "My Heart Belongs to Daddy" to Vincente. They knew that his health was failing and that he might be close to death. And long afterward, some of his closest friends would remember the evening with a mixture of sadness and wonder. Basking in the warmth of his friends' kindness, with his beloved Liza sharing the spotlight with him, the great director was momentarily suffused with happiness and strength. For a miraculous instant, he seemed young again and strong. But the audience instinctively understood that they were witnessing an illusion projected by a master illusionist. And as Vincente sang "Embraceable You" to Liza, they saw his frailty, her devotion to him, and they were moved to tears.

CHAPTER TWENTY-THREE

On March 8, 1983, a second tribute to Vincente was held at the Museum of Modern Art. Although Vincente was in the hospital and couldn't be there, two hundred and fifty guests, including Andy, Bianca, Dolores Gray, and Halston, attended the tribute and the subsequent dinner dance at the Pierre Hotel.

A week later, Liza and Mark were in Dallas, where Liza was appearing at the Majestic Theater. On the night of March 14, they had dinner with Judy Collins at their hotel, The Fairmont. After supper, Liza and Mark went to their room, where she began experiencing abdominal cramps and shortness of breath. Liza's spokesperson, Tony Zoppi, said, "It happened around 1:30 A.M. Gero became alarmed and called the paramedics. They rushed over and gave her oxygen and in a few moments, she was feeling better. But the paramedics suggested that she be checked out at a hospital, and after briefly objecting, Liza agreed. She could have been brought to the hospital by a bellhop, but since the ambulance was available, they decided to take advantage of it. After an hour, she was feeling really quite well. But the doctor insisted that she be admitted for observation. As I understand it, the whole thing was caused by a small piece of steak that would neither go up nor go down."

Another spokesman, Bill Mays, added, "Her doctor said she ate late last night and food lodged in her lower throat. She was having difficulty breathing and was apparently choking on the food." Zoppi's explanation, couched in the language of a circumspect publicist, contained contradictions in that abdominal pain was far more compatible with a possible drug-related anxiety attack than with choking on steak. The Dallas drama was later described in the press as "a brush with death," but whatever the cause, Zoppi later revealed, "She can't relax. She worked with sore throats and high temperatures. She'd do two shows a night and then find some small club and do some more."

In April 1983, journalist Bernard Barry interviewed Liza at Seattle's Paramount Theater. Chain smoking through the interview, Liza spoke in "a girlish machine-gun pace," according to Barry. In an expansive mood, she confided, "I've inherited a lot of that image of being some kind of pitiful, wounded creature. Certain people enjoy thinking of me that way. They prefer me vulnerable: They want me to be like my mother and I'm not like her. I'm really sorry to disappoint them, but that's the truth."

Up till that point, Fred Ebb had always advised her never to sing anything synonymous with Judy, but now he had a sudden change of heart, pointed to Liza's living room display of all her awards—an Oscar, four Tonys, countless others—and said, "It says Liza Minnelli on them, not Judy Garland. You've arrived. Now we can put some of her songs in the show. Maybe it's about time you said thank you."

He prevailed upon her and, for the first time, she sang "The Trolley Song." Although critics remarked on her uncanny resemblance to Judy, their reviews were primarily positive. On April 25, 1983, the *San Francisco Chronicle*'s respected music critic, Joel Selvin, reviewed Liza's show at the Golden Gate Theater. He wrote, "A ghost did hover over her entire show, Saturday, at the Golden Gate. It's in her face. It's in her voice. And when she wiped her sweaty hair back from her brow to sing 'The Trolley Song,' it became an almost palpable presence. But Minnelli long ago transcended the role of mere celebrity progeny and is, indeed, sculpting a legend all her own. Being Judy Garland's daughter is only a facet."

In April, too, Liza paid tribute to Judy offstage and said, "I think about her a dozen times a day. I think about her as a friend. I was lucky in that I was never robbed of love. Mom gave us her strength, her humor and her love."

In May 1983, Liza went to London, where she was booked for a three-week concert run at the Apollo Victoria. This was her first British show in three years and she gave a press conference at the Savoy. Asked about her miscarriages, she said, "I've come to terms with not having children. Sure I have. And I'm not obsessive about having children. And I have him [stroking Mark's arm] to take care of."

In a feature by journalist Andrew Duncan, an unnamed public relations person was cited as saying, "I find the easiest time to be around Liza is twenty-five minutes before she goes onstage. She is clearest during that period. Which means work is the very center of her life."

While Liza was in London, she visited the Institute for the Achievement of Human Potential, since she had always been very involved with the Institute's Wyndmoor branch. Without courting any publicity and keeping her participation secret from the press, Liza, a member of the institute's board, spends time at the institute every year working with brain-damaged children.

In contrast, on June 7, Liza attended the launching of the Halston III collection for J. C. Penney, held at the American Museum of Natural History. Despite her support of his new venture, there was, however, trouble in the formerly idyllic relationship between Liza and Halston.

On June 25, Andy Warhol recorded in his diary that Liza no longer stayed at Montauk, as she and Halston were not on good terms. Warhol's explanation was that Liza hadn't worn a Halston to that year's Academy Awards. Questioning her motives for slighting her valued old friend, Warhol's answer was that the Gero family felt undermined by Halston's control over Liza. And he observed, "I guess Mark knew that Liza was using Halston's to have assignations, too."

Fidelity had never been one of Liza's strong points, and the problems in her marriage had only encouraged her to stray.

In July 1983, the original uncut version of *A Star Is Born* was shown at Carnegie Hall, and the rift between Sid and Liza was healed. Lorna and Liza both hosted the screening; only Joey was unable to attend because he was working for a pharmaceutical company and couldn't get time off.

Lorna was happily married and working, having appeared off-Broadway in *Extremities*. The following year, she gave birth to her first child, Jesse Cole, but she still coveted stardom. Liza shared Lorna's happiness wholeheartedly, but the birth of Jesse also emphasized her own dwindling hopes of having a child herself. And, as a close friend of Liza's and Lorna's observed, "It is a tragic irony that Liza has everything that Lorna has ever wanted—stardom. And that Lorna now has exactly what Liza wants—a happy marriage and a child."

In 1983, columnists reported that Liza was romantically involved with actor Joe Pesci. In November, they were seen having a cozy dinner together at The Manor in West Orange, New Jersey. After dinner, Liza sang with the musicians there for over two hours. The restaurant's part-time pianist was, in actuality, a plastic surgeon named Dr. Hugh Feehan. He played requests for Liza and Joe, but when Hugh asked Liza to sing "You Made Me Love You," she refused, saying, "That's my mother's song."

Though the rumors of their romance persisted into 1991 both Liza and Joe consistently denied them. She remained married to Mark and, in December, the couple celebrated their fourth wedding anniversary by throwing a party at their apartment. Liza, having healed her rift with Halston and returned to the fold, wore one of his more eclectic designs—fashioned out of red chain mail—which fascinated the guests, who included Martha Graham, Deborah Harry, Cornelia Guest, Lucille Ball, Chita Rivera, Cher, Cheryl Tiegs,

Penny Marshall, Al Pacino, Robert De Niro, Bianca Jagger, Charles Aznavour, Steve Rubell, and Kevin Kline.

She was now in rehearsals for *The Rink,* a musical comedy by Terrence McNally with music and lyrics by the ubiquitous Kander and Ebb. The plot of *The Rink* revolves around Angel (Liza), who returns home to a dilapidated roller-skating rink once owned by her family and confronts her mother, Anna (Chita Rivera), about their relationship. Liza's role was far smaller than Chita's but required her to plumb every aspect of a mother and daughter's sometimes painfully recriminatory relationship.

When the show opened at the Martin Beck Theater on February 9, 1984, a few critics complained that the show was more akin to therapy than to entertainment and Liza herself later confessed that *The Rink* had unnerved her totally.

According to Liza, *The Rink* was an excruciating form of self-analysis. She said later, "I went very deep into myself for that character. I've never done that with any other character I've played. I didn't realize how painful it was until it was too late."

Amid the primarily negative reviews of the musical, Edwin Wilson in *The Wall Street Journal* wrote of Liza's performance, "Miss Minnelli comes off the better, because that forlorn mouse face of hers radiates a credible vulnerability and sometimes more pungent and positive feelings."

And Brendan Gill in *The New Yorker* complimented Liza, "I think Miss Minnelli is well worth going to see. I always felt like a happy puppet in her presence, tugged this way and that by her seemingly unself-conscious artistry."

Even Liza's old adversary, John Simon, failed to lace into her with caustic criticism, conceding that "Miss Minnelli can belt out a song in her plangent, vibrato-laden voice, and she does more than justice to the childish eagerness of the adolescent Angel as well as to the sense of rejection of the older one. What she lacks is something beyond the floppy-toy and tearful-clown qualities, beyond the painted smile and the hangdog pathos."

The general critical consensus was that, as a musical, *The*

Rink was a failure. Nevertheless, because of the drawing power of both Liza and Chita, tickets, even at $45 each, continued to sell.

But when the curtain fell and Liza went home, the pressure of *The Rink* took its toll. She and Mark spent most of their time either seething in silence (in what Liza later termed "a real bad period of not listening to each other") or having arguments that escalated into loud battles and intermittent separations.

Writer Paul Steiner says of their marriage, "Mark is quiet and unpretentious. He's very real, earthy and isn't a phony. He told me that he had to chauffeur Liza around. In many ways, he became her gopher and couldn't really do his own thing. He liked to go to his studio downtown and chip away at the stone and didn't want to go to too many events with her. He is a private person, although having her money to use meant a great deal to him."

Both Chita and Liza were nominated for Tonys for their performances in *The Rink*. Chita won, and on June 9, 1984, Liza gave a party at the Gotham Bar and Grill to celebrate her victory. Guests included Francis Ford Coppola, Robert De Niro, Gina Lollobrigida, Robert Culp, Mikhail Baryshnikov, Joe Pesci, and Lorna Luft, and the party went on until seven the next morning. One of the partygoers commented, "You'd have thought Liza was celebrating unless you looked closely at her. Then you could see the look of desperation in her eyes."

Although her part in *The Rink* was far smaller than her tour de force in *The Act,* the nightly repetition of the mother/daughter psychodrama played on her mind and she was racked by insomnia. Tortured by thoughts of the show and by her faltering marriage, she spent nights drinking coffee, watching television till sunrise, and then sleeping the days away.

But sometimes she went out, and on one of those nights, Bob Colacello saw her leaving Elaine's with Michael Jackson. According to him, she looked disoriented and "as her friend Michael Jackson helped her into a limousine—she collapsed with a loud, fake laugh." On other nights, after the show, she was at Elaine's with Sean Penn, at a party with Mickey Rourke, and at another party for Grace Jones, where she was protected from autograph hunters by a Sylvester Stallone lookalike bodyguard.

During *The Rink*, she also spent time with high-powered publicist Barry Landau, who had known Liza since she was fifteen. He had been a brother figure to her and she had encouraged him to go into public relations. After orchestrating the careers of Hollywood and Broadway stars, Barry became so successful that he was appointed National Entertainment Chairman for the 1988 Bush campaign and also worked on the queen of England's sixtieth birthday party.

Landau says, "Liza loves drama, she loves the outrageous, and she is wonderful at turning a negative into a positive. She is also the best friend anyone could ever have. One of her most endearing qualities is that she doesn't have two sets of manners. She has one set. She doesn't talk to the Queen of England one way and to the drummer another.

"When things are good for her, she pulls everyone up with her. If she is invited somewhere, she always wants her friends to go too. She is extremely, extremely supportive. I remember once I told her I couldn't see her because I had an important meeting at Elaine's with a potential new client and wanted to make a big impression on him.

"Liza held up her hand, declaring, 'Don't say another word. I know exactly what to do.' Later that evening, the prospective client and I were sitting down at Elaine's having dinner when Liza suddenly appeared and breathlessly said, 'Barry, darling, I must speak to you right away. I know I'm interrupting, please forgive me, but I must have your advice this minute. I just can't decide this without you.' She went on and on, the client was dazzled and I got the account. That's Liza!"

June 14 was Landau's birthday and Liza suggested taking him out to dinner at Elaine's to celebrate. On the morning of the party, Barry was in a taxi with his friend, Tyrone Power, Jr., and a bus drew up next to them carrying an advertisement for Liza in *The Rink*. Landau recalls, "Out of the blue, Tyrone asked me if I knew Liza and if I could introduce him. So I called Liza and asked her if she would mind my bringing a friend to dinner. She asked his name and I told her, 'Ty Power, Jr.' Liza gasped, 'Momma! Momma! Don't go away!'

"She dropped the phone and, the next thing I knew, was at my door, carrying a box of letters. Then she told me that Tyrone Power, Sr., had been the great love of Judy's life. Liza said that Judy had told her that she had become pregnant by Tyrone Power. At the time that she first discovered she was pregnant, Ty was thousands of miles away fighting the Second World War. Liza said that Judy told her she hadn't wanted Ty to marry her just because she was pregnant. She wanted him to marry her because he loved her for herself and not out of obligation. So she had the baby but then gave it up for adoption without telling him the truth.

"Liza told me that she had been looking for Judy and Ty's child, her sibling, for years, without success. So she was ecstatic to meet Ty, Jr. When they met, they ended up talking for hours, laughing and joking about how much they looked alike. Ty, Jr., played the piano and Liza, Ty, and I sang until dawn. Liza told me she felt really close to Ty—that he was like a long-lost brother."

Ty Power, Jr., says, "I had heard rumors that Judy had a baby by my father, but I never believed it. Liza and I did talk about my father and her mother that night and we got on wonderfully. But it wasn't really because of our parents, but because we just got on. We met a second time at Halston's apartment but apart from that, haven't seen each other for years. And I just don't believe the story about the child."

Watson Webb, a close friend of Tyrone Power, Sr., and Judy's during their relationship, does confirm that Judy was pregnant by Tyrone but says she had an abortion and emphatically denies that she ever gave birth to the child. Given Judy's stardom, status, and visibility at the time of her pregnancy, it seems highly unlikely that she would have been able to carry a child to term without detection. Yet Barry Landau categorically insists that Liza told him that Judy had revealed to her the existence of Tyrone Power's love child and that a second source, one who knew Power extremely well, confirmed to him that Judy definitely gave birth to his child, then gave it up for adoption.

CHAPTER TWENTY-FOUR

Liza and Mark were now separated, with the undercurrents of *The Rink* still preying on her mind. During the first week in July, she missed six performances of the show, sporting a black eye and claiming that she had been involved in a taxi accident. Another friend at the time said that, in reality, Liza had "drug jitters. She was acting paranoid."

Secretly, she consulted two doctors asking them to check whether she was suffering from mononucleosis or hypoglycemia. Both diseases were ruled out and, instead, she was prescribed Valium. Later she defined her mental state as being the outcome of the heightened pressure of her everyday life. "I have to be witty. I have to be glamorous, I have to be bubbly. Well, I tried to be those things for many, many years."

She was close to a breakdown. From her earliest childhood, she had been schooled in keeping up appearances no matter what the reality. During her mother's suicide attempts, she had remained calm and stable. While the public watched aghast as Judy stumbled from marriage to divorce, from drug rehabilitation to alcoholic stupor, Liza remained impassive. She had never betrayed her emotions, had always played the part of Pollyanna, had never revealed her true agony.

She had always hated her appearance—once referring to herself as "Queen of Ugly"—and she had never had any faith in her ability to be normal. Plagued by self-doubt, by insomnia, and forever haunted by her childhood memories that would often surge up and overwhelm her, she had become an escape artist par excellence.

Once it had been Eskimo Bars and dressing up in Vincente Minnelli's resplendent costumes that he had fashioned with love especially for her. As an adult, her chosen escape route was stardom, dancing, singing, sex, drugs, and drinking. She had hoped to find solace in her marriage to Mark. But that, too, had failed—as had her attempts to bear a child. She was racked by nightmares in which her life was reflected back to her, distorted, out of control, and ending in her bone-chilling death. It was inevitable that now, finally, her carefully constructed public persona would crack and the facade, at last, disintegrate.

On July 10, she attended a screening of *The Muppets Take Manhattan*. The next night she gave her performance in *The Rink* as usual. But somewhere in the course of that day, she called Jack Haley, Jr., sobbing and rambling on, culminating in an anguished, "I don't want to end up like Momma."

After the theater, on July 11, Barry Landau, Liza, and one of her friends, Pam Lewis, all went to hear some music at the club S.O.B. Barry remembers, "We went back to the apartment and everyone had a couple of drinks. Then Liza began obsessing about a growth she'd noticed that morning on her neck and insisted on dealing with it immediately. When she telephoned her doctor, Dr. Fishbein, she explained that her mother had had similar growths, and she was fearful of cancer. He said he would see her immediately.

"I took Liza to his office around six in the morning and, after examining her, he told me to take her to Beth Israel Hospital. When we got there, I filled in all the relevant forms for Liza and we couldn't stop laughing when the nurse asked Liza her mother's name. Before the operation, Liza begged me to get her some Chanel No. 5 so she would feel fresh. So I went down to the gift shop. But they didn't have it so I brought up what they did have.

"She was petrified and asked me to be in the operating room with her so I put on a green surgeon's gown. Then the doctor began the operation. But when he injected her with a local anesthetic, Liza suddenly went into shock and started having convulsions.

"I was frightened to death and called her assistant, Ronni Gallion. Ronni called Lorna and the two of them rushed over to the hospital. Around noon, I went home. Then, when Liza recovered, Ronni remembered I'd been involved in booking celebrities to support President Ford's 1976 election campaign and she asked me to call Betty Ford. I placed a call to Mrs. Ford's secretary and said I needed to talk to her about something urgently. Mrs. Ford called me back in ten minutes and I explained to her about Liza. She was very sweet and it was arranged for Liza to be admitted to the center."

On July 12, Liza broke the news to Vincente that she was going to seek treatment. In an interview for *People,* Lee Minnelli remembered, "Liza told her father she had to get help so she can continue living. She said she was trying to put her life back together and this was the only way. We were shocked and surprised by her decision but we were also very impressed by her strength."

Mark went to the airport to see them off as Ronni Gallion, Pam Lewis, Lorna, and a weeping Liza flew to Palm Springs together. And on July 13, the *Daily News* reported that Liza was not going back to *The Rink* (which was slated to run for a few more weeks) because of the removal of a cyst on her neck and that she was canceling her European tour. She was replaced in *The Rink* by Stockard Channing.

Naturally, the press soon discovered the truth, publishing headlines trumpeting, "DESPERATE LIZA BATTLES SAME PROBLEM OF PILLS AND BOOZE THAT KILLED HER MOM JUDY GARLAND" and "LIZA MINNELLI SEEKS TO BREAK A FAMILY LEGACY OF DRUGS AND ALCOHOL ABUSE BY CHECKING INTO A WEST COAST

CLINIC." Eventually Liza's spokesperson, Allen Eichhorn, was compelled to make a statement; he said on Liza's behalf, "I have a problem and I'm going to deal with it." He defined that problem as being induced by alcohol and Valium. Elizabeth Taylor had made admitting Valium addiction fashionable, and Liza followed in her very public footsteps.

She had now committed herself to seven weeks at the Betty Ford Clinic, paying $130 a night for treatment.

Lorna took her to Rancho Mirage, just fifteen miles outside Palm Springs. First, they went to the Eisenhower Hospital, where Liza was scheduled for detoxification. Next she was sent straight to the clinic. Crying and holding on to Lorna all the while, Liza said good-bye to her sister when they arrived at the clinic and walked in alone.

One of the first people who greeted her, an associate at Betty Ford Clinic (who spoke on the condition that her name would not be used), revealed, "I will always remember Liza when she first arrived. She was in a terrible state. She was desperate. Everything and everyone was pulling on her and I will never forget how she said to me, 'I feel like a suitcase that has been left at a railway station.' She is so open and so adorable. She is lovely."

By now the world knew that Liza was at the Betty Ford Clinic and the telegrams began pouring in. Bob Fosse, Sammy Davis, Jr., Chita Rivera, and Dudley Moore were all well wishers. But she was not permitted to receive telephone calls for the first five days of her stay to give her the opportunity of settling in.

A fellow patient said of Liza's first few days at the center that she looked as if she were at death's door, undernourished and physically exhausted from lack of sleep. She appeared frightened, confused, and almost beyond hope or help.

She shared a dormitory with another woman. Their day began with a 6:30 A.M. wake up call, after which Liza made her own bed, went on a brisk walk, and then ate a light breakfast in the communal dining room. The meals at the center were low-fat with an accent on fruit and vegetables.

The clinic's daily routine is based on the theory that drug-dependent people neglect run of the mill chores but that once these are mastered, the patient can begin working on the self. Therefore, most of Liza's day was spent doing chores. Apart from that, she joined in exercise classes, group therapy sessions of ten, and even submitted to the required bedtime of 10:00 P.M. She also diligently kept a diary, according to regulations.

Part of the center's process included asking the patient to write an intensely private letter to the one person who had made the biggest impact on his or her life. According to a close friend of Liza's, "Liza wrote to Judy because she's angry that the public loved her mother so passionately yet didn't care about her father at all."

Liza confessed, "I had one special thing to get rid of. I had to bury my mother. At last. I had never had the time—or taken the time—to mourn her or to really bury her, the sort of burial that doesn't take place in the ground but rather in the spirit."

And she also added, "I was overprotective. I saw myself as my mother's mother. What I didn't know was that I loved her too much."

When she arrived at the center, she had the air of a terrified little girl, galvanized with fear at being alone without her entourage. But she responded quickly to the clinic's routine and rapidly became a popular member of the sixty-strong community. After five days, Liza at last was allowed to make two calls from the pay phone in the dormitory lounge. Her calls were to Lorna and to Mark.

Elizabeth Taylor was the clinic's most famous patient, after admitting herself in order to beat her addiction to painkillers and alcohol. Previously, Liza's relationship with Elizabeth had been superficial, but now, in the heat of her trauma, Liza had turned to her for help and confided the truth. So, on July 18, Elizabeth visited her, congratulating her for following her example and taking the first step toward curing her addictions. She said, "I'm so proud of you now that you've agreed to get help. You should be proud of yourself, and the fact that you've had the courage to face up to your problems.''

Mark had called her repeatedly, but according to Betty Ford insiders, Liza was doing her utmost to avoid his calls. The rupture in their marriage appeared to be irrevocable, and Liza went as far as to summon her attorney to discuss drawing up divorce papers.

According to Tina Nina, "Liza used to say that Mark was protective and fatherly. But Lee told me that Mark took advantage of her. She would say that Liza worked like mad, worked her head off, while Mark would go to Lake Tahoe with his family and spend all his time playing tennis, poker, and gambling. And I heard that he was on drugs, too.''

In a last ditch attempt to rescue the marriage, Mark participated in Family Week at the center and, with Liza, began working on his own addictions. He gave up drinking, explaining, "I can't do what she's trying not to do. And I hope we can start afresh.'' He was not unaware, however, that a new rival for Liza's affections had appeared on the scene.

Gene Simmons, lead singer for the veteran band Kiss, had the reputation among rock insiders of being a sexual athlete. Once linked with Cher, he had now attracted Liza's interest on a personal as well as a professional level. He supported her wholeheartedly, uncompromisingly declaring, "There's nothing that Madonna's got that Liza hasn't.'' He visited her at Betty Ford, their romance intensified, and he also began giving her career advice, which, to this day, Liza still respects and often follows. But despite the attraction of Gene Simmons, when Liza left Betty Ford after seven weeks, it was Mark to whom she went home.

In the months and years that followed she was to talk repeatedly about her time at the center. Always very vocal about how her stay at Betty Ford had changed her life, she made a variety of statements that illustrate the demons with which she was consistently battling.

Liza only once admitted to having done what she referred to as "party drugs," insisting that this was only on the weekends. She claimed that her tolerance had been immense, that she could outdrink, outdance, outexhaust everyone around her and that she had never taken drugs before going on stage. She asserted that her addiction had been a disease, a disease from which her whole family had suffered, alleging that Lorna conquered her chemical dependency when she was only fifteen and that Joey, too, had been a victim of the same dependency. Neither Joey nor Lorna has ever publicly admitted to substance abuse, and Liza's reference is an isolated one. Their reaction to her revelation is not on record.

She thought back through her life and reiterated her tiredness and inability to complete simple tasks like shopping for food. She talked of being so tired and afraid, of her lethargy and her feelings of loneliness and abandonment. She spoke of days when she hid from the world, huddled under the bedcovers, convinced she was suffering from leukemia. And she swore that when she had finally faced up to her drug and alcohol problem, she felt relieved.

In the majority of interviews, she was consistently careful to attribute her addictions to Valium rather than to cocaine. Often specific, she confided that since Judy's funeral, she had taken five milligrams of Valium each day, coupled with a sleeping pill each night. She would take anything, she said, anything and everything that she thought would help her get through the hectic days and the long sleepless nights.

In an in-depth interview with *People* magazine writer Wayne Warga, published on November 26, 1984, she explained that she did drink wine and that she had taken Valium during the day. She confessed, "I'd find myself getting dependent on safe Valium, so I'd switch to Librium. And all the time I was taking the Librium, I'd be telling myself, 'See, Liza, you are not dependent on Valium. You just quit it. You fool yourself for years.' "

Liza denied that she had used cocaine, brushing away the possibility with "I'm too hyper as it is, so who needed help?" Her reason for lying by omission was clear: Unlike Valium, cocaine is illegal.

But Liza's self-censorship was redeemed by her unquestionable sincerity in coming forward and opening her heart so that she could help others who were chemically dependent. In a moving speech made in the London *Daily Mail* she said, "I'd like people to know that you don't have to face this alone—chemical dependency is an accepted disease and you can get help. With counseling, you can still go through withdrawal, but you won't have to go it alone. Dependency captures you in such cunning ways. I was always a nervous child and, when I was prescribed Valium, suddenly my hands stopped shaking and my muscles didn't hurt from dancing and I thought: 'Oh, there's a reason for this drug, it's valid.'

"It's a terrible, terrible thing to go through—the psychological damage, the guilt and the shame. There's a kind of sorrow where you feel you're standing on a corner and the wind is blowing through your stomach. It's that lonely. And you don't know what to do."

Invariably, she traced her Valium addiction back to the day of Judy's funeral, when, she always claimed, a doctor had prescribed it for her. But in a startling departure, she also once revealed that as a child her legs had trembled so badly that a well-meaning doctor had prescribed Valium. The discrepancy in Liza's story reminds one of Judy's tales of life at MGM, some of which were later refuted as being the product of an unbridled imagination owned and exercised by someone set on embellishing her personal mythology.

Liza's Valium use may well have begun when she was a child, or alternatively, on the day of her mother's funeral. But whatever the truth, one fact was indisputable: she was an adult child of an alcoholic, the product of a dysfunctional family who had never known normalcy and whose fate was set in stone long before her birth. And it is to Liza's everlasting credit that, by admitting herself to the Betty Ford Clinic, she began to fight the curse of her inheritance.

CHAPTER TWENTY-FIVE

She was scheduled to appear in August with Charles Aznavour at the International Red Cross Benefit at Monte Carlo, but she canceled the appearance and Charles followed suit. Instead, she checked in at the Palm Aire resort in Pompano Beach, Florida, where Liz Taylor had also gone to lose weight. Now thirty pounds overweight, Liza confided to a fellow Palm Aire dieter, "The only things I do now are smoke and eat. My life has always been in high gear, and I'm finding it difficult to change habits of a lifetime. I need something to do with my hands—so I've been using them to eat.

"I have the help of medication to ease me through withdrawal. Some days I'm very happy and everything seems like it will be all right. Other days, I feel like I'm under a cloud."

She had also joined AA and during the meetings discovered that she possessed a deep desire to turn to a higher power. Her religious education had been sporadic, and she vacillated between following the Episcopalian and the Catholic religions. But now, in November 1984, she began to attend Mass regularly and it was reported that she was granted a private audience with the pope in Rome.

Despite published reports of her renaissance, her redemption from drugs and alcohol, she was beginning to waver, to regress. On February 22, Liza threw a party at Los Angeles's Cafe Mondrian for Michael Feinstein. At the party, she was spied drinking wine and a source saw Elizabeth Taylor take her aside and demand to know the reason why she had stopped going to her AA meetings.

According to the *Boston Herald,* "Liz heard that Minnelli's doctor was worried because Liza hadn't been attending AA meetings as she should have after leaving Betty Ford." Another source alleged that Liza sobbed and said, "I'll do what you want, because I know it's my only chance. I'm determined not to slip back."

But on March 2, 1985, the news was made public that Liza had checked into the Hazelden Clinic in Center City, Minnesota. Her spokesperson Allen Eichhorn tried to defuse any suggestion that she had slipped back into her pre–Betty Ford state.

Whatever the truth, by June, she was fit enough to embark on her six-month, twenty-seven city concert tour, at which ecstatic audiences, thrilled that she was back with them again, rousingly applauded her rebirth and made it clear they were rooting for her.

Back in Manhattan, Michael Jackson was a constant companion, although Studio 54 had closed and she did her best to stay away from the trendier elements of New York's night life. Conscious that her fortieth birthday was looming, she turned her attention to her looks and began using Retin-A on her skin, explaining, "It's wonderful. People keep saying your skin looks so pretty and it helps. And I drink a lot of water. I think the best thing you can do, is stay clean in all senses."

That summer, she talked briefly about her struggles with addiction. Liza acknowledged, "I don't know if I could have made it if I had come back sober and Mark wasn't."

* * *

She had always cared passionately about children and had been deeply moved by author Mary Lou Weisman's book *A Time to Live,* the autobiographical story of her son's tragic fight with muscular dystrophy. When she heard that a movie of the week was being made, she campaigned heavily to play the part of Mary Lou and, to her joy, won it.

She projected heart-rending emotion in the role, drawing from her own tortured pain at her miscarriages. She said of the experience, "It was like having two miscarriages and knowing what it was like to feel the loss." Liza and Mary Lou Weisman spent three weeks together in Montreal during the making of *A Time to Live* and developed a rapport that outlasted the filming. Afterward, in an interview with *TV Guide,* Mary Lou commented, "I think Liza is as tough as nails. She may play roles that are flaky and emotional, but there is a strength somewhere in the center."

A Time to Live aired on October 28, 1985, and Liza's ardently dramatic performance garnered her second Golden Globe Award.

In February 1986, it was rumored that Liza once again had admitted herself to the Betty Ford Clinic. Two sources, including a board member of the clinic, claim that in an attempt to strengthen her resolve and prevent a regression into addiction, she spent another secret stay at the clinic on what is known as "a retread."

In March, she was slated to open at the London Palladium with all its memories. Before she left for London, she talked to award-winning playwright of *Sparky's Last Dance,* and *Daily Mail* writer, Richard Lay. She wore black slacks, a black jersey, a gold chain, and very little makeup and sipped tomato juice. Proudly, she revealed, "I think one of the biggest changes in my life is that I'm not afraid like I used to be. I'm not afraid of anything anymore." She was close to tears, then she added, "I'm not afraid of meeting new people and that free-floating anxiety that I used to always feel is gone, and what a blessing.

"When you are very sick, you lose sight of faith. You lose

sight of all the things you believed in as a child; my faith is back. The fast lane became normal, but things happened so slowly at first and then suddenly you say to yourself, 'How did I get there?' "

As always, insecure and defensive with the press, she insisted that the interview take place in the presence of Eichhorn. Richard remembers, "She came bouncing in, smiling a big nervous smile. But all through the interview she kept looking at the publicist for reassurance.

"She was quite charming, but she was clearly performing for me. The only time I saw her feathers ruffled was when I happened to say, 'I think Pia Zadora is doing very well,' as Pia had just made a couple of records. Liza bristled and flared, 'Well, I don't think she's very good.' I had dared to say that another singer was doing well and for the first time I saw that there was a fiery lady underneath Liza's sweet smile."

In London, as always, Liza stayed at the Savoy. There, now reconciled with Mark, she beamed, "I love him very much. Mark is strong and calm and he's also like a kid." Then, excitedly, she showed a group of reporters her hands, "See, I've been biting my nails for thirty-nine years and it's taken me until now to stop. At last, I've grown up."

She toured Birmingham, Brighton, and Manchester. Her Palladium opening on March 7, 1986, was a Hollywood-style extravaganza with a multitude of press and fans mobbing her before and after the show.

But she managed to momentarily escape from the spotlight and attend a London AA meeting. Afterward, a member who was at the meeting said, "Liza stood up and told everybody about her problems in the past. It helped a lot of people there and gave them a lot of encouragement."

She returned to America and began a triumphant show with Frank Sinatra at the Golden Nugget, Atlantic City, where they appeared together from April 30 to May 4. She was spellbound singing side by side with the legend who had known her from the moment she was born. Singing with Sinatra was tantamount to singing with her mother, and

Liza was exhilarated by the experience every time she sang with him.

Her Sinatra tour de force was topped by the spectacular response of the audience at the Liberty Weekend Celebration in New York Harbor, where she sang "New York, New York" and received a deafening ovation from 50,000 Liza-crazy fans.

It seemed that she had entered a period of unparalleled success, ripe with the potential for happiness. But then, when she went back on tour again, there was a disquieting incident in Indianapolis which may well have seemed to her to be a bad omen. One night, at 1:30 A.M., she was just leaving a party held in an Indianapolis townhouse. The parking garage next to the townhouse was being demolished to make way for a twenty-eight-story office tower, and the night crew was working until the morning. Just minutes after Liza left the party, flying glass from the demolition narrowly missed hitting her. John T. Irish, who hosted the party, said, "We thought the building was falling down. There was flying glass everywhere. Liza had a lucky escape."

Shortly afterward, she received word that Vincente was seriously ill, so she canceled the rest of her Indianapolis performances to be with him. He was eighty-three years old, and in the past few years she had endeavored to spend at least one day a month with him and to telephone him as often as possible. She and her father still took great comfort in each other's company. Their mutual love of films endured and, at one stage, Carl Reiner arrived at Vincente's house to find Liza in floods of tears. When she had regained her composure, she explained that she had been crying because, for the first time in years, she and Vincente had watched *Meet Me in St. Louis*, the film in which he had directed Judy.

He was suffering from a variety of terminal illnesses and exhibiting all the symptoms of Alzheimer's disease. His daughter Tina Nina remembers, "Everybody knew Daddy had Alzheimer's; it was hard for him to talk and he couldn't write. He sometimes said complete sentences, as if he could understand what was going on, but he couldn't really express himself.

"Liza told me about the time she took him to see a show. When they came out, he suddenly stopped, clutched Liza's arm, looked at her and said, 'You know, I live inside myself.' It had a great impact on Liza. He was so bright but suddenly he couldn't talk or write or cope with anything that was going on around him."

Liza spent July 23 and 24 with Vincente at his house, talking about his films and her plans for a baby and asking Vincente's advice on songs and clothes for future concert tours. Then, on July 25, believing that his condition had stabilized, she left for the airport, bound for Nice, where she had a concert date. That night, Lee cooked him his favorite supper of scallops and snow peas and then, after dinner, Vincente died.

When it happened, Liza was still mid-Atlantic, on the plane. Hearing of Vincente's death, a saddened Frank Sinatra, filled with dread that on landing in Nice, Liza might accidentally learn of her father's death from the media, personally contacted her on arrival and broke the news. In a state of shock, Liza flew back to Los Angeles.

Tina Nina heard the news of her father's death from her stepfather. "He called me at midnight," she remembers. "He said he had just heard it on VIP radio and he suggested that I fly to California to the funeral because, he said, 'They are probably not going to tell you.'

"No one called me. When Daddy had been in the hospital earlier in the year, Lee kept telling me everything was all right and that I didn't need to come. But I did. I became very friendly with his nurse, Brenda Moore, and when I arrived for the funeral, she said to me, 'I'm so glad you came. They weren't going to tell you anything until everything was organized.'

"I discovered that Lee and Liza were making plans for the funeral and I wasn't consulted. Then I found a note in Daddy's handwriting making it clear that when he died he didn't want any publicity and also saying something like, 'I ask of my two daughters, Liza and Tina, that when I die I will be cremated and I don't care what is done with the ashes.'

But Liza didn't take any notice and, instead, she and Lee planned a big funeral.

"I talked to Liza about it and reminded her that Daddy hadn't wanted a funeral or any service at all. But she said that Daddy's friends wanted that kind of a funeral and that Lee, too, wanted a big funeral because Daddy had been so important. I got the impression that it was all just part of show business."

Tina Nina's judgment fails to take into account Lee and Liza's burning dedication to preserve Vincente's reputation as a great artist—which they both would continue to pursue with a messianic fervor. To that end, they were naturally determined to give Vincente a glitzy Hollywood funeral befitting what they deemed to be his status in the community.

The invitation-only funeral service was held at the Wee Kirk of the Heather at Forest Lawn Memorial Park. Father George O'Brien of the Church of the Good Shepherd in Beverly Hills conducted the Catholic service. One hundred and twenty-five people mourned Vincente, including some of the biggest names in Hollywood, who had loved and been inspired by him: Bob Hope, Kenny Rogers, Jimmy Stewart, Henry Mancini, and Jack Haley, Jr., Kirk Douglas, and Gregory Peck, who gave the eulogy.

Liza, Mark, Lee, and Tina Nina left the house in a limousine together, but Tina Nina was stunned when the car made a surprise stop. "I was amazed when Michael Jackson stepped into the limousine. Then, all the way to the funeral, he and Liza had a long discussion about their next project, a film they planned to make together. Michael Jackson is a wonderful person but it was very strange to arrive at the church for my father's funeral with him—as if he were a family member, one of the mourners.

"Before we got to the church, Liza whispered to me that the funeral was so incredibly difficult for her to go through now as she was completely clean. Then, when we walked into the church together, she started breaking up and shaking all over. I held her arm tightly and said, 'Everything is OK. Take a deep breath and we'll get through this together.' Then she kind of relaxed."

In his eulogy, Kirk Douglas said, "I loved Vincente, but I found he was a difficult man to know. Enigmatic Vincente with that boyish laugh. He was a man of mystery: the mystery unfolds in his work, and the vivid memories he has given the world for generations to come."

Gregory Peck movingly referred to Liza's performance at the Statue of Liberty Celebration on July 4. "I've been thinking of how much of Vincente there was in Liza's performance, that sensibility that is beyond professionalism—to the point that transcends reality." Of Vincente, he said, "He was a man who literally gave his life to reach for the distant star, to create works that a hundred years later will glow with life and power."

Gigi co-star Eva Gabor, who attended Vincente's funeral, has never forgotten the final moments of a tragic day that was suddenly transformed by a strange and magical second that the great Vincente Minnelli himself might have conceived. "Vincente's favorite color was yellow and so he was dressed in a yellow blazer and buried in an open coffin. All of a sudden, a yellow butterfly flew out of his blazer pocket and flew over the congregation. It was as if it were Vincente's spirit taking flight."

As the mourners filed out of the chapel, the organist played "Embraceable You," the song that only three years ago Vincente Minnelli had sung to the love of his life, his daughter Liza.

After the service, the mourners were ferried in cars to Vincente's hilltop grave. Up till that moment, Liza had displayed perfect control and—as at Judy's funeral—had maintained her composure. But now, as her father's casket was lowered deep into the ground and she threw a flower into the grave, she was overcome with grief and broke down completely at the finality of her loss.

Then the sad procession of mourners retired to Vincente's house on North Crescent Drive, where Liza sublimated her own pain by comforting Lee. Once inside the house, her heart heavy with sadness, Liza performed her duties as a hostess. According to one guest, "She was as gracious as always and made sure everyone was comfortable and at ease. Despite the way she felt, Liza made an effort to talk to all of us and to say a few words to each of us about her father."

Tina Nina, however, was not impressed and later said, "The funeral was arranged like a big event. It was very hard for me, knowing as I did that Daddy didn't want there to be anything public at all. Yet it ended up being like a show business party with personalities and stars and a buffet and drinks at the house afterwards. I felt as if I were at a big cocktail party. But my father was dead and I knew he hadn't wanted this."

She stayed on with Liza at Vincente's house for a few days. She remembers, "Liza and I told each other things we were never able to while Daddy was alive. We told each other how jealous we had been of each other. And Liza confessed to me that she couldn't stand it when Daddy read her my letters."

As fate would have it, when Vincente died, his second wife, Tina Nina's mother, Georgette Magnani Minnelli, was visiting in San Diego, just a few hours away from Los Angeles. As soon as she heard the news of Vincente's death, Georgette flew to Los Angeles to be close to Tina Nina and to give her moral support. She says, "I didn't want anyone to know I was in town. It wasn't my place. I didn't come to Los Angeles for publicity but just to be there for Tina Nina.

"Tina Nina stayed at Vincente's house, I stayed with a friend and Tina Nina and I met for dinners. But after the funeral was over, Tina Nina told Liza that I was in town. She seemed thrilled and said she'd very much love to have a family dinner with Lorna, Jake, Mark, Sid Luft and his wife, Tina Nina, and me.

"We had the dinner at Le Dome but neither Jake nor Mark turned up. I asked Liza where Mark was. After all, her father had just been buried. And she told me that he was at a poker party. During dinner, Liza kept asking me, 'Was I a good girl to you? Was I a good girl?' I said, 'It's a bit late to ask. . . .' She laughed. In life, Liza is the same way as she is in movies. She never stops acting."

* * *

By now Tina Nina had two children whom Liza had never met. Her first child, a boy, was Vincente Minnelli's only grandchild and Tina Nina had named him Vincente. Yet his grandfather only saw him once during a visit to Mexico City and Liza never acknowledged his birth.

"But when my daughter Xeminia was born, I suddenly received a check from Liza. I felt as if a miracle had happened," says Tina Nina. "I wrote and thanked her and said I'd love to keep in touch with her. She answered and gave me her phone number, but then we lost touch with each other again."

Georgette takes up the story. "In those days after Vincente's death, Liza seemed lonely and she said she wanted to meet Tina Nina's children, Vincente's grandchildren. So they flew to Los Angeles. When the children arrived, they had ice cream and spent about a half hour at the Beverly Hills Hotel where Liza was staying.

"The children admired Mark's tennis shoes and asked where he had bought them. Liza said, 'Give them $30 each, so they can buy the tennis shoes.' Then she left and they didn't see her again. A few days later, Tina Nina and the children flew back to Mexico City."

Liza had tried to play the loving aunt to the best of her ability but the moment had passed and her attempt had ended in dismal failure. From the first, Liza's intentions had been good, but they had been negated by her own inability to concentrate, to focus on a situation with undivided attention, and to be consistent. Instead of gaining a devoted family, she left Tina Nina and her children feeling rather like disgruntled fans who had been momentarily seduced and then summarily discarded.

CHAPTER TWENTY-SIX

L iza was devastated by Vincente's death, but instead of turning to drugs and alcohol for comfort, she submerged her grief in food. As Tina Nina had noticed, at the funeral she was already overweight. But her friends were relieved that she didn't crack up entirely and sabotage herself.

They rallied round to help and, at the end of August, she took refuge in Monte Carlo, where she stayed as houseguest of lyricist Leslie Bricusse, who wrote *Stop the World, I Want to Get Off*.

On September 22, 1986, she held a memorial to Vincente at the Museum of Modern Art. A hundred guests attended the tribute, including Liza's old love, Scorsese, who co-organized the event with Stephen Harvey, a curator at the Museum of Modern Art Department of Film. Liza spoke last. "Whenever I see a film of my father's, I can't help poking the person I'm sitting next to and saying, 'Hey, my father thought of that.' " Tina Nina was not present at the tribute, nor had she been invited.

By November, Liza was turning her attention to Mark once more and, on November 11, threw a party for him at her apartment to publicize his painting. The usual crowd was on hand: Andy Warhol, Halston, Steve Rubell, and Bianca Jagger. Afterward, an unimpressed Andy compared Mark's paintings to Liza's life, remarking on the titles of the pictures—one of which was named "Death of a Baby."

She was more interested in Mark, in making her marriage work, than in drugs or high society. At a subsequent party in December (yet again attended by Andy, Halston, Bianca, and Steve), she made it clear that drugs no longer featured in her life and, at the stroke of midnight, asked everyone to leave as she was due to fly to Rome the next morning.

She was scheduled to work with Burt Reynolds again, on a film called *Rent a Cop,* in which she was cast as a hooker. This was her first feature film in six years (the last was *Arthur*), and she joked that the only reason she had accepted the part was "Burt's an old friend and he called and said, 'I'm doing this film in Italy, come, let's go.'"

But a shadow fell over the proceedings when, soon after shooting began, she received the news that Tina Nina was contesting her father's will, claiming that Liza had exercised undue influence over Vincente and that he had not been of sound mind when the last will was drawn up.

Tina Nina had been left a cash payment of $5,000 in the will, which Vincente had referred to as "In recognition of the fact that she is financially well taken care of." Vincente, however, had been mistaken. Although Tina Nina's aunt, Christiane, was married to a wealthy Mexican businessman and her mother to a leading publisher, Tina Nina herself, now divorced, was extremely short of money and struggling to support herself and her two children.

Under the terms of the will, Vincente's house was left to Liza, on the condition that she allow Lee to live in it for as long as she wished. The house was a two-story Regency mansion with three bedrooms, a drawing room, a dining room, and a very large garden big enough to build another house on. According to Georgette Magnani Minnelli, at the time of Vincente's death, the property was independently valued at around $3 million.

His cash flow had been minimal and in the last years of his life Liza had supported the household, made mortgage payments, bought furniture, and covered Lee and Vincente's travel expenses.

On the surface, it seemed incontrovertible that Liza had every right to inherit the house. But Tina Nina believed she, too, had a valid claim. The battle over the will between her and Liza began after Liza informed her that she was going to be appointed executor of Vincente's will. Outraged, the usually timid Tina Nina summoned up every iota of courage she could muster and refused to sign the papers appointing Liza executor.

She says, "Liza told me, 'Don't worry about a thing. I will look after you.' But I didn't believe her and I decided to fight the will. Liza's attorney had drawn up Daddy's will but Daddy hadn't signed it. He was unable to write and Lee had been signing all letters for him.

"Daddy couldn't write anymore and even on the phone, he would black out and forget who he was talking to. Lee always picked up the phone and spoke for him and answered all his letters for him. She was always there, translating for Daddy. Daddy and I could have communicated with our eyes, or through touch, or through a few words, but Lee never gave us the chance.

"I don't know how Liza felt about Lee, but I do know that she had arranged for her to sign a pre-nuptial agreement so she couldn't get the house. She didn't want someone else taking over the last thing my father had left, which was the house. He no longer had his MGM pension (which my mother had arranged for him) because he had signed it away and taken the proceeds in cash.

"I didn't question the will for the money, I questioned it because I wanted to do what Daddy wanted. And he always wanted Liza and me to share the house. Many times, my father told me, 'I want you to know that in my will, the house will be half for you and half for Liza.' Daddy wouldn't have just told me this, he said it for a reason, and he said it many times. He knew I was in financial need and that Liza didn't need money and that my children were his only grandchildren."

Her mother, Georgette, still wonders, "Why didn't Liza take half the house? She could have had the house valued and given Tina Nina half. Then she could have had a good conscience. She could have given Tina Nina what her father wanted for his grandchildren."

Although her suit was filed on the premise that Liza had exercised undue influence over Vincente, in reality Tina Nina blames both Lee and Mark for the inequities in his will. During the last three years of Vincente's life, he was cared for by the nurse with whom Tina Nina became extremely friendly and who gave her information relating to her case against Liza.

Tina Nina says, "Normally, Liza would spend less time with Daddy when Mark was with her. The nurse told me that Mark and Liza would sometimes go and see my father in the hospital but that neither of them were well. The nurse saw Liza get very sick, sometimes because of her drug problem.

"I think Mark wanted the house. As soon as Daddy had died, Liza told me, 'Mark loves Daddy's Cadillac and he is going to fix it so he can drive it. And he is going to clean out Daddy's studio so he can sculpt there.'

"My father was a painter and painted beautiful paintings—works of art. He painted in that studio and I couldn't stand the idea of Mark working there as well. Except that I couldn't imagine him doing anything except playing tennis or poker. Liza was so under Mark's influence and, I think, trusted him far too much.

"After I sued Liza, I heard from mutual friends that she was very worried. She felt guilty and called friends asking if she had been wrong, if she had done the right thing.

"Finally, we made an out of court settlement whereby my children were beneficiaries. It was nothing like I would have originally received. But I never blamed Liza because she was influenced by other people.

"There was always a power struggle between us. Liza

was always jealous of me because all her life she has wanted to be Vincente Minnelli's only daughter.''

In Rome, Liza continued filming *Rent a Cop* in subzero temperatures, doing her best to ward off flu by taking vitamin C tablets. She stayed at the Hassler, stuck religiously to Coca-Cola and cappuccino and her traveling companions, a teddy bear, a stuffed beagle, a stuffed seal, and a stuffed hound dog. As always, she and Burt Reynolds got on wonderfully. During *Lucky Lady,* he had treated her as a little sister and, once the film was released, fiercely defended her from critics and staunchly maintained, *"Lucky Lady* could have been a classic and meant another Oscar for Liza.'' But despite Burt's support and friendship, she had misgivings that *Rent a Cop,* too, would prove to be a disaster.

When she returned to Hollywood (via Paris, where she attended a special performance of *Cabaret*) on February 22, David Janssen's widow, Dani, threw a party in her honor. Liza was welcomed home by Sean Connery, Jack Nicholson, Swifty Lazar, and Lorna, who had just completed an engagement at the Hollywood Roosevelt Hotel.

She was constantly in the spotlight for the next month. On March 1, she appeared at a benefit for the Institute of Human Potential, didn't take a fee, sent the institute an additional $10,000, and picked up all production costs, estimated as running as high as $35,000. On March 18, Channel 13 broadcast a televised tribute to Vincente called *Minnelli on Minnelli,* produced by Jack Haley, Jr., with Liza introducing the program. And on March 25, *An Evening with Rodgers & Hart* was televised. The show had been recorded at the White House with Liza singing ballads with Vic Damone and Nancy Reagan.

In April 1987, Liza became the youngest recipient ever to receive the Friars Club Life Achievement Award and performed at the ceremony held at the West Coast Friars Club. The club's male-only members adored her and—after the April 21 Supreme Court decision that women should be allowed into the club—decided that Liza should become the first official lady Friar. So, on June 6, 1988, Liza was inducted—after a vote by seventeen male comics paying tribute to her popularity in the industry.

On May 28, 1987, she opened a three-week engagement at Carnegie Hall. The audience that night shone with celebrities all representing aspects of Liza's past and present, including Peter Allen, Lorna Luft, Lee Minnelli, Halston, Alan Pakula, Bob Fosse, Baryshnikov, Fred Ebb, John Kander, Mark Gero, Albert Finney, Carly Simon, Francesco Scavullo, Mia Farrow, Diane Sawyer, Candice Bergen, William Hurt, Dolly Parton, Calvin Klein, Steve Rubell, Cornelia Guest, and Anthony Quinn.

All the usual elements of a Liza Minnelli smash success were in place: Halston's costumes, Kander and Ebb's songs, and euphoric reviews by Liz Smith, who raved, "The super comeback of a girl who never really went away but who has had enough ups and downs to keep us fascinated for years. On stage came the same youthful looking gaminlike, innocent, wide-eyed Liza we have always known and loved."

And, of course, Clive Barnes, forever enthralled by Liza, waxed lyrical, describing the show in glowing terms: "Liza Minnelli at 41, is A number 1, cream of the crop, king of the hill, top of the heap. She comes on in a shiny, spangly Halston miniskirt, her hair all moussed up, in her customary pixie bouffant. She looks gorgeous, almost edible. Her eyes are black brilliance studded in a guileless doll's face of heartbreaking innocence, a vulnerability stretched by the scarlet gash of her mouth.

"Her beauty is as much of a child as a woman—it depends in part on character, on shifting expressions of trust, love, friendship and simple openness. It is a face you'd give your last penny to. It's a face where all the smiles have a subtext of tears, and all the tears are washed away on a rainbow. The very real gaiety has a very real undertow of sadness. The face is a map of contradictions. Liza wears her vulnerability on her sleeves."

The entire audience rallied to her, dispatching floral tributes to her dressing room, smiling compassionately as they read and reread the program entry that Liza herself had written, "I don't drink anymore," and applauding uproariously when they heard her sing, "When I go, I'm NOT going like Elsie"—the "Cabaret" lyrics she had rewritten to reflect the changes in her own life as well as her burning determination to sustain them.

Liza's 1987 Carnegie Hall season was the longest continuous engagement by a solo performer and broke all records in Carnegie Hall's ninety-six-year history. Afterward, Peter Allen observed, "She didn't really know how good she was until tonight."

After Carnegie Hall, her triumphal procession moved to Atlantic City en route to her national tour, which began on August 9 in Saratoga Springs. Everywhere, fans flocked to her show, applauding her more passionately than ever, their applause resounding with an admiration of Liza the performer and Liza the human being who had survived.

In September, *Liza at Carnegie Hall,* her first solo album in eight years, was released. Although her film career was in abeyance, her singing career was more successful than ever, and Jack Haley, Jr., commented, "I've known her since she was fourteen years old and I've never seen her more happy, or with a greater vision of where her career is going and what she is going to do with it. Liza's gift is her resilience, her knowledge, her experience. And that, whatever she says, comes from her mother."

On November 14, she flew into London for yet another series of concert appearances, this time at the Royal Albert Hall. Looking slim and sexy, dressed in a clinging miniskirt, a leopard skin jacket, black lacy gloves, black stockings, and high heels, Liza seemed rejuvenated to onlookers.

And while the ever-vigilant British press remained on the lookout for evidence that she had strayed from sobriety, her trumpet player at the Albert Hall, Dave Stahl, attested, "She may smoke too much for her own good but that's her business. I've never seen her touch a drop of drink, and I've been with her for one and a half years."

The success of her London performance was followed by a less than pleasant incident: the last-minute cancellation on December 4 of *Frank and Liza in Concert—The Night of*

Nights, just ten minutes before curtain time. Twenty thousand fans at the Brendan Byrne Arena in New Jersey were compelled to go home disappointed after it was announced that the sheet music had not arrived. There had long been rumors of Sinatra's memory lapses, and although Liza was willing to perform without the sheet music, Frank refused.

On January 1, 1988, *Rent a Cop* opened to negative reviews. In defense, Liza sadly said, "I wish we had been directed in that movie. I really depend on directors (being a director's daughter)." She and Burt had worked well together, but no matter how harmonious their relationship, Liza knew that they both needed a degree of guidance from their director.

Liza watchers held their collective breath, wondering whether yet another cinematic failure would precipitate a return to addiction. But Liza struggled gamely on and in March was even spied drinking nonalcoholic Moussy beer at Zanzibar in New York.

On March 15, she celebrated her birthday three days late at Columbus Restaurant, along with Sean Penn, Madonna, Cyndi Lauper, Joan Jett, Al Pacino, Drew Barrymore, Billy Joel, Christie Brinkley, and Melanie Griffith.

On May 31, in her first television drama since her Golden Globe Award–winning performance in *A Time to Live,* she appeared on the ABC Network in a series of three plays entitled *Sam Found Out: A Triple Play.*

The three plays, constructed around the line "Sam found out," were written by the team of Wendy Wasserstein and Terrence McNally, by Lanford Wilson, and, the last, a musical play, by Kander and Ebb. Liza garnered positive reviews; John J. O'Connor in the *New York Times* affirmed, "Liza Minnelli shows the kind of spunk that her fans, this one included, find disarming." Kay Gardella praised, "Minnelli, who has proven over and over again that she can handle heavy drama, light comedy and musicals as well, covers all bases here. Liza is absolutely first rate."

In a departure, in 1988 she made a commercial and also

took part in an advertising campaign. Until then she had only appeared in one of the "I Love New York" commercials, a series promoting New York, made with the no fee participation of celebrities. And when she took part in the print campaign, posing for photographer Richard Avedon for Revlon's Most Unforgettable Women, she donated her $50,000 fee to AIDS research.

That same year she was hired to sing a Kander and Ebb composition, "City Lights," in a television advertisement for Estée Lauder's new fragrance for men, Metropolis. Alvin Chereskin, the vice chairman of the advertising agency who had selected Liza, commented, "We thought Liza epitomized the big city singer. Like Edith Piaf represented Paris, we thought Liza was New York."

For once, Halston was not available to design her clothes for the commercial so Bob Mackie was asked to create her wardrobe instead. The clothes were flown in from California, but when Liza saw them, she was filled with consternation. Normally, she required Halston to incorporate big pockets in all the clothes he designed for her because she wanted the option of hiding her often nervously fluttering hands in them during a performance. To her relief, the situation was remedied at the eleventh hour, when Mackie arranged to have pockets flown in from California by Federal Express and sewn onto Liza's clothes.

Liza was reportedly paid a million dollars for the Metropolis promotion. The fee called for her to make personal appearances at department stores, and in June 1988, she took part in an hour-long promotion for Metropolis at Robinson's Department Store in Beverly Hills.

Dressed entirely in Chanel—a pink Chanel suit, Chanel flowers, Chanel chains, and a Chanel bag—Liza signed 8 by 10 glossies for eager fans. During that promotion, an adoring fan approached her and gushed, "You are just as good as your mother." Liza gulped momentarily, then thanked her graciously.

Arthur II opened in the summer of 1988 and although critics judged the sequel inferior to the original, Liza's performance and appearance were definitely superior. Although the first film had been made seven years earlier, she had then been in the throes of her addictions and now, in *Arthur II,* she looked younger, vibrant, and radiantly healthy.

She was happy working with Dudley Moore again and Dudley, a good friend, said of her, "Liza is very alive, very agreeable and very funny. And she understands these days what is important in life." During filming, he and Liza and Mark socialized a great deal and later dined together at off-beat restaurants in Little Italy, where both he and Liza, oblivious of the risk of putting on weight, could gorge themselves on vast servings of pasta smothered in rich cream sauces.

Although *Arthur II* was a comedy, the plot had painful significance for Liza. She had never dreamed that she would make a comedy about the two greatest traumas life had dealt her, infertility and alcoholism, but, in a way, *Arthur II* was somewhat of a catharsis for her.

The film begins after millionaire Arthur Bach and Linda Marolla (played by Liza) are married and living happily together. Then the millionaire father of Arthur's jilted fiancée fabricates a revenge whereby Arthur loses all his money. Arthur turns to alcohol and rapidly goes to seed. Linda discovers she is infertile and finally, when Arthur regains his fortune, the couple adopt a child.

The script called for Liza to say the poignant words, "It seems like without a baby, something really wonderful is being wasted." But no matter how searingly sad her emotions, she did not allow them to overwhelm her and didn't ham or overplay the scene. One can only wonder at Liza's secret anguish as she played scene after scene in which she decorated the nursery, bought toys, held a newborn baby in her arms, and smiled with a joy that, in real life, she will never know.

CHAPTER TWENTY-SEVEN

When *Arthur* was released in 1981, Liza had done very little publicity, it was whispered, partly because she was so wasted by drugs and alcohol. And it is a testament to her recovery to contrast the hectic schedule she willingly undertook in order to publicize *Arthur II*, starting in Nice, then flying to New York, from there to Los Angeles, then to Honolulu, and, after just one night, back to Los Angeles.

Then in September, she was slated to tour eleven cities with Frank Sinatra and Sammy Davis, Jr., in what came to be known as the Rat Pack Tour. For Liza, the experience was unique. As she enthused, "I mean can you imagine standing up there with two people you grew up with, your Uncle Frank and your Uncle Sammy, and suddenly you're sharing the bill with them!"

Sammy had always been as much of a father figure to her as Frank, calling Liza "Stuff," because, as he sentimentally put it, "She is the best stuff in the world, her stuff is really together." Of Frank, she said wryly, "He will always think of me as a kid." Yet it could not have escaped her that both her father figures were fading into the twilight of old age, as Sammy battled cancer and Frank all manner of ailments.

She was also worried about Halston. He had lost a great deal of weight but when she asked him about it, he refused to comment. Knowing his life-style and predilections, AIDS was a marked possibility, but Halston never betrayed his own fears or his illness to her.

Up till now, her albums had either been sound tracks of her films or recordings of her live performances. She turned to Billy Joel, Cyndi Lauper, and Michael Jackson for advice, quizzing them on how she could improve her chances of a hit record. But it was Gene Simmons, who was now managing the recording side of her career, who came up with what he believed to be an ideal formula. He proposed that she take a different direction and arranged a meeting with CBS records chief Walter Yetnikoff, who then initiated a collaboration between Liza and the innovative British group the Pet Shop Boys.

In April, while Liza was appearing at the Royal Albert Hall with the Rat Pack Tour, she took a break and cut a record, a dance version of Stephen Sondheim's "Losing My Mind," with the Pet Shop Boys. When she walked into the studio to start recording with the Boys (Neil Tennant, Chris Lowe, and Julian Mendelsohn) her first question was a bewildered "Why aren't the musicians here? When are they arriving?"

"Are you crazy?" countered an amused Neil. "There are no musicians. It's all done with machines, darling."

Chris and Neil, who were producing the record as well, felt honored to be working with Liza but still didn't hesitate to give her direction. Liza marveled at Neil's advice, "Sing like you're putting on a pair of silk stockings." Gently, he also asked her, "Why are you singing 'L-u-u-r-r-ve?' " counseling, "Sing it naturally like Charles Aznavour." His advice paid dividends and when "Love Pains" (the B side of "Losing My Mind") was released it became Liza's first hit record ever, climbing to number eleven on the *Billboard* dance singles chart.

Liza was understandably thrilled, but it soon transpired that she was also completely ill-equipped for pop stardom. When she appeared on the British television show "Top of the Pops" for a live performance, an amused Neil Tennant chided, "Don't smile. This is rock and roll!"

Liza and the Boys also cut an album, *Results,* which included "Losing My Mind" and "Love Pains" as well as new songs she and the Boys co-wrote. The album was not a hit. Nevertheless, the Boys were so enamored of Liza that they postponed their summer holidays in order to squire her to London hot spots like the bizarre club Heaven, to an Acid House rave, and to the film *Batman.* At the time, Neil Tennant said, "Liza is fabulous," then added cryptically, "but the thing about Liza is that she is fabulous all the time."

She reveled in her friendship with them and, also in the summer of 1989, traveled to Hollywood to make a video of "Losing My Mind." The video proved to be a relative failure, confirming Liza's secret fear that she was forever destined to sing songs that had been written before she was born.

Her fans seemed to prefer her in the role of crown princess, Hollywood's baby, petted and adored by tinsel town's aristocracy. Her participation in the Rat Pack Tour was a great success. Offstage, however, she encountered a series of problems. When the tour reached Finland during the first week of April 1989, an ear infection compelled Liza to cancel her Helsinki appearance. Once she had recovered, she encountered yet another obstacle.

At the time, she was traveling with her beloved dog, a pampered two-year-old Scottish cairn terrier named Lilly. In May, she checked into a five-star Stockholm hotel with Lilly by her side. Lilly was the quintessential pampered pet and by taking her into the country, Liza had blithely defied Sweden's stringent quarantine laws. Consequently, Lilly was put under house arrest. As Swedish customs inspector Stig Thelberg sternly pointed out, "Dog smuggling is a serious offense." In a comical series of events, customs agents took up guard posts at Liza's hotel to ensure that the little terrier didn't abscond. Liza retaliated by threatening to cancel her tour if the Swedish authorities deported Lilly as decreed.

After negotiations, Liza agreed to appear in the show with Frank and Sammy on condition that the authorities allow Lilly to stay in Stockholm overnight. Throughout the entire contretemps, Liza denied having smuggled Lilly into the country. In true Hollywood star fashion, she chartered a $50,000 jet to transport Lilly (escorted by Liza's bodyguard, Simon Scudera) to Paris. There, Liza's friend, Parisian socialite Pierre Billon, met Lilly and her bodyguard and boarded them in a luxury suite at the Meridien Hotel. The dog then spent a week being wined and dined by Scudera and Billon, who took her all over Paris, ordering gourmet rabbit stew for her edification, while a heartsick Liza phoned twice a day to check with Scudera on how Lilly was surviving the wrenchingly tragic separation.

Her life seemed to revolve round singing, Lilly, and all her friends, whom she needed desperately, now more than ever. She was lonely again; her failure to conceive a child had left a deep and painful void in her life. Her abiding desire for motherhood was further reinforced by Lorna's two children, Jesse and Vanessa. She lavished all her love on her nephew and niece and spoiled them outrageously. Yet no matter how much she loved Lorna's children they could never fulfill her yearning to bear her own.

She believed that a child wouldn't merely bring her fulfillment but would also cement her marriage to Mark. The marriage had simmered through the years, constantly in danger of self-destructing, and she was convinced that a child would ensure the marriage's survival. But now, after two confirmed miscarriages (and a possible third claimed by a source), Liza was distraught. Mark also professed to want a child, but only if it was biologically his. According to friends of the couple, although Liza was eager to adopt a child, he categorically refused to consider adoption as a viable alternative.

Driven by a sense of hopelessness, the previous year (on

March 25, 1988), she had checked into the Omega Institute of Health in Louisiana, a clinic specializing in reversing infertility. There, she had submitted to a barrage of tests and procedures, then waited. She felt adrift and helpless and said, "Inside every woman there is a little girl. I suppose I'm still very much the little girl I was at the age of ten, when I used to find all the answers to my questions in a song or a poem."

In 1990 she was forty-four and was increasingly conscious of her own mortality. She had lost her father and now, it seemed, was on the verge of losing her father figure as well. She was deeply saddened to learn that Sammy Davis was suffering from terminal cancer and did all she could for him, faxing him daily letters and poems of comfort.

Her world seemed to diminish month by month. On March 26, 1990, Halston died of AIDS in San Francisco. Conscious of Halston's promiscuity and acutely aware of the ravages of the AIDS epidemic, she had worried ceaselessly about his health. But, right until his death, he persisted in denying to her that he was ill. The news of his passing came as a terrible shock to her and she felt bereft of love and comfort.

On March 31, she attended Halston's San Francisco funeral. Then, just a few days later she entertained at a Police Athletic Benefit in New York, where she choked back tears when she was told by a group of police officers that Halston had saved the lives of many cops because his design for their jackets made it easier for them to carry their weapons.

Liza continued to mourn his death and to miss him bitterly. On June 6, she paid for Halston's memorial service, which was held at Alice Tully Hall at Lincoln Center in New York. That night, film clips and photos dating back to his long ago childhood in the Midwest were shown of Halston. Katherine Graham, Isaac Mizrahi, Marisa Berenson, Martha Graham, and Elsa Peretti witnessed Liza's moving eulogy to Halston. Photographer Roxanne Lowitt, who was also there, says, "I remember that her dedication to Halston was one of the most beautiful I've ever heard. She was a very loyal friend to him and when nearly everyone else abandoned Halston, Liza never did."

Her grief at Halston's death never subsided and, a year after the funeral, the mention of his name still made her cry.

She had lost her brother figure and, not long afterward, her father figure, Sammy Davis, Jr., as well. She was so desolate when he died on May 16, 1990, that during the first week in June, grief-stricken and unable to work, she canceled several appearances at the Sands in Atlantic City.

That same month, on Father's Day, she participated (in front of an audience of six hundred) in the opening of an eight-week retrospective, *Directed by Vincente Minnelli,* held at the Los Angeles County Museum of Art.

A stellar audience, including Bob Hope and Gregory Peck, dined in the museum courtyard, eating a gourmet meal ending with intricate individual desserts formed in the shape of chocolate grand pianos. Then guests viewed the newly restored print of *Meet Me in St. Louis,* after which Liza (accompanied by pianist Michael Feinstein) gave a spectacular forty-five minute performance. Toward the end of the performance, she touched the audience's hearts immeasurably by looking up into the sky and wishing Vincente a happy Father's Day.

Her frenetic pace continued all through 1990. She headlined at the Riviera in Las Vegas and, on a rare occasion, Mark accompanied her. She reserved a ringside table for him but, according to a source, was deeply upset when he didn't stay for the whole show and instead spent the evening playing poker. She had failed to conceive, and he hated traveling with her and was tired of his role as "Mr. Liza Minnelli." He also complained vociferously of her temperament. It was clear to Liza's intimates that after eleven years, the death knell for their marriage had at long last sounded.

There was a bitter irony in the fact that the final break occurred long after the days in which they had both battled their addictions together. But it may well be that it had been their addictions and their resultant fight to overcome them that had bonded them. Now the bond was broken and, according to friends of the couple, Mark's self-effacing facade had cracked fatally, and he had become highly critical of Liza, of her career strategy, of her clothes, and of her show business friends. In search of his own social life among the art crowd, Mark had too often left Liza alone and so had inflicted on her the deepest wound of all, and, for her, the most unbearable—that of loneliness.

In November 1990, Mark moved out of their apartment and into his Greenwich Village studio. On December 5, they made an attempt at keeping up appearances by going to a Whitney Museum opening. But they were unable to sustain the illusion and, on December 12, when Liza went to the New Jersey party following *The Frank Sinatra Birthday Concert,* Mark did not accompany her.

She was tired of having to explain his absences to friends, of listening to his criticisms, of traveling alone and being alone. During the Sinatra party, she broke down and confided to trusted columnist Liz Smith that she and Mark were separating.

Always generous, Liza did her utmost to exonerate Mark of any blame, perkily explaining that Mark, as a real man, had found it difficult to be married to a famous woman who wielded power. Claiming that she didn't want Mark to sacrifice anything for her, she conceded that, for any woman in her position, the price of fame and fortune inevitably seemed to be a happy marriage.

CHAPTER
TWENTY-EIGHT

She continued to find a great deal of comfort in Lorna's children, Jesse and Vanessa, once confiding to friends, "I am working for my nephew and niece." She spoiled them both extravagantly and seven-year-old Jesse adored her. And as for Vanessa, Lorna's new baby, it seemed, even to her mother, that she was Liza all over again. She looked like Liza, sounded like Liza, and acted like Liza, and Lorna herself admitted that Vanessa truly was another Liza Minnelli.

In divorcing Mark, Liza knew she would be alone in the world. It had been Mark's family and the promise of normalcy that had captivated her in the first place and now she knew she would no longer be a part of his family. Instead, she turned to a substitute family, spending New Year's Eve in France with Charles Aznavour, his wife, and his three children. Asked whether his wife was ever jealous of Liza, Charles defensively retorted, "Liza is like a big sister bubbling over with the joy of life. We all adore her."

In January 1991, Liza and Mark were still living apart and, in March, she filed for divorce. In the meantime, she distracted herself by rehearsing for her Radio City debut and spending time with female friends including top model Naomi Campbell, with whom she went one night to Edelweiss, an avant-garde drag club on Manhattan's 29th Street.

The previous year she had formed a close friendship with another, even more unconventional woman, country and western singer k.d. lang, whose self-confessed lesbianism, coupled with her masculine aura, once prompted Madonna to rave, "I met her and I thought, 'Oh my God, she's the female version of Sean. I could fall in love with her.' "

In August of 1990, when they were still together, Mark and Liza had gone to see k.d. open at New York's Beacon Theater and, after the show at the first night party at Cavaliere, k.d. and Liza talked animatedly together for most of the evening.

In a conversation with Liza, printed in *Interview* magazine, k.d. lang said of their friendship, "I think one of the great things about our relationship is that there is similarity between us almost because of our differences. You're experienced in the business, and I am just sort of just starting and we both feed off each other's excitement and knowledge, you know? Rebels. Well, I'd say there's a little bit of that in both of us."

Liza elaborated, "Our friendship is so funny. We talk on the phone from all over the world and see each other maybe twice a year! But oh my God, it's important."

A few days before she was due to open at Radio City, Liza took the unprecedented step of granting an interview to the controversial gay and lesbian news magazine *Outweek* for a cover story that appeared on May 15, 1991. Before submitting to questions by writer Matthew Davis, Liza stipulated that she would not talk about any inflammatory issues such as the practice of "outing" (publicizing the hitherto hidden homosexuality of public figures), which had been pioneered by the magazine.

In advance, she also adamantly refused to discuss any of the gay men in her life. Nor would she answer questions about Judy. Instead, Liza adroitly used the interview to promote *Stepping Out* (her Radio City show) and glibly defined what "stepping out" meant to her, explaining, "Sometimes 'stepping out' means risking being happy. A lot of people are scared of that, but it's wonderful when you do it.

"It means taking chances, doing something you've never done before, just trying something. Or something you always wanted to do and just didn't have the time, or you didn't have the nerve, or you didn't have the guts, or you didn't have the confidence."

The closest interviewer Davis (a committed Minnelli fan) came to asking Liza to discuss alternative sexuality was when he questioned her about a Charles Aznavour song about a female impersonator that she was planning to sing at Radio City.

Liza, first asserting that loneliness wasn't the sole prerogative of any one type of person, went on to say, "Everybody's afraid of abandonment or feeling different. And I think everybody at one point in their lives has felt ostracized and separate through whatever circumstance anybody's been through. Whether it's because you were born to movie stars or if it's because you're born gay—you can feel separate."

Gabriel Rotello, then editor in chief of the now-defunct *Outweek,* was dissatisfied with the interview, as were many on his staff. "We felt that Liza was less than forthcoming in her answers about gay and lesbian issues. I don't remember the exact questions that were posed to her but one centered around rumors that her mother had had a lesbian affair.

"Madonna's interview with *The Advocate* was all about gay issues. Liza is even more an icon in the gay community than Madonna, but she didn't want to talk about any of those things. All she wanted to talk about was her new show and her new act.

"Matthew, the writer who interviewed Liza, is a total Liza Minnelli fan. He worships her. That was one of the problems. We didn't think he was pushy enough, so we then called her publicist, and asked to do the interview again. Liza's publicist told us, 'Submit your questions in writing and I'll give you answers.'

"So, we submitted them and essentially we didn't get answers, only more evasions like, 'Oh, I don't talk about this, I don't talk about personal issues, I never talk about my mother, etc.' "

"We sort of expected that the whole reason she agreed to the interview was because she had something important to say to the gay/lesbian community. Our readers were angry that we printed an article where we essentially allowed somebody to 'get away with' the very kind of evasions which we are so critical of people getting away with."

She opened in *Stepping Out* at Radio City in a show that was the most ambitious and innovative she had ever attempted in her entire career. Act I featured Liza in Concert and Act II, Liza and Friends, a group of women dancers aged sixteen to sixty whom Fred Ebb and Liza had chosen out of a pool of five hundred women who had auditioned for the show.

Watching her concentration as she worked with the other dancers, Fred Ebb still had difficulty realizing she was no longer seventeen and found himself conscientiously avoiding swearing in front of her, while carefully shielding her from off-color jokes. She was forty-five, yet Fred Ebb sometimes found the fact impossible to grasp.

But now she was an adult, plainly in charge, and she applied herself with passion to the task of masterminding the Radio City show. First, she researched Radio City archives, where she unearthed examples of her father's works and designs, which only served to reinforce her feeling that he would be watching her perform at Radio City.

Then she perfected her routine "Seeing Things," the tribute to Vincente conceived as a dreamy ballad with music by John Kander and lyrics by Fred Ebb. " 'Seeing Things' is the most touching moment in a show crammed with brass, flash and old-fashioned show business sentiment," observed *New York Times* reviewer Stephen Holden after the show's first night.

Stepping Out was a tribute to Vincente, but in it Liza also paid homage to two of her other father figures in two routines that included a tribute to Bob Fosse (featuring "Pack Up Your Troubles in Your Old Kit Bag" and "It's a Long Way to Tipperary") and three of Charles Aznavour's songs.

Fortified by coffee and diet Coke, Liza attacked rehearsals with an energy that one cast member labeled as "scary." She treated them well, throwing a champagne party for the cast each week but never sipping anything other than diet cola herself.

The Radio City cast reciprocated and gave her a surprise backstage birthday party in March. On arriving at the theater to be confronted by cameras and flash bulbs, she screamed, "Oh my God! You scared me to death." Then she toasted everyone with Evian. She held her own birthday party later, with Joan Rivers, Sean Young, Naomi Campbell, Mary McFadden, Isaac Mizrahi, Marisa Berenson, and Diane Von Furstenberg.

The *Stepping Out* opening on April 23, 1989, was the event of the Broadway season. At the after show party at the Rainbow Room, Liza was escorted by *GoodFellas* actor Joe Pesci. Her entrance to the party glowed with old time Broadway pizzazz as she arrived to the throb of "New York, New York" and danced and sang her way down the Rainbow Room's art deco staircase and into the arms of her illustrious fans, who all idolized her.

The next day, although a few critics quibbled that the show was a bit long, the majority agreed that *Stepping Out* was a hit. Liza's number one admirer, Clive Barnes, raved, "Minnelli is the epitome of Broadway, the living heart of the show business that no business is like. She has the voice, the strut, the manner, the hair-breadth nervy confidence, the brashness, the charm, the deftness, the concentration, the focus—and the talent. The talent that brushes genius and comes two or three times in a generation."

Liza's *Stepping Out* show set a stupendous $3.8 million box office record at Radio City, and she went on to repeat her success during an eighteen-city tour of America.

* * *

Her stardom had been reconfirmed and her happiness was complete when her romantic life, too, was resolved. During rehearsals for the show, she had formed another alliance, with someone who was to eclipse k.d. in importance. The new object of her ardent affections, twenty-seven-year-old pianist Billy Stritch, was born in Texas and had been part of the vocal jazz group Montgomery, Plant and Stritch. Billy had received positive critical recognition and was Liza's vocal arranger at Radio City. She would even eventually compare him to George Gershwin.

"Billy is a really nice guy. He was always really popular and fun," said Lisa Branch, who went to John Foster Dulles High School in Sugarland with him. Billy thoroughly charmed Liza and, with stars in her eyes, as always when she first fell in love, she instantly incorporated him into her life, engulfing him utterly and completely. When the show opened, Billy was appearing at Bobo's restaurant on New York's 42nd Street. Each night after she had finished at Radio City, an ever effervescent Liza dashed over to the restaurant and, chain-smoking nervously, eagerly applauded the rest of the night away as Billy played the piano.

She encouraged and promoted his career as fiercely as any Pygmalion his Galatea. And while unkind hangers-on, jealous that Liza was devoting herself to Billy, might mutter that he was exploiting her, that he was just another version of Rex Kramer, an opportunist leeching on Liza's generosity and her fame, that was far from the truth. Billy was a consummate professional, a much praised performer who had appeared at the Algonquin and had his own following. And while Liza's interest in him did not go unnoticed in the press, it was not essential to the success of his career.

She demonstrated her new-born love for him in many ways. When he and Sally May opened at Tatou, in New York, she baked them a cake beforehand, carefully decorating it with "GOOD LUCK" in sugar icing. At the show, Liza sat by the stage, applauding loudly. And when Billy played at the Russian Tea Room, Liza sat through show after show, as always applauding passionately and, as a source who saw her there says, "She looked wonderfully in love with him."

In the summer of 1991, Liz Smith confirmed Liza and Billy's relationship, reporting on their joint appearance at Saks Fifth Avenue's Twelve Gala charity salute to American designers, "Yup, it's love!" Dressed in a Bill Blass design, her brown eyes melting with tenderness, Liza held Billy's hand throughout dinner and afterward raved to Liz Smith about her recent visit to Billy's home in Sugarland, Texas, where she was given a backyard barbecue by the Stritch family and also received the key to Sugarland from the mayor. According to Liz, "She's crazy wild about Billy Stritch, and he looks like the cat that swallowed the canary these days."

She was in love with Billy and looked ready to join another "normal" down home family in the Kulbeth-country mode, in Texas. But unlike the Kulbeth family, the Streichs (Billy's real name until he changed it) were not farmers and William Streich, Billy's father, taught journalism in Sugarland. Liza and Billy visited Sugarland together on many occasions (including Christmas 1991–92) and Billy's entire family were completely captivated by Liza's eagerness to belong. Billy's eighty-seven-year-old grandmother, Mrs. William Streich, Sr., says, "Liza is a wonderful person. She was just an ordinary person. I made her breakfast in my kitchen—eggs with rolls—and she seemed to love it and she loved my two poodles."

Liza was convinced that this time, she would be lucky, that this time she would finally get it right. To that end, on August 23, Liza returned once to the Omega Institute in Louisiana, where she and Billy were examined by a fertility expert, Dr. Joseph Bellina, co-author of the book *You Can Have a Baby*. The results of her consultation are not available, but her longing to have a child remains unrequited.

Then, in September 1991, Billy and Liza flew to London for the royal premiere of *Stepping Out*, her new film, which had not yet been released in America. There, she was interviewed by *Guardian* reporter Suzie MacKenzie, who observed, "You sense that she hates to be touched, physically as well as emotionally, and at one point when I go to light her cigarette, she recoiled into her chair. The laugh is forced, defensive and always ready, another prop. Such things you can rely on she seems to say, other things not. Dependency in different forms has always been her theme."

She had always felt lighthearted in London and this trip was no exception. She took Billy to Harrod's, showed him the sights of London, and, on September 20, they attended the charity premiere of *Stepping Out* at London's Empire Leicester Square Theater, in the presence of Princess Diana, the princess of Wales.

Before her presentation to Princess Diana, Liza and fellow *Stepping Out* actress, Julie Walters of *Educating Rita* fame, practiced their curtsies and giggled nervously. Dressed in white, with Billy by her side, Liza said she was very excited at meeting the princess. Her eyes shone as she took her place next to Diana at the theater and, during the film, she couldn't help casting nervous sidelong glances at the princess to see how she was reacting.

After the premiere, a party was held at London's Langham Hilton. Flouting tradition, for the first time ever, Princess Diana attended the after premiere party for an hour, enjoying Liza's performance of the song "Stepping Out" and her duet with Billy Stritch of "Come Rain or Come Shine." Only Luciano Pavarotti and Elton John before her ever serenaded the princess of Wales in an impromptu performance.

In London, in September 1991, too, Liza laid down the stipulation that she would no longer talk to the media about her mother. Always diffident, suspicious of the press, she picked her words carefully when discussing Princess Diana, describing her as "swell" on both Sally Jessy Raphael's and Regis Philbin's television shows.

At the end of October 1991, she and Billy were back in London again, where Liza was booked for a one-woman show at the Royal Albert Hall. On October 22, Billy gave a £10,000 cabaret performance at the exclusive Pizza on the Park jazz club in front of composer Andrew Lloyd Webber, Susan George, and other British stars. Liza led the applause and later, her voice racing with pride, said, "I think that he is a real star."

Then, on October 29, Liza and Billy were guests of honor at a Royal Variety Club tribute lunch for Liza held at London's Royal Lancaster Hotel. There, Billy accompanied Liza at the piano as, in front of a star-spangled audience that included Vanessa Redgrave and Michael Caine, she sang "Stepping Out."

She and Billy wore matching platinum friendship rings and Billy announced to the celebrity audience, "We met in March and since then we have never been apart. We have worked together and gone out together from that time.

"The question of marriage has come up. I don't really want to talk about what we have discussed—but who knows, we are taking one day at a time. I just adore her."

As always, London loved Liza, although critic Hilary Bonner pointed out, "She gets away with a level of sentimentality which would kill most other performers, and milks the willing audience for all she is worth. But coming from her, that's fine. There may be better singers than Liza Minnelli, there may be better dancers, but there are few greater stars."

She was the last of the great Broadway entertainers and her British audience paid tribute to her legendary appeal.

Her career in America, however, was not proceeding as smoothly. Liza had filmed *Stepping Out* over four months during the fall of 1990 in Toronto. Produced and directed by Lewis Gilbert of *Shirley Valentine, Educating Rita,* and *Alfie* fame, the film was a cross between *Rocky* and *A Chorus Line.* In it, Liza played dance teacher Mavis Turner, who gave tap lessons to an assorted crew of women, including Shelley Winters, Julie Walters, and comedienne Andrea Martin.

Liza was happy working with Julie Walters and the Oscar-winning American actress Shelley Winters and mothered the entire group of women, especially during the preproduction three-week period of eight hours a day tap training. Choreographer Danny Daniels was a hard taskmaster and Liza, thinking back to *Best Foot Forward* when she first worked with him, laughingly complained, "Danny was strict then but he's worse now. It's been like going back to school for all of us."

The cast of the film *Stepping Out* had nicknamed her "The Iron Woman" because she worked so hard. But she still found time to relax and, on Halloween, attended an end of filming cast party in a Toronto suburb where she led some of the actresses through an impromptu version of "Danny Boy" and "That's Entertainment."

Although she had taken a risk in selecting a script based on a relatively unknown play to be her fourth musical, everyone had high hopes for the success of *Stepping Out,* and Liza insisted of her part as Mavis, "It's the best role I've had since *Cabaret.*" Originally, *Stepping Out* was scheduled to open in conjunction with Liza's Radio City show (of the same name). But the opening was delayed a full nine months and, as a result, did not benefit from the Radio City show and the resultant publicity.

Varying reasons for the delayed release date have been put forward. Some blame the delay on a shake-up at Paramount, others on the flaws in the final edit of the film. Liza herself attributed it to the Gulf War. But whatever the reason, when *Stepping Out* opened in the fall of 1991, the film received a brief showing at scattered movie theaters throughout the country and although Liza promoted it on talk shows, evidently the Hollywood powers-that-be did not seem to want to support it. Yet again she had believed in a film and given it her all, but it had failed dismally. And, viewing Liza's solo production number in "Stepping Out," it is her tragedy that the film world no longer contains the genius of a Vincente Minnelli to create MGM-style musicals that would show-case her talent.

Nonetheless, she refused to remain disheartened by the failure of *Stepping Out.* And while rumors surfaced in the tabloids that she was drinking again, she did all in her power to stay true to everything she had learned at Betty Ford and Hazelden.

She stuck rigidly to her policy of never staying too long at functions where other people would be drinking, conscious always that the longer the night drew on, the stronger the danger of her straying into temptation.

Now she no longer tried to be perfect, no longer to be the life and soul of the party, the live wire whom everyone loved. Instead, she learned to spend many an evening at home, drinking tea, watching television, doing needlepoint, and just being with Billy.

She also religiously attended AA meetings, sometimes in London, where her presence inspired other members who knew of her struggle. And in America, in the summer she was often to be seen at the 4:30 Saturday AA meeting at the Whaler's Church in Sag Harbor.

On December 17, 1991, Liza filed divorce papers and, on January 27, 1992, her marriage to Mark Gero formally came to an end in an uncontested divorce granted by Manhattan State Supreme Court on the grounds of his abandonment on November 1, 1990.

She was still in love with Billy, and throughout 1992 she gave a good impression of being in the throes of passion and romance. Professionally, she lent him all her support and sang two duets with him (including "Come Rain or Come Shine") on his solo album, *Billy Stritch*. And her 1992 Radio City reprise was, as always, a stupendous success, establishing her conclusively as one of the greatest, most acclaimed cabaret stars of our time.

Off stage, however, loss appeared to be the leit motif for Liza's life in 1992. Early in the year, singer Freddie Mercury died of AIDS, and Liza flew to London to appear in the tribute to him held at the Wembley Stadium. There, dressed in black velvet and wearing a red ribbon proclaiming her support for the fight against AIDS, Liza led the rousing finale, singing "We Are the Champions." Fans noted that Liza, with her hair flying in the bitter wind, looked terrific. Yet, in her heart, she could only have been sad. Mercury, a Judy Garland admirer and a true original, was yet another one of Liza's close friends to die of AIDS.

Even as Liza sang, Peter Allen, too, had fallen prey to the

disease. At first, Peter, forever the optimist in love with show business, believed that he had throat cancer but would survive. Later, when he learned the truth—that it was AIDS—still believing in his survival, and that he would perform again, Peter adamantly refused to tell the public the truth.

From the first, though, Liza had known. In the words of Peter's personal assistant, Bruce Cudd, "Liza rallied around him. She really helped get him back in the swing of things so he wasn't sitting at home. She was real strong." Together, they went out on the town in Manhattan, where, when they had both been young, they had once played Zelda and Scott together. They saw Joan Collins in *Private Lives,* Ellen Green at Michael's Pub, and spent hours together talking about the past—about their lives.

When the end came, on June 18, 1992, Liza was on the verge of flying to London for a tribute to Sammy Davis, Jr., at the Royal Albert Hall in London, held to raise money for London's Royal Marsden Hospital and New York's Memorial Sloan Kettering Cancer Center. She heard the news of Peter's death from Bruce Cudd, who later said, "She was very upset, but I really admired her because the first thing she wanted to do was call Peter's mother and sister in Australia." Liza added that Peter had helped her get ready for Albert Hall. "Even though he was ill he was still thinking about me and Sammy. Peter was a wonderful man. I knew he was ill and we stayed close, but no matter how much you prepare, it's still a shock."

Despite her relationship with Billy, her world was now smaller and, perhaps, sadder. Peter was gone, so were Sammy, Halston, her father, and her mother.

Also in 1992 there were more shocks, yet none so terrible as Peter's death. After eighteen years of marriage, Lorna's life with Jake Hooker ended abruptly after she allegedly fell in love with British pianist Colin Freedman. By now, too, Liza was forced to confront the sadness that she would never be able to bear a child. And like many childless women, somewhere in her soul she would always remain the eternal child herself; the Director's daughter, Vincente's princess, Daddy's girl, Judy's baby.

More tragedy struck in 1992, this time hitting one of her dearest, oldest friends. Ben Vereen, who many said had been her lover, was struck by a truck and critically injured. After a series of painful operations, Vereen survived, vowing that despite pins in his leg and hip, he would one day dance again.

Liza, too, could never live without show business. For show business had always been her life, her oxygen, the bedrock of her very existence. Yet even in this arena, in the realm of show business that she so loves and of which she is a product, Liza's career is not all she would wish it to be.

Her chances for a hit record seem increasingly slim. Her detractors theorize that Liza is too tied to the past, to the semiautobiographical songs of Kander and Ebb, and that she isn't sufficiently contemporary in style to make the hit parade.

When it comes to her acting career, Hollywood's princess appears to be far more beloved by Broadway than by the tinsel town of her birth. The camera has never loved Liza unreservedly and she has never been able to establish herself conclusively as a film star. Some Liza watchers believe that part of the reason for her lack of success in films is that Liza, to this day, remains a victim of her own good nature. Forever loyal to her family of co-workers, she is loath to fire anyone, to refurbish her team, or to purchase her own cinematic projects to star in. Just as Liza (unlike Natalie Cole) could never release a duet with a dead parent, neither could she (like Streisand) direct her own picture.

Duetting with Judy would probably fracture the emotional facade she has so painstakingly created, and directing would evoke all her inability to confront or to take charge completely. Yet despite everything, Liza will continue to survive.

She may never again win the Academy Award, nor scale the hit parade, yet her legions of fans will never desert her. And it is clear that her career will endure, just as Sinatra's has endured, partly because of her talent to entertain, but also because her story and the memories her songs evoke have become inextricably enmeshed in our stories and in our lives. Today she is an icon, a star who is redolent of another era, another time, yet who exudes the hope and resilience of tomorrow.

In 1993, Liza will be exactly the same age as Judy was when she died. And although Liza has survived and has clearly emerged from her mother's shadow and sometimes transcended her professionally, her life is still lit by the brilliance that was Judy Garland. And even Liza, the mistress of avoidance, has finally acknowledged the truth. She was once asked to define the difference between them, and, after a moment's reflection, she eventually answered, "I had Judy Garland as a mother." Indeed she did: the legend, the curse, the gift, and the blessing.

BIBLIOGRAPHY

Bacall, Lauren. *By Myself*. New York: Alfred A. Knopf, Inc., 1979.

Bogarde, Dirk. *Snakes and Ladders*. New York: Holt, Rinehart & Winston, 1979.

Colacello, Bob. *Holy Terror: Andy Warhol Close Up*. New York: HarperCollins, 1990.

Crane, Cheryl (with Cliff Jahr). *Detour: A Hollywood Story*. Arbor House/William Morrow: 1988.

Deans, Mickey and Ann Pinchot. *Weep No More My Lady*. New York: Hawthorn Books, 1972.

Finch, Christopher. *Rainbow: The Stormy Life of Judy Garland*. New York: Grosset & Dunlap, 1974.

Frank, Gerold. *Judy*. New York: Harper & Row, 1975.

Gaines, Steven and Robert Jon Cohen. *The Club*. New York: William Morrow, 1980.

Gaines, Steven. *Simply Halston*. New York: G.P. Putnam's Sons, 1991.

Hackett, Pat (ed). *The Andy Warhol Diaries*. New York: Warner Books, 1989.

Harvey, Stephen. *Directed by Vincente Minnelli*. New York: The Museum of Modern Art/Harper & Row, 1989.

Lawford, Patricia Seaton. *The Peter Lawford Story*. New York: Carroll & Graf, 1988.

Minnelli, Vincente (with Hector Arce). *I Remember It Well*. New York: Doubleday, 1974.

Parish, James Robert (with Jack Ano). *Liza!* New York: Pocket Books, 1975.

Petrucelli, Alan W. *Liza Liza! An Unauthorized Biography of Liza Minnelli*. Walled Lake, Mich.: Karz–Cohl Publishers, 1983.

Phillips, Julia. *You'll Never Eat Lunch in This Town Again*. New York: Random House, 1991.

Rothschild, Guy de. *The Whims of Fortune*. Granada Publishing, 1985.

Sanders, Coyne Steven. *The Rainbow's End: The Judy Garland Show*. New York: William Morrow & Co., 1990.

Smith, David and Neal Peters. *Peter Allen: "Between the Moon and New York City."* New York: Delilah Books, 1983.

Spada, James, with Karen Swenson. *Judy and Liza*. Garden City, New York: Doubleday, 1983.

Spector, Ronnie, with Vince Waldron. *Be My Baby*. New York: Harmony Books, 1990.

Torme, Mel. *The Other Side of the Rainbow with Judy Garland on the Dawn Patrol*. New York: William Morrow, 1970.

ACKNOWLEDGMENTS

In the text, some interviewees are referred to as confidential sources, and I am grateful to them for talking to me and enhancing my perspective on Liza.

I am equally grateful to the following people who were among the many who granted me interviews:

George Abbott
Mario Arboleda
Pia Arnold
Jim Bailey
Lisa Branch
Dr. Calcroft, principal of
   Dixon and Wolfe
John Carmen
David Sorin Collyer
Tom Cooper
Alma Coustelaine
Mrs. Daly
Elizabeth Elliott

Jerry Fischer
Robert Fitch
Eva Gabor
Zsa Zsa Gabor
Katherine Grayson
Anthony Haas
Anne Hamilton
David Hamilton
Mac Hayes
Robert Hazeltine
Richard Heard
Francesca Hilton
Victor Hugo

Anne Jeffreys
Eve Johnson
Schuyler Johnson
Peggy Kulbeth
Barry Landau
Ron Lewis
The late Doris Lilly
John Lloyd
Georgette Magnani-Minnelli
Christiane "Tina Nina"
  Minnelli
Michael Medwin
Mark Miller
Roger Minami
Ronald Neame
Lester Persky
Tyrone Power, Jr.
Denise Prentis Cobb Hale

John David Ridge
Ray Rogers
Donald Royall
Lee Schrager
Charles Schramm
Michael Sellers
Dorothy L. Silverstone
Suzanne Soboloff
Ronnie Spector
Mrs. William Streich, Sr.
Bill Thomas
Theadora Van Runkle
Andrea Vereen
Ingrid Von Anke
Trudie Von Trotha
Watson Webb
Holly Woodlawn

I also owe a debt of gratitude to Gail Gabert for her impeccable secretarial work and to the following editors, writers, journalists, and photographers for their help in making the book possible.

Oscar Abolafia
Christopher Anderson
Agnes Ash
Chris Bowen
Kathy Brady
Tim Carroll
Sharon Churcher
Gerald Clarke
Gerald Davis
Ingrid Divita
Lydia Encinas
Guy Flatley
Gerold Frank
Steven Gaines
Cathy Griffin

C. David Heymann
Marvene Jones
Richard Kaplan
Celine La Frenais
Patricia Seaton Lawford
Richard Lay
Skip E. Lowe
Roxanne Lowitt
Sophie Malik
Ann Pinchot
Gabriel Rotello
Joel Selvin
James Spada
Noreen Taylor
Russell Turiak

Mary Vespa	Beverly Willisden
Joyce Wadler	Lee Wolfurt

I am indebted to my editor, Christopher Schelling, for his vibrant creative input. With special thanks to Elizabeth Kaplan of Sterling Lord Literistic.

INDEX